GRACE
GOES TO
PRISON

An Inspiring Story of Hope and Humanity

Melanie G. Snyder

Brethren Press

Grace Goes to Prison: An Inspiring Story of Hope and Humanity
Melanie G. Snyder

© 2009 Melanie G. Snyder

Published by Brethren Press®. Brethren Press is a trademark of the Church of the Brethren, 1451 Dundee Avenue, Elgin, Illinois 60120. Visit www.brethrenpress.com for publishing information.

Library of Congress Cataloging-in-Publication Data

Snyder, Melanie G., 1961-
    Grace goes to prison : an inspiring story of hope and humanity / Melanie G. Snyder.
        p. cm.
    "Bellefonte, Pennsylvania."
    "CentrePeace."
    Includes bibliographical references.
    Summary: "Tells the story of Marie Hamilton and her volunteer work in the Pennsylvania prison system. For more than thirty years, Marie used principles of nonviolence and restorative justice to create unique programs for inmates"–Provided by publisher.

    ISBN 978-0-87178-128-4 (pbk.)
 1. Hamilton, Grace Marie. 2. Volunteer workers in corrections--Pennsylvania. 3. Prisoners--Pennsylvania. 4. Prisons--Pennsylvania. I. Title.

    HV9305.P3S69 2009
    365'.661092--dc22
    [B]

                                                                                    2009031423

13 12 11 10 09   1 2 3 4 5

Printed in the United States of America

A portion of this book's sale will be donated to CentrePeace, Inc., the nonprofit organization founded by Marie Hamilton. CentrePeace, based out of Bellefonte, Pennsylvania, works to decrease victimization and crime in our communities by improving the attitudes and capabilities of prison inmates through productive work and training in job and interpersonal skills. For more information, visit www.centrepeace.org.

For Jerry, Bear, Yusef, Butch, Hawk, and countless other incarcerated men and women who had been forgotten.

And for Grace Marie Fortney Hamilton and many other VAC and CentrePeace volunteers, who remembered them.

Whatever the question . . . love is the answer.
Virginia Fortney (1910–2007)

CONTENTS

PREFACE

The day after the April 2007 Virginia Tech shootings, when one angry college student killed thirty-two students and faculty members, I received an unexpected phone call from Jon Singer, executive director of the Lancaster (Pennsylvania) Area Victim Offender Reconciliation Program (LAVORP).[1] Jon asked if I would develop and teach a conflict resolution and anger management course for troubled youth. I was a mediator for LAVORP's restorative justice program and had a full slate of other volunteer and family commitments. And I was busy trying to expand my freelance writing business. Adding another commitment seemed crazy. Yet, after the devastation caused by one angry and troubled young man in Virginia twenty-four hours earlier, the timing of that out-of-the-blue request seemed like more than just coincidence. Perhaps this was something I was meant to do.

I had taught conflict resolution courses in business settings, and I had worked with at-risk kids in various volunteer roles. But I quickly discovered that trying to engage angry, court-referred teens who'd rather be anywhere but in my class was intimidating. Feeling desperate after one especially rough Saturday class, I stood up in church the next morning and asked for prayers for myself and the teens.

After church, my friend Jean Moyer told me that, years earlier, she'd met a woman named Marie Hamilton who taught conflict resolution skills to prison inmates. "I visited one of her classes and wrote an article about her. Maybe she could help you," Jean said. She offered to look for Marie's contact information. I scribbled the name on a scrap of paper and took it home. However, Jean couldn't find her contact information, and my note with Marie's name on it was soon buried on my desk.

I struggled through a few more classes, but knew I needed help to connect with my students. I thought again of Marie Hamilton. If she had been able to get through to hardened criminals, surely she could give me some tips for reaching tough teens.

Through the Internet, I found Marie and CentrePeace, the non-profit organization she'd started in Bellefonte, Pennsylvania. I learned that, in addition to teaching conflict resolution classes in prisons across Pennsylvania, Marie had started an annual statewide prison runathon that had enabled inmates to raise over a quarter of a million dollars to help at-risk youth, a program that allowed children to create Christmas cards for inmates, a family visitation assistance program for inmates' families, and restorative justice[2] initiatives to provide "avenues to peace, healing, responsibility and accountability for offenders."[3] I really wanted to meet this woman.

In another miraculous twist, Marie visited our church soon afterward. Jean happened to sit next to her, though didn't recognize her. But when Marie put her name on the attendance pad in the pew, Jean excitedly reintroduced herself, saying we had wanted to contact her. Jean told her about my class and Marie offered to talk with me and share her training materials.

Then Marie shared amazing news of her own: she was looking for someone to write a book about her restorative justice work in the prisons. Both Jean and I had writing experience. It seemed once again that larger forces were at work.

On a blue-skied day in October 2007, Jean and I drove to Bellefonte to meet with Marie, learn more about her work, and discuss the possibility of collaborating on a book about her life. We sat at a picnic table outside the CentrePeace offices, sipping sun tea and listening to some of her stories—stories of despair and raw hope, of violence and forgiveness, of struggles and miracles. By the time Jean and I climbed back into the car for the two-hour drive home to Elizabethtown, we knew this book had to be written.

That initial conversation was to be the first of hundreds of interviews with Marie, current and former inmates, prison staff, judges, community leaders, and others who have known her. Through those conversations, we learned that Grace Marie Fortney Hamilton has been a prison *volunteer*—not a prison employee, not officially part of the "system"—for over thirty years. She's had no formal education or background in criminal justice. Everything she's done challenges conventional wisdom about how we should deal with criminals, even those who have committed the most reprehensible crimes. Yet she became a trusted insider in many of Pennsylvania's prisons. Wardens, corrections officers, and inmates all came to rely on her. Programs she created by collaborating with prison administrators and inmates have become an integral part of Pennsylvania's prison system.

As we were learning about Marie's work, the Pew Public Safety Performance Project released a report[4] on their landmark study of the American criminal justice system. The report revealed that more than one out of every 100 American adults are now in prison or jail. The United States incarcerates more citizens than any other country in the world, including nations commonly considered police states. Mandatory sentences, stringent parole regulations, "three strikes" laws, and tough-on-crime attitudes have contributed to the burgeoning U.S. prison population.

According to the Pew study, all of this comes at a staggering cost. Between 1987 and 2007, the U.S. prison population has nearly tripled and state spending on corrections has increased 127 percent. State spending on higher education has increased only 21 percent during the same period. Yet the sharp increases in corrections spending and incarceration rates, says the report, are "failing to have a clear impact either on recidivism[5] or overall crime."

In the face of such complex issues and deeply entrenched attitudes about crime and criminals, we wanted to know: how could a soft-spoken Brethren homemaker and former Avon lady break through barriers of mistrust, hostility, and shame to bring hope, humanity, and grace into prison? Throughout the process of writing this book, we have uncovered the simple, yet profound answers to this question—answers that are revealed in the story you're about to read.

I must confess that writing a book about Marie's life and work has become infinitely more than I ever imagined. As I've gone into the prisons myself, to talk with some of the men and women whose lives Marie has touched, my own views have been challenged. Learning about crime and those who perpetrate it and those harmed by it has opened my eyes to the capacity of the human spirit, for both good and evil, and it has plumbed the depths of my own heart. I have felt both shocked and saddened as I've started to get a rudimentary grasp on the realities of our so-called criminal justice system. This book certainly isn't the story I thought I'd be writing when we first met Marie that autumn afternoon. Nor is it a story in which I could have ever envisioned myself getting involved. Yet through a series of what Marie says were, without a doubt, miracles—here it is.

Marie, through her own example, has inspired me to dream big. In that spirit, my hope is that reading the stories of the incarcerated men and women who have been a part of Marie's life will challenge your own thinking about crime and justice, prompt you to ask probing questions about our current criminal justice system, and inspire you to get involved at whatever level feels right for you in addressing the needs of our nation's most forgotten citizens. Because in the end, though this is Marie's story, it is also theirs.

A NOTE ABOUT THE TITLE

Though she was born Grace Marie Fortney, from a young age she has been called "Marie," and this is the name used for her throughout the book. But as we considered possible titles for the book about her life and work, we liked the double meaning of *Grace Goes to Prison*. *Webster's Revised Unabridged Dictionary* offers this definition of *grace*: "The exercise of love, kindness, mercy, favor; disposition to benefit or serve another."[6]

When we talked with Marie about her name and the possible book title, she said, "I don't feel I'm worthy of the name 'Grace,' so I don't use it." But as we learned her story, we thought that her life and work were the very essence of grace, and that both grace and Grace had, indeed, gone to prison.

SPECIAL ACKNOWLEDGMENT: JEAN MOYER

Though Jean decided early on in this project that she preferred to do background work rather than being a coauthor of the book, she has been a tireless behind-the-scenes partner, a constant source of inspiration, and a fount of knowledge. She has conducted background research, crafted the discussion questions, supplied Church of the Brethren perspectives and history, and proofread numerous drafts of the manuscript. Most of all, Jean offered wise and loving counsel throughout the project and has become one of my most cherished friends. And of course, it was Jean who heard my plea for prayers for myself and my students and suggested that I talk with a woman named Marie Hamilton. Little did either of us know the miraculous journey that would unfold from that simple prayer request and Jean's response. For all of this and much more, I am deeply grateful to Jean. Simply put, this book would not exist without her.

Melanie G. Snyder
Elizabethtown, Pennsylvania

EDITORIAL NOTE

This book contains stories about persons living in the Pennsylvania prison system from 1975 through 2009, and does not focus on the details of the crimes committed. Special care was employed in protecting the identity of inmates, the crimes for which they are charged, and the families of victims as well as inmates.

Prison inmates are identified in the book by first name only, at the discretion of the author and publisher. When they are first mentioned, an endnote indicates whether this person's name is a pseudonym or their real name (or a given nickname). Permission to use real names was sought from inmates who are still alive and mentally aware.

The faces of inmates in some photographs have been intentionally blurred to protect the anonymity and in accordance with a Pennsylvania Department of Corrections request.

In the research and editorial work, every attempt was made to depict fairly and accurately the details about each person's life. Each story in this book is shared with a deep level of respect and humility.

And, finally, personal letters and correspondences quoted throughout the book have been reprinted exactly as they were originally written, including spelling and grammatical mistakes.

GRACE
GOES TO
PRISON

PROLOGUE

Marie Hamilton stared up at the man holding a knife to her throat. Crazed brown eyes glared back. In their brief struggle beside Marie's car, she had landed hard on her back. His intentions were clear: rape. If she struggled: murder.

He had turned into someone she didn't recognize—someone ugly, violent. He was no longer Tony,[1] the natural-born charmer who'd had a room full of Brethren church ladies blinking back tears an hour earlier as he told his story. He wasn't even Tony, the hustler and former prison inmate Marie had taken under her wing.

Her mind churned as Tony ranted. She'd seen rage like this before, but not from him. She tried to focus, to think. To recall something—anything—from the training she'd had in principles of nonviolence. During classes, they'd tossed ideas around like confetti. Now Marie couldn't remember any of them.

Afraid to look away, she searched Tony's face. His eyelids flickered, shifting something in Marie's mind. Suddenly she saw everything as though she was hovering above it. His body over hers. The slump of his shoulders. The tilt of his head. The quivering hand clutching the knife. Movements in slow motion. Unexplainably, she was him. Inside his head. Comprehending. Her own breathing slowed. Time stopped. One confetti idea floated down: disarming statements.

"Do you really want to hurt someone you want to love?" Marie asked softly.

Tony froze. Stared at her. His Adam's apple bobbed once.

Marie shifted slightly on the sharp gravel.

Tony recoiled like someone electrocuted. Leaped to his feet. Cursing, spewing rage, he threw his knife to the ground. He paced the length of the gravel parking lot. Back and forth. Back and forth.

Cautiously, Marie sat up. Watched him. Smoothed her hair. Adjusted her blouse. When he reached the edge of the woods, she shuddered. *That's probably where they would have eventually found my body*, she thought. She got to her feet. Waited. Foul words spilled out of him.

She studied the lights of State College, winking yellow and white far below. She tried to pinpoint her quiet neighborhood, the comfortable house where her husband and sons were probably watching TV. A breeze rattled the few remaining autumn leaves across the top of Tussey Ridge. A thin sliver of moon dangled overhead.

How stupid and naïve, she thought, *to stop here at night with him to look at the view*. It was maybe even more stupid and naïve to stay there, instead of driving away and leaving him behind. But she believed so strongly that there was good in everyone, no matter what evil things they might have done. That belief was what had gotten her through all these years as a prison volunteer. Even when it had proven to be dangerous, Marie refused to give up on anybody.

Since Tony had first walked into the Voluntary Action Center, soon after his release from jail, Marie had been determined to see his potential. Even as she'd interviewed him for a volunteer position, when he had admitted that his recent jail term hadn't been his first, Marie saw hope. After all, he wanted to be a volunteer and serve others, didn't he? That had to count for something.

"So, you're a hustler," she'd said to him back then.

He had nodded, grinned a little sheepishly.

"Well, then, why don't I help you learn how to hustle for good?"

And so, Tony had become one of her cherished volunteers. She'd taken him to banquets, civic groups, and churches to tell his story and garner support for her Volunteers in Prison programs. That's where they'd been tonight, before winding back north along the narrow mountain road that crossed Rothrock State Forest. Before stopping here.

Suddenly, Marie realized Tony was no longer pacing—or cursing. He stood a few feet away, staring glumly at the region that locals called Happy Valley. In the distance, beyond State College, a rectangle of lights outlined the complex of the Rockview State Correctional Institution, another of Tony's former residences.

He finally turned toward Marie. He glanced at her, and then stared at the ground.

Night sounds traveled on the breeze. Crickets calling, nocturnal creatures scrambling in the undergrowth, an owl hooting. And from the streets far below, the hum of cars, trucks, and motorcycles. The sounds of people going about their lives.

"Let me take you home," Marie said quietly.

Tony nodded.

1

PATH TO PRISON

*The degree of civilization in a society can be judged by
entering its prisons.*
         —Fyodor Dostoevsky (1821–1881)

As a young girl, Grace Marie Fortney could never have envisioned this life for herself, spending time in prisons working with rapists, murderers, thieves, and drug dealers. Many came from dangerous inner-city neighborhoods. Some had abusive families, some had no family at all. Their world was a long way from Curryville, Pennsylvania, the one-street town in the foothills of the Allegheny Mountains where the blonde, pig-tailed girl everyone called "Marie" had grown up. Her father, Robert Fortney, was a truck driver and her mother, Virginia Wineland Smith Fortney, served as the church pianist at the Curryville Church of the Brethren. Like most of the locals, the Fortneys' social life revolved around their church. There, Marie and her brothers, Dean and Fred, learned Brethren principles of simple living, compassionate service to others, and nonviolence. At home, they lived those principles, doing without indoor plumbing and growing enough vegetables and fruit in their garden to feed themselves year-round. Transient men who rode the trains that ran through the center of Curryville knew they could count on a hot meal and a bit of paying work from the humble Brethren family that lived in the white clapboard house along Main Street.

Marie had always imagined she would live the same kind of simple life her parents had. By the time she was twenty, in 1958, she'd gotten a good start on that life by marrying Joe Hamilton, her high school sweetheart. Marie adored Joe and poured all of her energy into trying to run a perfect home. She invested so much of herself in domestic duties—sewing thirty-five neckties for Joe by hand, cooking gourmet meals every night, and keeping everything in order to meet Joe's exacting standards—that Marie soon began struggling with the stress of married life. Joe didn't want Marie to go anywhere without him, except to her secretarial job or to church. He even had Marie do her grocery shopping during his lunch hour at the A&P store where he worked. Marie worked tirelessly to meet his demands.

Five years later, when their first son, Steven, was born, Marie quit her job and immersed herself in motherhood. Their second child, Michael, followed in 1965. But Marie soon found that staying home all the time didn't agree with her, especially when Steven and Michael were old enough to be in school all day. Because of Joe's job, they moved five times in six years. In each new community, Marie got involved in the nearest Church of the Brethren congregation, teaching Sunday school and directing the choir. However, it was a challenge for Marie to find and keep close friendships outside the home. Joe was often jealous of the time Marie spent with others. He wanted everything at home to be perfect, and Marie felt like she never measured up to his standards. Eventually, Marie's unhappiness led to serious bouts of depression.

Once, on a family camping trip, Joe had shown Marie how to operate the gas-powered heater in their camping trailer. He warned her that turning on the gas and extinguishing the pilot light could fill the trailer with deadly fumes, and said that some people even committed suicide that way. In the depths of Marie's depression, she remembered Joe's explanation and it seemed like the ideal solution.

She planned for it the way she planned everything. She decided on the date and marked it on her calendar. She cleaned the house and made sure everything was in order. She even cleaned the garden tools, sanded the wooden handles, and painted them blue. She wrote good-bye letters to her sons.

The night before, Marie prayed, "If you're there, God, and you don't want me to do this, give me a sign." She lay in the dark and waited, but there was no sign. She fell asleep envisioning the gift of freedom she was about to give Joe.

The next morning, Marie saw Steven and Michael off to school, hugging each of them tightly until they wriggled away with an embarrassed, "Mom!" As she started washing the breakfast dishes, the phone rang.

It was a dear old friend with whom she had lost touch. He told Marie that he'd gotten a very strong feeling that he needed to find her. They talked on the phone for several hours. Afterward, Marie felt peaceful and content. It wasn't until hours later that she remembered what she had planned to do that day. It had completely slipped her mind. *Thank you, God, for sending someone who could make me forget*, she prayed. She had gotten the sign she'd prayed for.

GROWING UP IN CURRYVILLE, Marie had been known as an enterprising and compassionate young woman with a "can-do" spirit. She had developed a knack for sales, selling magazines, candy, and gift items to raise money for various causes. She even became an Avon lady for a while, breaking numerous sales records. Marie had been heavily involved in church activities, too, becoming a counselor and music leader at Camp Harmony, a Church of the Brethren camp, and then serving a year with Brethren Volunteer Service[1] at a Native American school in Arizona. Through all these formative experiences, Marie knew she was happiest when she was helping others. So, after moving to Joe's hometown of State College in the early 1970s, she decided to search for volunteer work at a Pennsylvania State University volunteer center, hoping to find a way to serve in the community. It was at the volunteer center where Marie met Ann Cook, an energetic sixty-one-year-old community activist who recruited Marie to join a team of women to start the Voluntary Action Center (VAC) of Centre County. Their team included Myrna Feller and Nancy Desmond, both committed community activists, and Dr. Rose Cologne, a seventy-one-year-old Quaker and former Penn State sociology professor who had been a tireless, long-time advocate for people living in poverty. They surveyed every human service agency in the county regarding their mission and volunteer needs, and then recruited, matched, and referred volunteers to address those needs. If they discovered an unmet human service need in the community, they tried to address it.

Marie and Ann Cook in the early days of the Voluntary Action Center (April 1973). Photo courtesy of Centre Daily Times (State College, Pa.).

It was at the VAC, on a blustery afternoon in January 1975, when a local engineering executive named Larry Ruffner asked the question that was to change the direction of Marie's life.

"Do you have any volunteer opportunities at the Rockview prison?" Ruffner asked. "I drive past the prison every day on my way to work and think about how dismal it must be for the people in there. I'd like to do something to help."

Coincidentally, Marie had spoken with a Dr. Mazurkiewicz at the prison a few days earlier. "I was calling doctors for a Health Council meeting," she explained to Ruffner. "He promptly told me that he's not an MD. He has a PhD and is a prison superintendent. Why don't I call him right now?"

Ruffner nodded and Marie placed the call.

After reintroducing herself to the superintendent, she explained, "I'm calling for another reason today. I'm with the Voluntary Action Center here in State College, and we're wondering if you'd like some volunteers to work with your inmates."

Mazurkiewicz chortled, then cleared his throat. "No, ma'am, we don't want volunteers. The only people who try to get into prisons as volunteers are religious fanatics, university researchers, reporters, or lonely women."

"Oh," said Marie, flustered by his refusal. "Well, if you ever need volunteers who just want to help inmates, I can recruit them for you. In fact, I have someone in my office right now who'd like to volunteer there and I'm sure he doesn't have any motive other than to help."

"Then he can contact one of the churches that are approved to run religious services here or organizations that help inmates after their release," Mazurkiewicz said brusquely. "I'll send you information on those groups. If we ever need other kinds of volunteers, I'll let you know. Thanks for the call."

Marie hung up and shrugged. She shared with Ruffner what Dr. Mazurkiewicz had said and asked if his counteroffer would be of any interest.

Pennsylvania Governor Milton J. Shapp (in office from 1971 to 1979) signs a declaration during National Volunteer Week as Voluntary Action Center members Carolyn Freark and Marie Hamilton look on (circa 1975). Photo courtesy of Marie Hamilton.

Ruffner shook his head. "I really hoped I could do something in the prison. Thanks for trying, though."

As he left Marie's office, she felt discouraged. It was the first time she'd ever had someone turn away volunteers.

ALMOST NINE MONTHS later, Marie received an unexpected phone call from Rockview's Dr. Mazurkiewicz. "Is your volunteer organization connected with the university?" he asked abruptly.

"Uh, no. . . . " Marie replied, confused.

"Good. We've started up a separate housing unit for inmates who are about to be released from prison. They could use face-to-face contact with ordinary, everyday typical citizens—someone other than parole officers or the people they'd usually come into contact with."

"So you want some volunteers?" Marie asked.

"Yes. You said you could recruit volunteers if we needed them. Maybe four or five people who would visit these inmates, talk with them about the current price of hamburger and what's going on in the outside world, things to help ease their transition back into the community once they're released."

"Men and women, both? You had mentioned concerns about women going into a prison."

"Well, let me think about that," Mazurkiewicz conceded.

"We'd need to know any stipulations you have about who could volunteer. We don't screen volunteers. We just find people willing to do the work, then refer them to you."

"I'll work out the details and have John McCullough, our director of treatment, call you to arrange a time when you can come here to the prison to discuss it."

Marie couldn't help smiling, though she was glad he couldn't see it. "Okay, Dr. Mazurkiewicz. Just tell us what you need and we'll be happy to recruit volunteers for you."

After hanging up, she gathered the VAC staff to discuss the new Rockview opportunity.

"The prison? We can't send volunteers in there. How do we know they'd be safe?" one staff member objected.

"Assuming we could even find anyone willing to visit with criminals," another added.

"And what about the liability? VAC can't be taking that on."

Marie felt blindsided by their resistance. "Well," she said, "I'll meet with people at the prison to discuss how to set it up and, of course, I'll ask about any liability issues. But I don't want to go in alone. Who can come to the prison with me for this meeting?"

Suddenly, everyone was intently studying their fingernails or the floor. "Anybody?" Marie pleaded. No one responded.

As Marie turned to go back into her office, Ann Cook spoke up. "I'll go with you."

Marie smiled gratefully. She was learning that she could always count on her fearless sixty-three-year-old mentor when she needed Ann the most.

A few days later, John McCullough called Marie to arrange their visit to Rockview. She and Ann made the seven-mile trip north along Benner Pike to the five thousand-acre prison complex. Rockview had opened in 1915 as a prison farm branch of Pittsburgh's maximum-security Western Penitentiary. As the two women wound along the curved entrance road to the prison, the lush acres of rolling hills and thick stands of autumn-colored trees surrounding the prison were a surreal contrast to the stark guard towers and high fences topped with barbed wire. Marie parked in front of a gray stone building that looked like a medieval fortress.

She glanced nervously at Ann as they approached the entrance. After a guard buzzed them through a barred gate, they were asked to sign in and take a seat in a small waiting area.

A few minutes later, a lean man with long brown hair framing a boyish face came out and greeted them.

McCullough introduced himself and led them across the prison yard, pointing out different buildings, called "blocks," and explaining what types of inmates were housed in each. The pre-release unit where they were headed was called "B Block North." Catcalls, whistles, undecipherable comments, and monkey-like sounds came from the tiny barred windows. Marie later learned that the monkey calls were an expression of the inmates' disgust when they saw anyone who looked like a researcher or reporter coming through to see the "monkeys in cages."

When they reached B Block North, a guard opened the heavy door to the block. Marie jumped at the echoing clang as it slammed behind them. They entered a long, narrow passage with dimly lit cells that looked like cages on both sides. Above them, more cages lined a second tier. Men stared out through the bars at the two slender blondes passing by in flowered dresses and high heels. Marie felt like she was in a zoo, with a bizarre role reversal—she and Ann were the exotic creatures and the men were the ones straining to catch a glimpse of them. She prayed that her face didn't register the shock she felt at seeing humans in cages. *We do this in America?* she thought, feeling nauseated and ashamed. She'd had no idea what to expect, but never imagined anything so barbaric.

"This is the first time we've ever allowed women to come into the block," McCullough explained. "A lot of these guys haven't seen a woman in years."

His explanation left Marie feeling even more appalled.

Everything echoed in the block—footsteps, voices. A toilet flushed loudly in one of the cells as they passed. The toilets were in plain sight in every cell. Marie's face grew hot as she grasped the humiliating lack of privacy that was the norm here. Besides the incessant noise, Marie noticed the smell—a mix of disinfectant, cigarette smoke, and bodily odors that she found unnerving. She stared straight ahead until they reached the control desk.

A sign overhead read "Houser's Hall." McCullough explained that the inmates had named the block in honor of Sergeant Robert Houser, the widely respected head of the unit. As if on cue, Sergeant Houser appeared and greeted Marie and Ann with a friendly smile. Houser's white hair, horn-rimmed glasses, and the pipe that dangled from the corner of his mouth gave him a grandfatherly appearance—a sharp contrast to the tough-looking inmates he supervised.

A scrawny man with intense blue eyes, shaggy brown hair, and an oversized mustache stepped forward.

"This is JT,[2] one of our residents[3] here in B Block," Houser said, putting his hand on JT's shoulder. "He'll show you around, then we can talk."

JT was a charming tour guide, clearly relishing his special role. He explained that some of the men had jobs at the prison and were out working for most of the day. He showed them a few unoccupied cells—tiny spaces that held only a cot, a small desk, and a toilet. The cells were just as stark and gray inside as the buildings were outside. A few had a picture or two on the wall or a colored towel draped carefully over the desk. Most were so tidy that Marie couldn't believe anyone actually lived in them.

Marie told JT about the planned volunteer visitation program.

"Sounds good," JT replied. "We could all use a few squares to talk to."

"What are squares?" Marie asked.

"You know, people like you ladies appear to be—straight arrows, upstanding, model citizens, pillars of the community."

From JT's tone, Marie wasn't sure it was a compliment, but she simply said, "Oh, thank you."

They stopped to talk with some of the men in their cells. Marie was struck by how young most of them were. She asked JT about this.

"I'm thirty. Most are in their twenties or thirties, a few are just teenagers. I think the oldest guy is about thirty-six," JT replied.

They're all younger than me, Marie thought. She wondered how many of them were married, had children. She thought about her husband and her two boys, and about how awful it would be to have a husband or father in prison.

Something else surprised her—the vulnerability and humanity she saw in the men's eyes. She'd never given much thought to who was in prison. But chatting briefly with a few of the men pulled at something deep within her. The men were clearly surprised to see women on the block, and even more surprised to hear that volunteers from the community, both women and men, might soon be visiting them regularly. *They'd better not allow me to be one of the volunteers, though*, Marie thought. *I'd find the key and let all of these men out.* Each man they met thanked Marie and Ann for taking time to stop and talk with them.

JT chatted breezily with the women as they walked, telling them about different places he'd lived and about his dream to be a rock guitarist. What he didn't mention was that he had a lengthy police record of car thefts and burglaries that had started at age eleven. He'd been incarcerated so often that his adoptive parents, wealthy New Englanders, no longer wanted anything to do with him. JT had been a central figure in a prisoners' strike at the federal penitentiary in Lewisburg, Pennsylvania.[4] Despite having come to Rockview with a reputation as a troublemaker, he'd be eligible for parole by April 1976.

After the tour, JT delivered the women back to the sergeant's desk with a gentlemanly flourish, expressing his hope that the residents of B Block North would soon have the pleasure of regular visits from Ann, Marie, and others.

McCullough and Houser led Marie and Ann to a tiny converted cell that served as a meeting room on the second tier of the block. There they discussed the possible scope of a volunteer program. McCullough started by giving an overview of the pre-release unit, a therapeutic community (TC) where staff attempted to create an atmosphere of family life for the residents. It was a fairly complex program, combining a wide range of treatments including reality therapy, behavior modification techniques, encounter groups, traditional group therapy, and simulated exposure to community living. The goal was to encourage residents to show concern for each other, take responsibility for themselves, and examine and change their self-defeating behaviors in preparation for their release from prison.

McCullough was Rockview's resident expert on therapeutic communities, which had most commonly been used for substance abusers throughout the 1960s and early '70s. He had been trained in the TC concept by ex-inmates and junkies at New York-based Daytop, Inc., the oldest and largest drug-free, self-help program in the United States. He had then directed two therapeutic communities for narcotics addicts in the federal penitentiary in Danbury, Connecticut, before coming to Rockview and adapting the TC model for use with pre-release inmates.

As McCullough and Houser talked, Marie took notes, trying to keep up with all of the new terminology they used.

Sergeant Houser explained that many of the inmates had assigned roles within the "house," ranging from cleaning, maintenance, and clerical work to organizing events to encourage positive interaction among residents. One "department," called "Expediting," was responsible for enforcing rules and addressing infractions of the rules through a "pull-up" system where inmates reported the misbehavior of any of their peers. Residents also received rewards or punishments from their peers. Any resident's eventual release from prison would depend, in part, on his behavior while in the program. Most would be in the program for six to eight months.

"These men need contact with some square people from the outside community to provide positive relationships," McCullough explained. "The volunteers would have to be emotionally mature enough to interact with inmates in a prison atmosphere. They have to have a strong character and they have to be shock-proof. These guys will try to con them, play them, manipulate them. The volunteers will hear about things they might rather not even know about, like the crimes some of these guys have committed. We don't want any prison reformers, no psychiatrists, reporters, or ministers, no curiosity-seekers. No university researchers either, coming in here to evaluate what's going on. We've had bad experiences with people from the university coming in here, treating this place like a laboratory and all of us like lab rats. Anyone you recruit will have to have an interview and orientation with me first. We'd want them to commit to coming here once a week, for at least a year."

Marie and Ann scribbled notes furiously as McCullough laid out the requirements.

"What about women as volunteers?" Marie asked. "Dr. Mazurkiewicz had some concerns about that."

"We discussed it and decided it would be good for the men," McCullough conceded. "Might be a little awkward at first, but they need to be able to interact positively with women, and we have ways

Judge Paul Campbell with Marie Hamilton at a volunteer recognition event (circa 1975). Photo courtesy of Marie Hamilton.

of dealing with any inappropriate behavior. So, yes, some female volunteers would be a good idea. But again, they need to be emotionally mature and able to deal with this environment. They've got to be strong and shock-proof," he repeated.

Marie and Ann asked for assurances that their volunteers would be safe and that the VAC would not bear any liability for safety issues that might arise. McCullough didn't have immediate answers for them, but promised to take the matter up with Dr. Mazurkiewicz.

By the end of their meeting, Ann and Marie had a clearer

understanding of what they'd be asking of their volunteers. But Marie wondered where she'd find enough "shock-proof" people willing to do it. She expressed her concerns to Ann on the drive back to the office.

Ann nodded thoughtfully as Marie shared the unsettling mix of emotions she felt after their brief visit: disbelief, pity, and, she had to admit, shock.

"This will certainly be one of the most unusual volunteer opportunities we've ever had," Ann acknowledged. "I think it will also be one of the most important. You have a gift for finding the right volunteers for every project, Marie. I know you'll find the right people for this program too. And I'll support you in any way necessary."

Starting the next morning, Marie immersed herself in the search for prison volunteers. She asked Ann Cook and Rose Cologne for recommendations. She made nearly a hundred telephone calls over the course of a few days. The first call, to Larry Ruffner, was easy. He was pleased that the prison superintendent had changed his mind and quickly agreed to volunteer. Other phone calls proved more challenging. Finding people who were willing to go into a prison and work directly with inmates was the toughest sale Marie had ever had to make.

Finally she had a list of people willing to visit the residents of B Block North. Following standard VAC procedure, Marie called John McCullough at Rockview to give him the volunteers' names and their contact information. The VAC left it to each agency to contact the volunteers to make logistical arrangements. Marie made a note on her calendar to contact the Rockview volunteers in a week to see how it was going. Then she breathed a sigh of relief.

The following week, Marie made follow-up phone calls to each of the Rockview volunteers.

"I'm sorry. After talking with the man who called me from Rockview, I've changed my mind about volunteering at the prison," one told her.

On the next call, Marie heard, "After hearing more about it, I've decided it's really not for me."

When Marie called Larry Ruffner, he said that the prison staffer who had called him gave a pretty grim picture of conditions and seemed to be trying to talk him out of volunteering. But Ruffner wasn't deterred. He still wanted to volunteer. All of the other volunteers Marie had recruited had backed out. But Marie had given Dr. Mazurkiewicz her word and wasn't about to admit defeat. She started another round of phone calls and conversations with everyone she knew who might have the right skills and a possible interest in addressing needs in the prison. This time, she told prospective volunteers about her first prison visit and her own reactions. She wanted anyone who was going to do this to understand what they were getting into.

When she had a new list of volunteers, instead of simply giving their contact information to Rockview, Marie called John McCullough and said she wanted to personally bring the volunteers in to meet with him.

"You don't need to come in with them," he told her. "We'll contact them."

"Well, apparently I didn't recruit the right kinds of people the first time," Marie replied. "I want to bring these new volunteers to the prison, have you meet them, and make sure they're right for the job."

McCullough acquiesced and they set a date for a group orientation at Rockview. Marie and the four volunteers—Larry Ruffner, Terry Fagley, and Jim and Debbie Mullen—drove to the prison together for the meeting.

McCullough met them and escorted them to a room called the Rotunda. It reminded Marie of the police interrogation rooms she'd seen in movies—empty except for one long table, a few chairs on either side, and one light fixture dangling down over the middle.

Another impossibly young-looking man who didn't even appear old enough to shave joined the group. "This is Mr. Jeffrey Beard, the counselor supervisor here," McCullough explained.

McCullough started the conversation. "This place isn't for the faint of heart. You'll be working with guys who have committed some pretty terrible crimes. Rape, armed robbery, assault, murder. One guy even chopped somebody up." He paused a moment, as though to let that sink in. "Awful stuff," he emphasized. "These men will try to take advantage of you in any way they can. They're very needy emotionally. You might find yourself having to be counselors to them."

Marie interrupted. "I had told these volunteers their role was to befriend the men, not to be counselors. Perhaps I misunderstood?"

Beard jumped in. "No, you're right, the volunteers would just be here to befriend the inmates. We don't expect them to be counselors. We have our own counseling staff."

"Sorry," McCullough said. "I just meant that sometimes the men will want to talk about pretty intense stuff. The main thing you need to understand is that you'd be working with guys who have a lot of problems."

Beard detailed the behavior issues they were trying to address with the men, including aggression, defiance, withdrawal, lying, stealing, covert drug use, and other illegal behavior. Many inmates were unwilling to accept responsibility for their own actions and constantly blamed others, the "system," or the raw deal life had handed them. Many had little to no self-esteem and others showed complete indifference to everything and everyone around them.

Then Beard reviewed the rules to which volunteers would have to adhere. "Volunteers should not bring anything in or take anything out of the prison when visiting, not even a letter that an inmate might ask you to mail. Anything brought in or out without permission could be considered contraband. You are not to relay messages for the inmates to anyone, either. The inmates are only allowed to contact certain people and they must do so themselves."

Marie took notes as quickly as she could, trying to keep up.

"Inmates who are due to be released soon are allowed to take furloughs[5] of up to one week," Beard continued. "Furloughs are an opportunity for them to get reacclimated to life outside of prison for a little while. Volunteers may take inmates out on furlough, but if you do you should only plan to take them for a maximum of six days, in case of any delay getting them back to the prison. If an inmate goes out on furlough and doesn't return by the seventh day, they're considered 'escaped'—a serious offense. As volunteers, you wouldn't be *required* to take men on furloughs, it's just an option. If you decide to do that, we'd provide you with a complete list of the furlough rules and regulations. Whatever activities or programs or services you might want to offer to the men, you must get approval from us first."

Beard also mentioned that the pre-release program was underfunded and they needed radios, magazines, newspapers, books, and many other things for the men. If the volunteers were willing to donate any of these items, it would be appreciated, as long as the volunteers got permission first.

By the time McCullough and Beard had finished running down the list of program needs, requirements for volunteers, restrictions and possible consequences of any infractions, Marie felt overwhelmed. She looked around the table at the volunteers trying to gauge their reactions, but couldn't read their faces.

McCullough concluded, "Why don't you all just go home and think over whether you really want to do this? If you decide to go through with it after all, you can call me."

Suddenly, Marie understood what was going on. At their first meeting, McCullough had said volunteers must be "shock-proof." He was *trying* to shock them. She wondered if the Rockview staff would prefer not to have volunteers coming in, even though Dr. Mazurkiewicz had requested them. If the staff went back and told Mazurkiewicz they'd tried to get volunteers, but no one was willing to do it, the whole concept would be scrapped. Marie saw all the work it had taken to get to this point disintegrating right in front of her. But she had no idea how to salvage the situation. She prayed silently for help.

Then Larry Ruffner spoke up. "I don't need to go home and think it over. What you're telling me doesn't bother me in the least. I know I'm interested in volunteering here and I'm ready to start any time."

Beard and McCullough both looked surprised.

"I'm ready too," Terry Fagley added.

"Yes, let's do it!" Debbie Mullen agreed. Her husband Jim nodded enthusiastically.

Beard and McCullough hesitated, so Marie took charge.

"It sounds like these volunteers are ready," she said firmly. "Let's get a visit set up."

Though they seemed reluctant, Beard and McCullough agreed to schedule the first visit for December 4, from 1 to 3 p.m. The volunteers would spend one hour in group discussions with the inmates about various topics that might be useful as they prepared for their release. During the second hour, volunteers and inmates could mingle and socialize. They decided to call the second hour "free time," though the irony of that moniker didn't occur to Marie at the time.

With the arrangements finally made, their orientation was over.

"Could we meet Dr. Mazurkiewicz while we're here?" Marie asked. "I've talked with him several times on the phone, but never met him."

"I don't know if he'll see you without an appointment, but I'll take you up to his office," McCullough replied.

They crammed into an elevator and went up to the second floor. McCullough tapped on the superintendent's office door, stuck his head in for a minute, then opened the door wide and motioned to the volunteers to go in. A serious-looking, portly man with white hair, thick glasses, and ruddy cheeks came out from behind an imposing desk.

"These are the new volunteers for B Block," McCullough said.

Mazurkiewicz looked over each volunteer like a general reviewing his troops.

Marie stepped forward to introduce herself. "We have our first visit scheduled already," she added enthusiastically.

Mazurkiewicz nodded brusquely. "Mr. McCullough and Mr. Beard have reviewed the rules with you?" It seemed more like a command than a question.

"Oh, yes, we've covered all of that and we're ready to go," Marie said with a smile.

Mazurkiewicz didn't smile back. "All right, then. Thank you for stopping by." And they were dismissed.

Everyone was silent in the elevator on the way back down, but Marie's thoughts were swirling. Most agencies were overjoyed to have volunteers and gave them a warm welcome. Here she sensed wariness and reluctant tolerance. She suspected that if the tiniest thing went wrong in the first few weeks the volunteer program would be shut down. Her mouth was dry as they stepped out of the elevator, said goodbye to McCullough, and left the prison. She suggested to the other volunteers that they gather at a nearby restaurant to debrief.

"So, what do you think?" Marie asked as they settled into a booth.

Larry shook his head. "After that meeting, I'm not sure how welcome we're going to be, Marie."

"The superintendent didn't even seem like he wanted volunteers," Debbie observed. "Wasn't he the one who contacted you in the first place?"

"Yes, he was," Marie replied. "I think today was a test. John McCullough warned me that our volunteers would have to be 'shock-proof'—and I think they were trying to shock you. I was definitely shocked when Ann and I visited Rockview for the first time." She shook her head, remembering those first horrifying moments when she'd walked into the cellblock. "But when you meet the men, you realize they're human beings who crave positive attention. I think that's what all of you can bring to them." She looked around the table at each of the volunteers. "Dr. Mazurkiewicz definitely thought there was value in having people from the community spend time with the men, and I think John McCullough and Jeff Beard see the value too. But first, they had to be sure you were all up to the task."

"What about you, Marie? Will you come in with us on these visits, at least until we feel comfortable with all of this?" Terry asked.

Marie took a sip of tea. She hadn't planned on being one of the volunteers. And after all of the warnings and stipulations the Rockview staff had laid out, she wasn't sure she'd meet the "shock-proof" test over the long haul. But she'd gotten them into this. And after all the work that had gone into setting it up, she wanted to be sure it succeeded.

"I'll come in with you for a while, until you're all comfortable. But I know you're going to do just fine."

At home that evening, Marie told her husband, Joe, that she was going to accompany the volunteers to the Rockview prison for a few weeks.

"Why would you do that?" he asked bluntly.

She described the needs of the men in the pre-release unit and the role of the volunteers. Joe's face darkened when he heard she'd be working directly with inmates.

"I'll just be going in temporarily, until the new group of volunteers gets comfortable," she said, trying to appease him. But she realized the obstacles she'd had to overcome with VAC and prison staff to get this program started wouldn't be the only ones she'd face.

THOUGH THE VAC's liability and safety questions were still unanswered, Ann and Marie agreed that the volunteers should go to Rockview as scheduled. In the group discussions during the first hour, some of the men were outspoken, some soft-spoken, and some never spoke at all. A few seemed leery, even suspicious of the volunteers. Marie and Debbie generated stares, whispers, smiles, and nods of approval, along with a few whistles and catcalls. But other residents put a quick stop to inappropriate behavior from their peers. Marie was impressed with how the men kept each other in line. She gathered that most of them understood that having volunteers coming right into the cellblock was unprecedented, a privilege that needed to be carefully protected.

During the second hour of their visit, the oddly-named "free time," Marie sat and talked with residents one on one. She was surprised at how deeply moved she felt as she listened to their stories.

A few days later, a pile of thank you letters from the men they'd visited arrived at the VAC office. Marie had to blink back tears as she read each one. The last letter especially touched her:

> Dear Mrs. Hamilton:
> On behalf of all of the residents . . . I extend to you our thanks and appreciation. . . . If more citizens were as interested and concerned with men and women who are incarcerated, I am certain that a lot of the second and third offenders would not be breaking the law and thereby coming back to jail. . . . I would like to let you know what it means for me personally to be able to be in a program of this kind. I am not from this area, and because of the long distance my family can not come to visit me too often. . . . I have been in jail for three years. . . . I hope that you can imagine how starved I am for any and all outside contact. . . . Thank you for the work you are doing to make other people aware of the need for this kind of program and to list their support for it. . . . Thank you.
> Sincerely, Marvin[6]

After reading the letters, Marie looked forward to her next visit to Rockview.

During the first tentative weeks of visiting B Block North, Marie tried to spend a few minutes with as many of the men as possible, to offer some words of encouragement and to hear their stories. Many of them told her they felt forgotten and alone in prison and feared they might die there. As she got to know some of the men, she felt a call to serve them that she couldn't explain. Marie had always thought that someday she'd become a missionary and serve in a foreign country, perhaps when her sons were grown and on their own. But as she listened to the Rockview inmates and saw how desperately they yearned for even the smallest gesture of kindness, she wondered whether there was something else she was meant to do. She prayed for answers. *There's a tremendous need right here, God . . . in a place that feels very foreign . . . is this meant to be my mission field?*

2
LIFE BEHIND BARS

What word of grace in such a place
Could help a brother's soul?
    –Oscar Wilde, "The Ballad of Reading Gaol" (1898)

With every Thursday afternoon visit to B Block North, Marie became more aware of just how foreign the inmates' world was. Many were from Philadelphia or Pittsburgh where they'd grown up in inner-city neighborhoods filled with violence, drugs, poverty, homelessness, and other horrors Marie had never known. *No wonder they've lost their way*, she thought.

Meanwhile, she and the volunteers were struggling to *find* their way. They met before and after each week's visit to review how things were going and to figure out together how to navigate this uncharted territory. Fortunately, they didn't know that several guards at Rockview had placed bets that the "naïve blonde and her idealistic band of do-gooders" wouldn't last a month. But they did know that they needed more than five volunteers to allow ample weekly visiting time with each of the sixty men on the block.

A month into the program, Dr. Mazurkiewicz responded to the VAC's liability concerns. In a letter to Ann Cook, Mazurkiewicz explained that the VAC would be considered only a referral service and would bear no responsibility for the volunteers' safety or actions while at Rockview. Prison staff would be responsible for screening and accepting volunteers. However, volunteers would have to sign a notarized waiver releasing the prison from any liability for their safety. Shortly afterward three of the five volunteers dropped out, leaving only Larry Ruffner and Marie.

Recruiting more volunteers for Rockview became Marie's top priority. Though prison staff would screen them, she knew she'd have to be careful about who she recruited. In those days before criminal background checks, all she had to rely on were her own instincts and recommendations from people she trusted. Ann Cook dug into her extensive list of community contacts to make additional recommendations. Marie called Rose Cologne and expressed her concern about finding volunteers who didn't have ulterior motives for going into the prison.

"Don't worry about motives," Rose counseled. "Every volunteer's motives change over time as they do the work. Yours will too. Pay attention to the small particulars. Find compassionate people who are willing to help, and the rest will fall into place."

Then Rose hung up without saying goodbye—one of her trademarks.

Once again, Marie put on her sales hat and started to make calls. She'd just hung up from one of these calls when her phone rang.

"John Brighton will join your group." Marie recognized Rose's voice. Phone conversations with Rose also never included hello. She'd just dive in wherever the previous conversation had left off.

Rose had personally called Brighton, a fellow Quaker and Penn State engineering professor, and asked him to volunteer for Marie's program at Rockview. It was hard to say no to Rose Cologne.

"John's a good man—you'll like him," Rose told Marie, before abruptly hanging up again.

Soon Marie had a crew of nine new volunteers. The group included a couple of nurses, a housewife, two professors, an accountant, a statistician, and an insurance agent. One of the professors, Ken Wilkinson, a Penn State sociologist, was a serious researcher. Marie talked with him about the prison's "no researchers" rule. Ken promised to keep his prison volunteering and his research separate.

She decided an orientation program was in order, though they'd also be briefed by John McCullough, as well as by Officer Lou Matsick, one of the guards on B Block.

The first thing she told the new volunteers was not to let the prison's exhaustive list of rules intimidate them. Of course, they did have to follow those rules to the letter, as the slightest infraction could shut down the whole program. But she also wanted them to look beyond rules, to breathe humanity into what they were doing.

She emphasized that many inmates had been repeatedly let down by other people. "So, never tell an inmate you'll do something if you aren't absolutely sure you can do it. Not even something as basic as saying you'll listen to the inmate's favorite radio program, because they'll hang on to that, and the following week, they'll want to talk with you about it. If you haven't kept your promise, they'll lose their trust in you."

"Most importantly," she added, "be the kind of volunteer you'd want visiting you, if you felt alone and forgotten by society."

Finally, Marie shared the story of important lessons she had learned years earlier in Brethren Volunteer Service and how they were shaping her ideas about the prison volunteer program.

"Back in 1956, right after I graduated from high school, I visited my friend Pat Holsinger, who was in training for Brethren Volunteer Service. Pat introduced me to Dan West, one of the leaders of the BVS unit. Dan West was quite famous in Brethren circles and beyond as the founder of the Heifer Project.[1] Dan told me all about the different BVS opportunities and said, 'Marie, I think you'd be a good person to go into BVS.'

"Well, I was so excited that I phoned my parents immediately and asked my mother to pack my clothes because I had decided to go into BVS for a year and would be leaving in a few days." Marie laughed and

Brethren Volunteer Service, Unit 31 (June 1956). Photo courtesy of Marie Hamilton.

shook her head. "My parents were in shock, of course, that I had made such a sudden decision, but they were very supportive.

"I was assigned to the Phoenix Indian School[2] in Arizona, as the assistant to the Reverend Harold B. Lundgren, the director of religious education. This was a boarding school for Indian children. They had missionaries from different religions there who would convert the children away from their native beliefs. One of my duties was to assign each student to one of the approved religions, then give each missionary a list of their assigned students.

"Well, I thought the school needed Brethren missionaries who would teach the students principles of nonviolence and peacemaking. So I wrote to the BVS director, Ora Huston, to make the suggestion. But Mr. Huston wrote back and said, 'It's not your job to convert the Indians.' Then, as I learned a little about the students' own native religions, I wrote to Mr. Huston again and told him that the Indian children had beautiful religions of their own and maybe the school shouldn't be trying to make them change religions at all. Mr. Huston told me to just stick to my assignment.

"When any of those children got into trouble at the school, their teachers would send them to my boss, Rev. Lundgren, so he could discipline them. The students would show up in our little basement office holding a note from their teacher describing some terrible thing they had done and asking that the student be punished. But Rev. Lundgren would shove that note into his pocket and invite the student to sit down and he'd just talk with them. He would ask them about their family or what life was like back on their reservation. Rev. Lundgren listened to the students and showed interest in whatever was important to them. He looked for the good in each student and never mentioned whatever offense had brought them to his office. But he did make it a point to tell students that they could come to him at any time. If they had problems or needed to talk with someone, he said they could simply tell their teacher they had to go to Rev. Lundgren's office.

"'And while you're here,' he'd say, 'you can

Marie with a Navajo student and the Reverend Harold B. Lundgren at the Phoenix (Ariz.) Indian School (October 1956). Photo courtesy of Marie Hamilton.

teach Marie how to speak your native language and tell her about your tribe's customs.' Since students were forbidden to speak anything other than English or to practice their native traditions at the school, this was his way of letting them know that our office was a sanctuary and that they could trust us.

"After students returned to class, their teachers often told Rev. Lundgren, 'I don't know what punishment you carried out, but you must have really put the fear of God into my student. He's really shaped up since I sent him to your office.'

"But of course, it wasn't punishment that helped those students shape up. It was the compassion and respect that Rev. Lundgren had shown them. He never focused on what they had done wrong. He just looked for the good in each student. I think that was the greatest gift he could have given them."

Marie looked around the room at her volunteers. "I think that looking for the good in the men at Rockview is the greatest gift we can give them, too."

DESPITE HER PEP TALK for the new volunteers, Marie was grappling with her own issues. Though she never asked inmates about their crimes, many confessed to her the awful things they'd done. She felt overwhelmed by the secret burden of their confessions and struggled with shocking stories she'd rather not know.

In the weekly discussion groups led by Rockview's staff psychologist, Greg Gaertner, the men sometimes shared painful stories of terrible things that had been done to them, including physical, emotional, and sexual abuse. Most had grown up in a world far removed from Marie's idyllic childhood. She was at a loss for what to say to ease their hurts at the horrors they had suffered.

She tried talking with her husband, Joe, about all that she was seeing, hearing, and feeling about the inmates and their plight. He didn't like her spending time with prison inmates and simply wanted her to stop going to the prison.

Desperate for a listening ear, Marie went to her pastor, Mike Scrogin, at University Baptist and Brethren Church in State College, to talk about her work in the prison. In what soon became weekly counseling sessions, Scrogin listened as she recounted the men's stories and pondered how best to help them.

"I don't know anything about prisons or the world these men live in," she admitted. "Maybe I should go to school to learn."

"Well, how would that feel to you?" Scrogin asked.

Marie didn't know how she felt about any of it. She hadn't even planned to continue volunteering in the prison once the program got going. Yet, week by week, she felt more strongly drawn to do whatever she could for the men of B Block North.

Scrogin encouraged Marie to let her heart be her guide, learning as she went. That seemed like good advice to Marie, since she had always learned best through experience.

She was reminded constantly of just how much she had to learn. The Rockview staff and inmates organized an evening social and invited the volunteers to join them for the special occasion. They served hoagies, chips, and soda—special treats for the men. The inmates had borrowed a record player from the Education Department to provide soft background music. The volunteers dressed up for the festive evening, with the men in dress shirts and slacks, and the women wearing dresses and heels, jewelry and perfume. Each inmate had clearly taken care with his own appearance, too, wearing clean, neatly pressed clothes, hair carefully styled. The atmosphere on the block was transformed for that evening.

At the social, Marie approached a staff member whom she had never met and introduced herself. "What do you do here, sir?"

"I'm a CO," he replied.

Though she thought it odd that a conscientious objector would work in a prison, she replied, "I used to train with COs when I was in

Brethren Volunteer Service. BVS was originally set up as an alternative for men who objected to war and the draft."

"You mean conscientious objectors?"

"Yes. Didn't you say you're a CO?"

"It stands for corrections officer, ma'am."

As she made her faux pas with the CO, across the cellblock, something that would become known as the "dancing scandal" was unfolding.

Several female volunteers and inmates were dancing in a small group. Though physical contact between volunteers and inmates was forbidden, the prison staff didn't see any contact in the dancing and allowed it to continue. The evening concluded on a pleasant note. However, reports of dancing in the prison leaked out to the local community. Within a few days, Superintendent Mazurkiewicz had received a barrage of phone calls from outraged citizens wondering why their tax dollars were being wasted on such inappropriate frivolity. A "no dancing" rule for volunteers was quickly added to the list.

The next week, John McCullough told Marie that some of the staff felt it wasn't appropriate to have women coming into a men's prison. Marie wondered whether the objections were really coming from the staff or whether they'd been raised by people from the community.

She told McCullough, "Actually, I think you're very smart to have women coming in. But let's test it out to be sure. I'd like to propose a little experiment. Next week when we come in, give me the names of five of your toughest inmates—the ones you just can't get through to. The ones who are belligerent, won't do what they're supposed to, won't even come out of their cells to get a shower. I'll have the women volunteers be sure to talk with each of those five men next week and let's see what happens."

McCullough looked dubious, but agreed to go along with Marie's proposal.

The following week, Marie had each of the female volunteers make special requests to the guards to see a few of the men on McCullough's list during "free time." As the guards told each man that a volunteer had specially requested to see him, Marie observed subtle shifts in the men. They stood a little straighter and spoke a bit more carefully. The other inmates treated those who had been called out as though they had won an award.

The week after the experiment, the inmates who had received special treatment the previous week were out of their cells, neatly groomed, and ready to participate in the discussion groups.

When Marie saw McCullough, she raised her eyebrows and tipped her head toward his "belligerents."

McCullough shook his head and smiled wryly. "You proved your point. The women volunteers can stay."

A few of the inmates, though, had concerns of their own about women coming into the cellblock. They didn't want to be near the female volunteers for fear they'd be tempted to say or do something inappropriate that would land them in trouble.

During one Thursday afternoon visit, JT told Marie, "I think the way the women volunteers interact with us can make all the difference. You've helped me think about women in a more wholesome way. Heck, I think your 'wholesome squareness' might even be rubbing off on me a little!"

"But you'd rather not turn into a total 'square'?" Marie asked, smiling.

JT grinned and shook his head.

Marie decided it was time to address the issue with the female volunteers and arranged a special meeting.

"Many of these inmates haven't even seen a woman in years," she reminded them. "They may say, 'Oh, you smell so good' or 'You look so fine' or 'Mmm, it's been a long time since I've been with a woman.' It may catch you off guard and make you uncomfortable. But it's to be expected. Never belittle them or put them down in any way. Be professional at all times and don't ever feed into suggestive comments. Simply say thank you and then ask about their family or their prison job or some other topic."

She had the women practice different responses to the types of comments Marie had heard herself. Then she tackled an even thornier topic.

"It's natural to feel a tug at your heart when you talk with these men. They're lonely and vulnerable, and many of them have had such difficult lives. They'll be so appreciative, complimenting you and thanking you for spending time with them. You may start to feel protective or motherly toward them. Or . . ." She paused to look at each of the women. "It's possible that you might feel like you're falling in love with one of them. If that happens, if you even think it might be happening, you must tell me immediately and you must stop volunteering in the prison."

AS THE FEMALE VOLUNTEERS tried to help the inmates adopt healthier attitudes toward women, John Brighton was breaking new ground by helping an inmate with his parole plan. When inmates were eligible for parole, they had to have a job and a place to live lined up before parole would be granted. Brighton had been meeting weekly with JT, who was up for parole, and found him bright and articulate. So Brighton offered to help him get a fresh start on the outside. JT had a tentative promise of a job with Keystone Legal Services, where he'd help process the numerous requests for legal assistance that they received from inmates. Brighton asked fellow Quakers to consider providing living quarters for JT, but soon decided to offer him a home with his own family. JT was paroled and moved in with the Brightons in April 1976. The arrangement lasted two months.

Repeating the pattern he had fallen into for more than two decades, JT committed yet another burglary. Though he'd once admitted that he liked the cat and mouse game of committing a crime, then hiding out and eluding the police, this time he'd seriously miscalculated. He robbed a coin shop located right across the street from the police station. Worse, the shop had an alarm system that was connected directly to the police. JT was caught shortly after fleeing the shop and taken to the Centre County Jail. From there, he called Brighton, asking his host to fabricate an alibi that would get JT released. Brighton refused. It was the end of their relationship.

B Block North staff (left to right): Sergeant Kline, Sergeant Houser, John McCullough, Captain Pratt, and Jeffrey Beard (1976). Photo courtesy of CentrePeace, Inc.

WHILE MARIE, BRIGHTON, and the other volunteers wrestled with these issues, the inmates and staff on B Block were beleaguered with serious growing pains in the program. The therapeutic community (TC) concept was new to staff, administration, and inmates alike, and the B Block North program was the first implementation at Rockview. It was viewed with suspicion by some and trumpeted as a model of progressive rehabilitation by others.

The men had published a detailed resident handbook for them-selves, outlining house rules, daily schedules, disciplinary procedures, and resident roles and responsibilities. All B Block residents were to be guided by the philosophy and principles they'd crafted together:

> We, in order to help ourselves through helping each other, have bound ourselves together into one common body: A body of men who contribute to each others' growth and well-being, individu-ally and as a whole, through honesty, communication, and deter-mination for the betterment of all concerned. For freedom to be truly enjoyed, it must be interrupted, and our purpose is to use this opportunity to better ourselves through each other, so we may have a better and more productive freedom when it arrives.[3]

However, in the bicentennial summer of 1976, the path to free-dom for the men of B Block North turned out to be filled with land-mines. B Block's sixty residents were a motley mix of young and old; educated and illiterate; black, white, and Hispanic; Christian, Jew, Muslim, and atheist. They were serving sentences ranging from two to five years to life for crimes including rape, armed robbery, drug deal-ing, drug possession, burglary, murder, and car theft. With staff-assigned monikers like "Viper," "Hound," "Misfit," and "Devil," they were as unique and challenging as their nicknames. And the group was constantly changing as men who had fulfilled the program re-quirements were released, paroled, or transferred to community-based residential centers, and others were brought in from the general prison population to fill vacancies. A few inmates who had been unable or unwilling to play by the TC rules were kicked out and sent back. Group dynamics among residents and staff were in constant flux. And they faced their first major loss of a staff member—their beloved Ser-geant Houser would soon retire.

Since the pre-release program had started, the men had gone through cycles of aggressive infighting and backbiting, bored indif-ference, and repentant striving to do better. This was the environment in which John McCullough, Greg Gaertner, and others worked daily, between the volunteers' weekly visits.

The visitation program's structure meant that volunteers spent most of their time listening to inmates, which made them naturally sympathetic to the men's issues and complaints. They knew little of the staff members' perspectives or even of what really went on in the block from day to day, making it easy for a few experienced con men on the block to manipulate this situation to their own advantage. On an unseasonably cool afternoon in July 1976, things heated up in B Block North.

When the volunteers arrived for their weekly visit, they were stopped immediately. After a long, awkward moment, the guard let them in and told the volunteers to sit at the tables that ran down the middle of the block. The inmates were lined up along one side of the block and staff members lined the other. None of the inmates would look at Marie or the other volunteers. The staff looked tense.

McCullough cleared his throat before addressing the volunteers. "We understand that some of the inmates have talked with you about things they want that will make life more comfortable for them here, and you've agreed they should have those things."

"Yes, that's true," Marie replied cautiously.

"Have you discussed these matters with the staff for their input and approval?" McCullough asked.

Marie took a deep breath. "Well, no."

"Exactly whose side are you on, then?" McCullough demanded. "The side of the staff or that of the inmates?"

Suddenly, Marie grasped what was happening, but had no idea what to say. She slowly got to her feet, stalling for time while she uttered a silent prayer: *This one's for you, God.*

She felt the eyes of inmates, staff, and volunteers on her. "We care about the inmates," she said, "*and* we care about the staff . . . we are neutral." She sat back down.

A long beat of silence passed before McCullough responded. "Okay. Your visits may continue."

During the afternoon's group discussion, the inmates asked what could be done about the requests they'd made to the volunteers.

"We'll be happy to provide things that could make life more comfortable for the men," Marie offered.

"We can't have you volunteers playing 'Lord and Lady Bountiful,'" McCullough argued. "If you give them every little thing they want, it will set an undesirable and antitherapeutic precedent of dependency. I don't want a rampant 'gimme' culture developing in here."

"That's not fair!" one inmate retorted.

"The staff here doesn't care about us the way the volunteers do!" another added.

The meeting quickly escalated into a series of increasingly personal attacks and counterattacks until the dissension reached fever-pitch, with inmates confronting staff in front of the volunteers, an unpardonable and serious breach. Abruptly, McCullough told the volunteers they needed to leave.

Too shocked to reply, Marie stood and quietly left. The other volunteers followed. No one said a word as they were escorted back across the prison grounds to the gate. Once outside, all their pent-up emotions spilled over—frustration at being dismissed so abruptly, confusion about how their simple offer of help had become such an explosive issue, disappointment that the conflict was left unresolved.

"What a messed up system," said Ken Wilkinson.

"We should stop going back in there," Brighton suggested. "That would make a real statement to the administration."

"I don't think the prison administration would miss us for one second," Marie answered. "The men are the only ones who would be hurt if we didn't go back."

"Yes, but the prison isn't really helping them," Ruffner argued. "The whole place should be shut down."

Everyone murmured in agreement.

"You're right, Larry. Unfortunately, I don't think that will ever happen until there's some kind of alternative to prison." Marie suddenly felt exhausted. The looks on the others' faces indicated that they felt the same way.

"Why don't we all go home, cool off, and try again next week," she suggested.

During the week, John Brighton and Marie talked at length about the volunteer program, about what had happened with JT, and about the previous week's showdown. Brighton thought it was time to address some of the issues the volunteers saw with the program, and Marie agreed.

The following Thursday, the volunteers returned to B Block. When the inmates, volunteers, and staff had all gotten situated at the long tables that filled the center of the block, John Brighton stood up.

"I'd like to read a letter I've written to all of you," he said. Marie prayed that what he was about to say would be well-received.

Brighton cleared his throat, and started reading.

I have been concerned for some time about the Pre-Release Program. I have been trying to determine what it is all about and what my role is in it. I have met with some frustration with both of these. One factor which has been of growing concern for me is that I recently heard that the volunteers are not supposed to be into prison reform. It just doesn't make sense to me that anyone who is working as a volunteer in this program would not be interested in trying to understand and improve the program. The very existence of a new Pre-Release Program is a kind of prison reform. In my opinion, we should all be trying to make it better.[4]

As Brighton continued reading, he urged the inmates to focus on helping themselves, to avoid blaming "the system" or other people for the mess in which they found themselves, and to continue trying to improve the system when necessary, through reasonable, well-thought-out, written requests. He encouraged John McCullough to be responsive to requests made by the men, and to assume that the men were making those requests responsibly and in good faith, rather than as a cover-up for their inability to deal with their own shortcomings. He pointed out that the volunteers were "safely in the middle," where they could get out any time (unlike the residents) and didn't have jobs to protect or order to maintain (unlike the staff).

"The purpose of the therapeutic community is for each of us to learn to be straight with ourselves and others—to become healthy so we can have a more fulfilling life. Why don't we all work together with mutual respect to try to achieve that?" Brighton concluded, then sat down.

The room was silent. Marie saw a few men nodding in agreement, while others looked surprised. In their discussion groups that afternoon, the men of B Block concluded that what they needed more than

Volunteers and staff at Sgt. Houser's retirement party. Back row, left to right: Bill Schrader, Ireene Jones, Elmore Browne, Cindy Duffee, and John Brighton. Front row, left to right: Ken Condo, Marie Hamilton, Marrianne Schrader, Sgt. Houser, LaVonne Ruffner, Deborah Hennehan, and John McCullough (July 1976). Photo courtesy of CentrePeace, Inc.

trinkets and goodies was more cohesion, care, and concern among themselves, and they promised to work harder at supporting each other. They also drafted an agreement with the staff and volunteers that, if the volunteers were still willing to donate a few things to make life more comfortable on the block, the men would decide what would benefit everyone and staff would review and approve reasonable requests. In the end, their requests were simple: subscriptions to *Field & Stream, Psychology Today,* and *Newsweek*; two floor fans to help alleviate the often unbearable heat in the cellblock; and a portable blackboard to use in discussion groups, classes, and house meetings. The volunteers were happy to provide the requested items. By the time Sergeant Houser's retirement party rolled around in late July, relative calm reigned between the B Block staff, residents, and volunteers.

Then Marie received a request that wasn't so simple.

RONALD[5] WAS A NEW resident in B Block. Marie had noticed during group discussions that he was unusually quiet, almost withdrawn. One Thursday, when she made a point of seeking him out, she discovered why.

"My wife died in a car accident a few months ago," he said, struggling to get the words out. "I didn't get to say goodbye or go to the funeral or anything."

He cleared his throat, then continued. "My little girl was in the car too and was hurt bad. She had to be in the hospital a long time. Now she's in a foster home. They told me she thinks I'm dead too. She's only seven and she hasn't seen me in such a long time." He stopped suddenly, staring out through one of the narrow barred windows. "I know it's a lot to ask, but . . . could you get someone to bring her here to see me—so she knows I'm not dead?"

Marie nodded, swallowing past the tightness in her throat before speaking. "Yes, Ronald. I'm sure the prison will have some way to get her here to see you."

When she went to John McCullough to plead Ronald's case, her optimism was quickly deflated.

"We only deal with the inmates, Marie. We don't do anything with the families," McCullough explained.

Marie's eyes widened, but she'd learned to stifle her reactions to prison policies. As she left Rockview that afternoon, she was stung again by her own ignorance, but determined to follow her cardinal rule for volunteers—deliver on your promises.

Ronald had given Marie the name of his daughter's caseworker in Pittsburgh. Marie's mind was already swirling with ideas when she returned to the VAC office. She shared Ronald's story with Ann Cook, then called the caseworker to discuss how to get Ronald's daughter to Rockview for a visit—nearly a three-hour drive from Pittsburgh.

"The foster mother is an older lady and I don't think she could make that long drive with the little girl herself," the caseworker told Marie. "But if you can find someone who would do the driving, I'll ask the foster mother to accompany Ronald's daughter."

Marie knew that local churches often provided drivers for the VAC's transportation program for the elderly. So she searched for phone numbers of churches near the Pittsburgh neighborhood where the girl lived. However, an afternoon of long-distance calls and telling Ronald's story countless times yielded nothing. Marie understood. Six hours in a car with two strangers, and several hours of waiting while they visited someone in a prison *was* a lot to ask.

Late that afternoon, Ann stuck her head into Marie's office. "How's it going?"

"No one's willing to drive here all the way from Pittsburgh," Marie said glumly.

"What about Greyhound?" Ann asked.

Marie laughed out loud. She could always count on Ann to see right to the heart of a situation and offer the simplest, most elegant solution.

"That's a brilliant idea! Thanks, Ann."

Ann shrugged. Marie found the number for the local Greyhound station in the phone book and placed the call. It would be a five-hour bus ride each way and would cost thirty dollars for the little girl and one adult. An early morning bus departing from Pittsburgh would get them to State College in time for afternoon visiting hours.

Although volunteers were to only make donations that would benefit all of the B Block residents, Marie thought Ronald's case was worthy of an exception. The other volunteers agreed and each of them contributed money to cover the bus fare. Marie called the girl's caseworker and offered funding and logistical coordination for the visit. The caseworker put her in touch with the foster mother.

On a sunny Wednesday afternoon in early September, an exuberant seven-year-old and her father, Ronald, were reunited for a few happy hours. When Marie visited Ronald the next afternoon, he was a changed man. Eyes twinkling, the proud father recounted everything his little girl had said and done in their afternoon together.

Marie wondered how many other inmates' families were unable to visit their loved ones. She asked prison staff about family visits and was shocked to learn that fewer than one-fourth of Rockview's inmates ever had visitors. For most families, money and distance were significant barriers. After talking with the other volunteers, and with Ann, Rose, and the VAC board, Marie called Dr. Mazurkiewicz to propose that the VAC create a program to help fund family visits to the prison. The superintendent heartily endorsed Marie's idea.

Rose Cologne suggested that they seek donations from Christian Mission, a coalition of local churches. Rose served on their board and offered to take a funding request to them. Working with John Mc-Cullough, Marie put together a three-page proposal outlining the need, the estimated number of families and inmates to be served, and the cost. They requested $1,000 for the first year of the program, and the board of Christian Mission agreed to fund it.

The Family Visitation Assistance program quickly became a bright thread of hope for dozens of men who had been cut off from their families. Through the program, wives, parents, children, fiancées, brothers, and sisters from Philadelphia, Pittsburgh, and numerous towns and rural areas in between visited their relatives at Rockview, many for the first time. One family traveled all the way from Buffalo, New York, to see their loved one for the first time since he'd been incarcerated years earlier.

Even the usually taciturn Dr. Mazurkiewicz wrote a heartfelt thank you letter to Christian Mission for funding the program.

IN DECEMBER, MAZURKIEWICZ wrote another letter—this time to the volunteers, inviting them to join him and the residents and staff of B Block for a Christmas social. They were also invited to bring their spouses. Marie asked Joe to come with her, but he refused. She went alone, determined to try and enjoy the evening anyway.

The residents had decorated the block, borrowed a record player and a selection of holiday records, and donated their own money to pay for a spread of sandwiches, chips, and soft drinks. Their pride in what they had achieved, individually and together, was evident in the way they carried themselves, their animated conversations, and the gallant way in which they welcomed their guests.

The evening's festivities included a play written and performed by the residents telling the story of a fictional inmate who is helped by the therapeutic community of B Block North. Poignant and funny, the play clearly mirrored the men's own feelings about the program.

Afterward, they served coffee, along with cookies and cakes that had been donated by the volunteers. As Marie looked around at the men's now-familiar faces, she was simultaneously exuberant, amazed, and relieved that the volunteer program had survived for a full year.

In a letter to the men a few weeks earlier to mark the first anniversary of the program, she'd written:

> Frankly, at first I had intended to visit only until I was familiar enough with the program to make proper volunteer referrals. . . . As I visited with you and you honestly shared your feelings and concerns . . . preconceived ideas disappeared one by one. . . . You welcomed the volunteers and made us feel comfortable and appreciated. There was an air of pride in Houser Hall and your dedication to helping each other sent me back to the community a more aware and dedicated person. . . . I wish to express my sincerest thanks for the most rewarding volunteer experience of my life. God bless you all.[6]

Toward the end of the evening, as she chatted with John McCullough, Marie couldn't help but smile, remembering their long-ago meeting in the Rotunda where he'd tested her and the other volunteers

Marie with inmates at a holiday social (circa 1976). Photo courtesy of CentrePeace, Inc.

to see if they were "shock-proof." The truth was, she had been shocked by much of what she'd learned about prisons and inmates in the last year, and if she'd had a crystal ball, she would have seen that there were many more shocks yet to come. But for the moment, it seemed safe to say, they were passing the test.

3
BREAKING BARRIERS

It is generally the [wo]man who doesn't know any better who does the things that can't be done. You see, the blamed fool doesn't know that it can't be done, so [s]he goes ahead and does it.

—Charles Austin Bates (1866–1897)

After the tumultuous first year of volunteering in prison, Marie and the others settled into a rhythm. Gradually they progressed from sitting in on group discussions to leading them, addressing topics like listening skills, family issues, values clarification, assertiveness, even a Dale Carnegie course taught by long-time Carnegie instructor and Rockview volunteer Joe Kirby. The inmates spent ten weeks in each group, then rotated to the next one.

Though Marie was starting to see tangible results of their volunteer efforts inside the prison, she realized the best solution would be to find alternatives to incarceration that would provide real help to those who committed crimes, so they wouldn't do it again. She knew that Ken Wilkinson, Rose Cologne, and John Brighton felt the same way.

The volunteers had been warned in no uncertain terms by Dr. Mazurkiewicz and John McCullough that prison reformers weren't welcome at Rockview. So, Marie, Rose, John Brighton, and Ken Wilkinson decided to address the issues from outside the prison. They gathered a few like-minded people, including Marie's pastor, Mike Scrogin, and Jim Fox, a professor in Penn State's Administration of Justice program.

Together, they formed an organization they named Community Alternatives in Criminal Justice (CACJ).

One of their first priorities was educating others about criminal justice issues. Several newspaper articles had been published about the prison volunteer program and responses from people in the community revealed that many knew little or nothing about what went on behind bars. Of course, the volunteers hadn't either until they'd started going into Rockview. But meeting and talking with inmates had changed their attitudes about who was behind bars and how they should be treated. They thought perhaps attitudes within the larger community would change too, if people were given the opportunity to meet some inmates and hear their stories.

The most dramatic example for Marie was an inmate named Rocky.[1] Rocky was serving time for rapes he'd committed in particularly heinous fashion. Among prison inmates, there's an informal but powerful class system, based on the type of crime each man has committed. Sex offenders are at the bottom of the prison hierarchy, considered by most other inmates to be the worst kind of criminals. Because of the horrifying nature of Rocky's crimes, even Officer Lou Matsick, who had extensive training and experience working with all kinds of inmates, had a hard time dealing with Rocky.

Rocky's family visited him only once. Marie helped them to make the arrangements through the Family Visitation Assistance program.

Afterward, Rocky's mother talked with Marie.

"I don't understand how my own son could have done what he did," his mother said, tears streaming down her cheeks. "I just can't come see him anymore. Would you please look after Rocky for me?"

Marie blinked back tears of her own and took a deep breath, quickly weighing what she was about to promise. She thought of her own two boys, now twelve and fourteen, and all of the hopes and dreams she had for them. Her heart quivered as she thought about the pain Rocky's mother must be feeling.

"Yes, I'll look after him for you," she told his mother quietly.

Marie had visited Rocky weekly ever since. She'd found that once she got to know him and heard his story, he was no longer Rocky the rapist, but Rocky the man with deep, internal scars. Rocky confided that his father's warped attitudes and abuses of women had distorted Rocky's thinking. His father had taken him along on numerous visits to prostitutes when Rocky was just a teen. Through all this, Marie saw Rocky desperately trying to relate to her in a healthier way.

Rocky told Marie that he had written a play about the path from life on the streets to life in prison. He and a group of inmates who had dubbed themselves the "Rockview Players" were rehearsing it. Marie asked John McCullough whether they could be brought out of the prison to perform somewhere in State College. Fortunately, protocols had already been established for such events, as the Rockview men's Glee Club performed at the Bellefonte High School each year. Dr. Mazurkiewicz approved Marie's request as long as four prison staff members would volunteer to chaperone the inmates on their own time.

The CACJ committee planned a community event for the Rockview Players to present their play. Mike Scrogin offered to host it at University Baptist and Brethren Church, which had a long history of involvement in social reform; pastors had conducted services at the local jail as far back as the 1940s.

Despite his uneasiness around Rocky, Lou Matsick volunteered to chaperone him and the Rockview Players. John McCullough and two other officers also volunteered, and the event was officially approved. Excitement mounted for the inmates as well as Marie and her fellow members of CACJ.

On a Sunday morning in April 1977, the Rockview Players performed their play, *Patches*, on the Fireside Room stage in the church basement. The lead character was an inmate named Patches, played by Rocky. Patches was released from prison and thrilled to get back home to the big city. But he was soon suckered into selling drugs and rearrested. Through street slang and realistic depictions of life on the streets, the men gave their small-town audience a poignant glimpse into the harsh realities of the urban world where most of the men had grown up. The play ended with Patches back in prison, where concerned fellow inmates in a therapeutic community helped him confront his behavior and taught him how to become a better person. The curtain closed to enthusiastic applause.

Afterward, the church hosted a potluck luncheon. Several inmates sat at each table with members of the community. Marie smiled as she watched Rocky across the room, in animated conversation with a group of church ladies. *How wonderful that they know nothing of his past and can get to know him simply as "Rocky,"* she thought.

The inmates seated at her table discussed religion with members of her church. Though Marie felt her role was not to try to convert inmates, but simply to model Christian principles, she said to these men, "I often wonder how someone who doesn't have a relationship with God can handle the kinds of things you've had to deal with."

"I don't know either," one inmate replied. Several others shook their heads.

Over lunch, the men shared their stories and answered questions with frankness and good humor. Even the four prison chaperones seemed touched to see their charges sitting side by side with local citizens, talking and even laughing. As Marie looked around the room, she prayed that a day would soon come when gatherings like this would happen regularly, and the walls of fear and suspicion between the imprisoned and the community would come tumbling down.

As people left, they thanked the CACJ committee profusely for the moving, eye-opening event. The overwhelmingly positive response inspired the committee to think even bigger.

Rockview's policies allowed for inmates to be furloughed for specific preapproved activities, assuming the inmates met all of the furlough criteria. Several of the volunteers had taken B Block inmates out to speak to civic groups. Marie had taken inmates with her to speak to church groups. She suggested that the CACJ committee request a group furlough for a larger number of inmates and invite the whole community to a day-long event.

They planned an ambitious itinerary with help from members of University Baptist and Brethren Church and Black Christian Fellowship. The day's activities would include individual families taking several inmates each to morning church services and then hosting them for lunch in their homes, followed by a community-wide afternoon gathering for softball and horseshoes and an evening picnic at Sunset Park. Hoping to eliminate the need for prison guards to accompany the inmates this time, seven of the prison volunteers offered to serve as chaperones and transport the men from the prison to each of the day's activities.

Marie wrote a letter to Dr. Mazurkiewicz, requesting a group furlough for twenty inmates. Knowing the prison's security concerns, Marie included with her letter a detailed agenda for the day, listing exactly which volunteers would be transporting inmates, where they'd be going, and when they would return to the prison.

Ten days later, Marie received a two-page reply from Jeffrey Beard, the young counselor supervisor she'd met at the first volunteer orientation at Rockview. Beard was now deputy superintendent for treatment at Rockview. In his letter, Beard explained that the primary purpose of furloughs was to help inmates and their families prepare for their return to the community. He questioned the therapeutic value of the event Marie had proposed. He said that the prison couldn't allocate staff time to process the necessary paperwork or prepare inmates for such an outing. Finally, Beard was concerned about the local response to having a large group of inmates out in the community. "I believe that the local authorities specifically and the community in general would frown upon such a proposal," he concluded.[2]

In a word, the answer was no.

DISAPPOINTED, BUT UNDAUNTED, the CACJ committee turned their attention to advocating for alternatives to incarceration. They had a ready-made case with JT, who was still in the Centre County Jail, awaiting sentencing for the coin shop robbery he'd committed while living with the Brightons. The CACJ committee knew that, given JT's history, he was likely to be sent back to the state prison. But they crafted an alternative plan for him, including housing, a job, and a network of people who would provide support and guidance to keep him on the straight and narrow. Though John Brighton's prior experience with JT was an unpleasant memory, he helped draft the plan.

Marie wrote a letter to Dr. Mazurkiewicz. She asked him to use his influence to recommend that JT be given another chance. Then they approached District Attorney Charles Brown to discuss the case and alternative sentencing.

Meanwhile, JT had contacted Marie to ask for help with issues at the county jail. Jail staff had refused to allow him access to the jail library, where they housed law books that he wanted to use. He also complained about the shoddy living conditions, food, and treatment of inmates at the jail.

"They could use a couple of squares like you in here to straighten things out, Marie."

Marie didn't know anyone from the jail, but she promised JT she'd try to help. She asked her mentors, Ann Cook and Rose Cologne, for advice. Rose suggested that she contact the Pennsylvania Prison Society.[3] The society had been established through the Pennsylvania General Assembly in 1787 to monitor prison conditions throughout Pennsylvania. Official Visitors, members of the society, investigate inmate complaints regarding treatment, living conditions, and other issues, and advocate for just and humane treatment. By law, Official Visitors are guaranteed access to all Pennsylvania correctional facilities and have the legal right to visit privately with any inmate in any Pennsylvania prison, any day of the week, without prior notice or approval.

Marie contacted the Prison Society and was put in touch with Major John Case, their field director, who asked Marie to set up a meeting with the wardens at the Centre County Jail. Marie and Major Case met with the wardens there and reported the issues JT was experiencing. The wardens knew of Marie's work at Rockview and assumed she wanted to start a similar volunteer program at the jail. Though that wasn't quite what Marie and Major Case had in mind, they concluded that getting volunteers into the jail on a weekly basis might be just the thing to prompt improvements there.

Marie and Major Case decided to set up the program as a branch of the Prison Society so that the volunteers couldn't ever be denied access to the jail.

With help from Rose, Marie recruited another group of volunteers and gave them an orientation to prison volunteering. She, Rose, and the volunteers began to visit the Centre County Jail every Tuesday evening. The jail staff agreed to allow any interested inmate to attend the weekly sessions. JT was a regular participant and seemed to relish educating the volunteers on jailhouse politics and offering "inside" advice on how they could get issues addressed. Initially, the volunteers simply held group discussions with the inmates, in a format similar to the Rockview program, but were soon organizing seminars and guest speakers on any topic of interest to the inmates. However, the Prison Society's regulations stipulated that a written report of every visit had to be sent to their headquarters in Philadelphia. Marie was designated the "convener" of the Prison Society branch and filed the required reports to the Prison Society.

JT finally had his own day in court. Despite all the effort Marie and the others from CACJ had put into advocating for JT, the alternative sentence they had requested for him was denied. JT was sent back to Rockview. Though he wasn't on B Block North, JT stayed in touch with Marie through frequent letters.

With all of the correspondence from inmates, two volunteer visitation programs, and the Family Visitation Assistance program to manage, Marie had little time left over to carry out her general volunteer recruiting duties at the Voluntary Action Center. She suggested that the VAC designate a coordinator specifically for the prison programs. The board asked to accompany the Rockview volunteers on one of their weekly visits to see the program firsthand. Marie made the necessary arrangements with Dr. Mazurkiewicz, and seven VAC board members visited B Block for an afternoon. Hearing from inmates about the importance of volunteer visits from inmates solidified the VAC's commitment to the prison programs. They agreed to formally change Marie's title to coordinator of Volunteers in Prison.

Marie also continued to play a significant role in the work of CACJ. They met regularly with local attorneys and judges to advocate for alternatives to incarceration. Marie met Richard M. Sharp in the fall of 1977, when he was running for a Centre County judgeship. Sharp asked for Marie's vote.

"I'll vote for you if you'll promise to come do some time in prison with me and our volunteers once you're elected," she countered.

Sharp laughed, never imagining that she was serious.

District Attorney Charles Brown was also running for judge and Marie invited him to visit B Block North and talk with the inmates. Brown agreed and spent a Thursday afternoon in the cellblock with the volunteers and inmates. The inmates asked tough questions about his stand on various criminal justice issues, and he answered each one.

The local elections for judge generated a lot of community discussion of criminal justice issues, and the CACJ committee members saw another opportunity to further educate the public. They organized a five-part Criminal Justice Forum, with a series of speakers. Pastor Mike Scrogin offered once again to host the forum at the church.

Major Case from the Prison Society kicked off the forum, talking about his experience during fourteen years as the warden of the Bucks County Jail and the prison volunteer program he had started there. A local attorney explained the criminal justice process, from the point of arrest to sentencing. John Brighton talked frankly about the ups and downs of prison volunteering and his experience with JT during his brief parole.

Marie obtained permission from Dr. Mazurkiewicz for three Rockview inmates to speak at one of the forums about their prison experience and the value of volunteers. One of those inmates was Butch,[4] who had come into B Block earlier that year. He was in the ninth year of a twelve- to thirty-six-year sentence. Butch had initially been cold, suspicious, and defensive toward Marie and the other volunteers. "I wondered about their motives and intentions," he said. "Then, I watched, amazed, as other inmates flocked around the volunteers, openly smiling, laughing, and talking with genuine trust and delight." It had been a turning point for him, Butch reported.

The final forum addressed the big question: "Crime and Punishment: What's Wrong and What Can Be Done?" Once again, the community response was very positive. Marie felt good about the light they were shedding on the problems in the system while chipping away at those problems from the inside.

Several of the inmates had become such an important part of her life that she couldn't imagine stopping the prison work. Rocky was quickly becoming one of them. Despite his terrible past, Marie cared

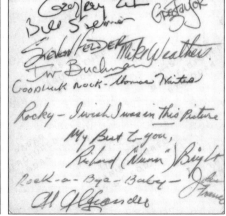

In November 1977, Superintendent Mazurkiewicz allowed the filming of "On the Yard," a documentary based on a book by Malcolm Braly, inside Rockview. Marie's friend, Rocky, assisted the film crew and asked them for a signed photo to give to Marie as a gift. Photo courtesy of CentrePeace, Inc.

deeply about him and delighted in all of the ways she saw him opening up.

December's holiday social marked the second anniversary of the B
Block volunteer program. Rocky and Butch both played important
roles in the evening's festivities—Rocky as coat checker and disc
jockey, and Butch as part of a singing trio that performed a musical
tribute to the volunteers, showing the men's profound appreciation
for the time and effort they gave so generously.

Soon after the new year, Rocky left B Block North to return to a
regular cellblock. Marie knew he hadn't liked B Block's "pull up" system and felt there was a lot of favoritism in the way things were handled in the therapeutic community.

"I know I have let some of you down and I'm sorry," Rocky wrote
in a letter to the volunteers, "but I couldn't take a lot of the under-
handed stuff that was going on over there. I have the opportunity to
return, but I don't think I will. I just want all of you to know that you
have helped a lot and I will always remember you as the world I have
always dreamed about. You have taught me what it means to be loved
and to return love, something I've never known. You have given me
the part of my life that was always missing."[5]

True to her promise to Rocky's mother, Marie continued to visit
Rocky every week after he left B Block, using her Prison Society Official Visitor card to get in to see him. Within a few months, Rocky said
he missed the volunteers and returned to B Block.

Later in the spring of 1978, Marie met up with Richard Sharp
again, in his newly elected position as president judge of the Centre
County Court of Common Pleas. She asked how he liked the new job.
Sharp was generally happy, but was really struggling with one of his
newest cases.

"There's this young man who has been in and out of court so many
times, and he's caused a lot of trouble," Sharp explained. "I just don't
know what to do with him, how to get him to straighten out. So, I'm

thinking about sentencing him to the state prison. Maybe he'll finally learn a lesson and will get some help there."

"Have you ever been inside a prison, Judge Sharp?" Marie asked.

"No, I never have."

"I hope you don't think anyone gets rehabilitated or gets any real help in prison," Marie told him. "Sending people to prison doesn't do *any* of the things you think it does. Why don't you come along into the cellblock at Rockview with me and see?"

That summer, he accompanied Marie into the cellblock. He spent a Thursday afternoon on B Block North with fifteen inmates who were in Marie's weekly discussion group.

"Tell me about your prison experience," Sharp said to the men. "Don't tell me about the bad food or the administration of the prison. I want to know about *you*. Tell me your name and tell me what being in prison has done for you or to you."

One by one, the men shared their stories.

"I can't make decisions any more. All the decisions are made for us here and I don't remember how to make them on my own," one man told the judge.

Another said, "I've lost all contact with my family. They've forgotten me. I don't even know where they are. I don't know where my children are."

"I've been here so long I'm afraid to go out into society. I didn't do too well before I came in and after being in here so long, I'm afraid to go back out there and try to make it on my own now."

"Least you got a chance of gettin' out," said another. "I been here since I was seventeen years old, sentenced to life in prison. Judge told me if I kept my nose clean and worked hard, I could hope to have my sentence reduced someday. But I already been here twenty years. Been denied commutation[6] every time I tried. I'm afraid I'm going to die here. And I never even got to have a real life on the outside."

Finally, Butch spoke up, offering a carefully crafted speech about his own observations of prison life. It was a speech Butch had continually refined and given to everyone who would listen during his ten years in prison. "Prison doesn't rehabilitate—it assimilates. Prison alters the qualities of a man's character that allow him to feel special about himself, that allow him to be a creative, effective, viable human being— leaving in its stead a dull, bitter, resentful man, bent on the self-destruction of his own humaneness. Prison takes away the essence of human experience—the choices, the decision making, even the sense of wholeness he has with his family. It punishes him *and* his loved ones. It destroys his confidence and distorts his sense of trust in others. The only thing worse than prison is the misguided motives of those who advocate and encourage imprisonment."

There was a long silence after Butch finished. Judge Sharp nodded thoughtfully, then summarized what he had heard from the men.

"Gentlemen, thank you for your willingness to talk with me." As he stood up to leave, Sharp looked around the circle at each man one more time. "I promise you that never, ever again will I send anyone to prison believing that he will receive help here."

Sharp's promise was more than Marie had dared to hope for.

WITH JUDGE SHARP'S visit, Marie and the volunteers had logged over 125 weekly visits to B Block, touching the lives of several hundred inmates. The inmates touched the volunteers' lives as well and they celebrated with each man who was released. The letters of appreciation they received from the men were the only evidence the volunteers needed of the importance of their work, despite all the barriers and frustrations. One inmate, a leader within the block, spoke for many of the men in a letter he sent to the volunteers just before his parole:

> There are many of us who have never had anyone to care about us the way that you do. It is very hard for us to understand—some of us say 'Why? Why are they doing this for us?'

To see and feel real love and concern sometimes is a hard thing to accept when you have never had it before. Some of us are frightened to open up because the love and concern has always been taken away and the only thing that is left is the hurt of how it was—so we close off and say 'I don't want to be hurt again' or 'I will push them away so that they can't hurt me, if they don't like me, they can't hurt me.' But we are learning because of this program and your organization. Thank you for caring about us and thank you for being concerned about what happens to us. You are making us feel again.

Tyrone[7]

Between the Rockview and Centre County Jail visitation programs and the CACJ initiatives, Marie felt good about their progress—helping inmates develop important skills, inspiring prison and jail staff to make improvements, changing perceptions within the community about the prison system, even making small inroads toward alternatives to incarceration. But she was also exhausted. She came down with the flu in the summer of 1978 and missed weekly visits in B Block for the first time in two and a half years. It took her weeks to recover.

4

Maxed Out

He that can have Patience, can have what he will.
—Benjamin Franklin (1706–1790)

Dear Marie, Hope you're feeling better soon. . . . I feel the pain when you are sick. From all your friends in BBN," the card read. It was signed by each of the men on B Block North. Rocky's signature was at the top of the list. Marie sighed as she leaned back in the easy chair in her darkened living room.

She closed her eyes, trying to ignore the dust, clutter, dirty dishes, and laundry that had piled up. She'd always prided herself on keeping an immaculate house. But with two teenage boys and a nearly full-time volunteer position, it was a challenge even when she was healthy.

For now, the housework would have to wait. Marie had to get to the VAC office.

She needed to contact the Rockview volunteers and let them know she'd rejoin them for the next afternoon's visit to B Block. They'd done a wonderful job of keeping things going in her absence. Several Penn State University students had joined the volunteer group over the past few months and Marie had welcomed their youthful energy and enthusiasm. Most were criminal justice majors and seemed anxious to learn about the prison system.

She also had to respond to letters from inmates that had piled up while she had been sick. Marie received an average of eight to ten letters a day. When she reached the office, she quickly skimmed through the stack.

Most were requests for help with furloughs and parole plans. Marie had compiled a list of agencies around the state that provided services to inmates, parolees, and their families, so that she had a qualified place to which she could refer them.

One inmate asked for legal help and enclosed documents from his case file. Marie responded as she always did to such letters: "I am not trained in the legal field and would probably do more harm than good." She gave him the name of a legal services agency that served inmates.

An inmate she'd never met had written to ask her to contact the parole board on his behalf and recommend him for parole. Marie wrote back, saying she was sorry she couldn't do so, since she didn't know him. She was careful never to promise anything she couldn't do.

Another asked to be matched with a pen pal. Marie sent him a list of pen pal programs. She had told her volunteers not to agree to be pen pals with inmates. She'd learned that pen pal letters from inmates often morphed into requests for money, favors, or gifts, or attempts by the inmate to develop a more intimate relationship with a volunteer.

As usual, there were a few love letters in the pile, one from an inmate she'd never even met. She had learned that among every prison's network of underground entrepreneurs were professional "love letter writers" who would craft flowery prose to a lady of one's choice in exchange for a pack of cigarettes. Many of the love letters she'd received were astonishingly beautiful; all were touching. She understood that profound loneliness was at the root of the inmates' declarations of love. In her replies, she always thanked the men for their kind words, then said that her commitment was to the Volunteers in Prison program. She never breathed a word about these letters to Joe.

Regardless of the type of letter, she responded to each one. She typed each response using two sheets of typing paper with carbon paper in between, then filed the inmate's letter along with the carbon copy of her response in the burgeoning file cabinet in her office.

There was only one letter she would not answer. It was from an inmate she'd never met, but who wrote to her regularly, asking her to help him get out of prison. Over many months, his letters had vacillated bizarrely from sweet and flattering to rude and threatening. After receiving numerous letters from him, she was able to recognize his handwriting and didn't even open his letters any more. She had told John McCullough about her concerns. McCullough had admitted that he thought that particular inmate, who was serving time for murder, would probably kill again if he was released and that, given his history, he was most likely to kill a woman. McCullough had assured Marie that they'd let her know if the inmate was to be released from prison.

It was one of the few situations in her prison work that had made Marie uneasy. She felt safer inside the prison than she did in some places on the outside. And she knew that, inside the prison, she and the volunteers were safer than the guards and staff, because the inmates respected and trusted the volunteers and would protect them. Over the years, a few guards had told her that their biggest fear was that they might die inside the prison. Many inmates were afraid of the very same thing.

Some inmates tried to end their own lives. Snooky[1] had been one of them. He had a drug problem, and he had been in and out of jail so often that his wife said she couldn't see him through another jail term. He was at the Centre County Jail now, awaiting sentencing for another round of drug charges. This time he'd become suicidal, swallowing broken pencils trying to end his life. His wife had called Marie and asked her to go in and talk with him.

Marie's own experience with depression and suicidal thoughts early in her marriage had helped her to understand Snooky. She felt a special kinship with him and, despite his depression, the two of them usually found something to laugh about.

After finishing her correspondence, Marie went to visit Snooky. When he shuffled into the crowded visiting room at the jail, she was shocked to see what bad shape he was in. Though Marie had decided early in her prison work not to talk about religion with inmates unless they initiated the conversation, she felt she needed to make an exception when she saw Snooky's condition. She didn't know how else to help him.

"Tonight, I want you to talk to God, Snooky, whether you believe in him or not. Just say 'If you are real, make yourself known to me. If you are real, help me.' You must ask and you will get a response," she told him. "Will you do that?"

Snooky nodded. Marie gave his hand a quick squeeze, looking around to be sure the guards didn't see her. If caught, they might reprimand her or, worse, put Snooky under heavy surveillance fearing he'd received contraband in that quick exchange. Marie knew Snooky would be strip-searched after leaving the visiting room—standard procedure for every inmate after contact with outsiders. What she really wanted to do was give him a hug. If anyone ever needed a hug, Snooky surely did. But such physical contact between inmates and outsiders was forbidden.

She told Snooky she'd be back to visit him again soon, then headed home, exhausted.

The next afternoon, when Marie met the other volunteers for their usual lunch before going to Rockview, none of the Penn State students were there. Over lunch, the volunteers brought Marie up to date on what was happening with the inmates. They shared who was out on furlough, who had been in trouble for one issue or another, and who was getting ready for their parole hearings. Then they gathered their belongings and piled into cars to drive to the prison.

As they walked across the prison yard and approached B Block, Marie saw dozens of inmates standing at the entrance. She thought perhaps they were there to greet her after her absence, but as they got closer she realized something was wrong. None of the inmates was talking or smiling as they usually did when they saw the volunteers coming. Most had their arms crossed over their chests and stood with their feet wide apart. Marie moved to the front of the group of volunteers. She looked first at one inmate, then another. Their expressions were cold, angry.

"Hello, Marcus,"[2] she said gently. "It's nice to see you again, Larry."[3] She smiled and nodded, looking each man in the eyes, and continued slowly walking toward them.

"William,[4] how have you been? Hi, Robert."[5]

She greeted the men, one by one, and one by one they stepped aside and allowed her and the volunteers to pass. The other volunteers followed her lead, quietly acknowledging each man as they walked into the crowd. Once they were inside the cellblock, there was a tense silence.

JT was the first to speak.

"We got letters from the student volunteers, saying they weren't coming in any more," he explained. "They said one of their professors told them that by volunteering here they were supporting a corrupt prison system, and that if they stopped volunteering, the prison would finally collapse under the weight of its own corruption."

Other inmates were nodding and murmuring.

"They said we shouldn't let the rest of you come in here anymore, either," JT concluded with a shrug.

Marie sat quietly for a few moments, trying to decide how to respond.

"Well, what do all of *you* think?" she asked the men. "Should we stop coming in?"

A chorus of "no's" and emphatic headshaking answered her question.

She looked around at the other volunteers. The tension seemed to be draining from their faces. She took a deep breath and smiled.

"Okay, then," she said brightly, "let's get started with our discussion groups, shall we?"

As the volunteers left Rockview that day, Marie reminded them, as she often did, that each visit to the prison could be their last. So many things could go wrong. Any one of them might say something that would be misinterpreted or do something that would cause problems, or an inmate might report something that would raise concerns among the staff about the volunteer program. What had just happened was a vivid reminder of how quickly the program could disintegrate and how tentative their hold was, even after nearly three years of dedicated service.

The following Thursday afternoon, John McCullough pulled Marie aside.

"Dr. Mazurkiewicz heard about what happened with the Penn State students. Effective immediately, he said there are to be no more Penn State student volunteers. I've contacted each of them and told them not to come back."

Marie nodded, though inside she felt like they'd all just taken a big step backward from the progress they'd made in tearing down the walls between corrections and the community.

PART OF HER ROLE as convener of the Prison Society branch at the Centre County Jail was to document inmate complaints and send detailed reports to the Prison Society. She and Rose often went to the jail together for the weekly visits, and then went back to Rose's house afterward to do some brainstorming about the best way to address the issues.

Sometimes they found that simply listening to an inmate's concerns and helping them come up with possible solutions was enough to put the issue to rest. They often tried to help inmates look at situations from the staff's perspective. At other times, they'd talk with the staff to see what could be done to improve things for the inmates.

Inmate concerns ranged from small matters related to food and daily routines to more serious issues such as violations of inmates' civil rights or other abuses.

One Tuesday evening's visit to the county jail was consumed by inmates' complaints about their socks.

"Every pair they've given me has holes in the toes," one inmate reported.

"It's not just the holes. . . . I can't get two socks that match," another added.

"Maybe it seems like a little thing, but it's just one more humiliation we have to put up with in here," said a third.

As they always did, Marie and Rose listened carefully, took notes, and said they'd see what they could do.

Sometimes inmates asked Marie and Rose to visit them privately to discuss more personal issues. When they received these requests, they were allowed to visit the inmate in his cell. The inmates were often surprised to see Rose and Marie walking right into an inmate's cell. Soon inmates were referring to the two women as "Batman and Robin." Rose and Marie never knew which one of them was Batman and which was Robin, but they loved their nicknames.

On one such visit, an inmate told the women, "I haven't been allowed to see my little girl in months and months."

"Why not?" Rose asked.

"The jail only allows visitors one night a week, and they have to be eighteen or older."

Rose Cologne at a Voluntary Action Center meeting. Rose said her epitaph should read, "Off to another meeting" (circa 1975). Photo courtesy of Marie Hamilton.

That was a clear violation of the state's "Minimum Standards and Operating Procedures" for family visitation. Marie made a note to bring it up, along with several other serious issues inmates had reported, at the next meeting of the Centre County Prison Board. Judge Richard Sharp, the wardens, the county commissioners, and the local sheriff served on the board.

At the Prison Board meeting, Marie raised the family visitation issue and cited the state-established minimum standard that inmates' children were to be allowed to visit with an accompanying adult. She and Rose had also been told that inmates were not getting access to the jail library, as required by the state. At first the warden denied it, but then said that if he had more staff he could get inmates to the library. Other inmates had reported that, for several months, they hadn't been allowed outside for daily recreation. Their only recreation time had been on weekends, in a small room in the jail's basement. Marie knew that a lack of structured recreation and outdoor time could lead to more fights among inmates, so she cited the state's guidelines of at least two hours daily of physical exercise outdoors, weather permitting.

"We don't need you to tell us how to run the jail," one warden said bluntly.

"I'm merely quoting from the state's 'Minimum Standards and Operating Procedures' for Pennsylvania jails," Marie replied.

Judge Sharp turned to the warden. "Do you have a copy of those standards?"

"No," he replied.

"Marie, can you see that the warden gets a copy of the standards?" Sharp asked.

"I'll see to it right away."

At the next meeting, the warden announced that he'd hired additional guards to accompany inmates to the library. He had also reinstated outdoor recreation time and changed the visitation policy to allow inmates' children to visit.

When necessary, Marie and Rose involved the Prison Society in resolving issues, but they preferred to handle problems locally, without outside intervention. They tried to balance the needs of both staff and inmates, and were usually able to find amicable solutions. Once, when inmates complained that their bedding and clothes weren't being washed, Marie got permission for the Prison Society branch to get a washer and dryer installed at the jail for the inmates' use.

Word spread about the volunteer visitation programs, and Marie received requests to start additional programs. Inmates in Rockview's "Unity House" cellblock next to B Block North asked if volunteers could visit them every week as well.

Snooky had been sentenced to the Huntingdon state prison and told the leaders of Community First Step (CFS), an inmate organization at Huntingdon, about the weekly volunteer visits at the Centre County Jail. The president of CFS wrote to Marie and asked whether she could start a volunteer program at Huntingdon. Marie contacted Major Case at the Prison Society, and Case made the arrangements with Huntingdon's superintendent, Ronald Marks, to establish another Prison Society branch there. Marie recruited volunteers from Stone Church of the Brethren in Huntingdon, and the new Prison Society branch at Huntingdon was up and running.

Pastor Ray Hill from the Lewistown congregation also contacted Marie and asked for her help setting up a Prison Society branch there. With three branches in place, the society asked Marie to act as an area representative to oversee the branches, and invited her to serve on their board of directors. Marie agreed, and Rose took over as convener of the Centre County Jail branch.

Outside the prisons, CACJ focused their efforts on alternative sentencing programs, working with local judges to implement them. Their Pre-Trial Intervention program enabled people charged with first-time and minor offenses, referred by District Attorney Charles Brown, to complete a program of community-based supervision and supportive services. If the offender successfully completed the program, their charges would be dismissed. Judge Sharp helped CACJ establish a Community Service program where certain types of nonviolent offenders could be sentenced to community service instead of jail time. CACJ established agreements with local nonprofit organizations who agreed to accept such offenders as volunteers, and instituted a process to match offenders with appropriate volunteer assignments.

Marie invited people from the newly established Prison Society branches to attend CACJ meetings to discuss expanding these alternative sentencing programs to other places. Superintendent Marks drove up from the Huntingdon prison to attend one meeting and talked with Marie afterward.

"I'm impressed with what you're doing here, Marie," he told her. "I really believe in finding alternatives to prison. If there's ever anything I can do to help advance your efforts, please let me know."

"Oh, I surely will," Marie told Marks with a laugh.

Marks laughed too. "Knowing you, Marie, I have no doubt I'll be hearing from you."

MARIE'S VOLUNTEER WORK was now more than a full-time endeavor. She needed help to keep up with all of it. Bob Gross, from the Church of the Brethren's Death Row Support Project, visited Marie and she briefed him on the work of CACJ and Volunteers in Prison. Bob recommended that Marie apply for a BVS volunteer to serve as her assistant for a year. BVS approved her request and her new, young assistant, Gary Dean, arrived in November 1978. Local church members offered free room and board for the BVS volunteer. He quickly jumped in to help Marie with every aspect of her prison work. Gary joined the Prison Society and became an Official Visitor so he'd have ready access to the prison and the jail.

With all of the travel and other expenses associated with her prison work, Marie also needed funding. She approached several organizations and was able to secure small donations to help defray expenses. Marie's prison efforts were becoming widely recognized within the Church of the Brethren, and in 1979 she was asked to serve as the criminal justice reform representative for the Middle Pennsylvania District. She traveled all over the district, speaking at churches about the need for prison reform and urging other Brethren to get involved. The district was very pleased and offered to help fund her work. Marie gratefully accepted.

Many Quakers had also been deeply involved in Marie's prison work, from Rose Cologne and John Brighton to Rockview volunteer Warren Smith. Warren had told Marie about a course called "Alternatives to Violence" that some Quakers had designed to teach in the New York prison system. The program had been designed so that inmates could teach it to other inmates. Warren suggested inviting the Quakers to come to State College to teach the program to the Rockview volunteers. In March 1979, Marie and several volunteers spent two full weekends taking the course and learning how to teach it to others. On the last day of the course, the volunteers were asked to write some short- and long-term goals for what they'd like to do with the course. Marie wrote that she'd like to teach the course in every prison in Pennsylvania. She realized how ambitious it sounded when she shared her goal with the others, but they agreed to start with Rockview and see how it went. Marie promised to draft a proposal to the prison administration, though she wondered how she'd find time to add one more thing to her long list of obligations.

Time wasn't Marie's only challenge. She was so emotionally drained trying to meet the needs of inmates and volunteers, that when she got home each evening she barely had enough energy left over to focus on her own family.

One evening, Marie noticed that Steve was wearing one blue sock and one gray one.

"Why are you wearing two different socks?" she asked.

"I can never find two clean socks that match, so I've started a new trend," he said with a laugh.

"At least yours don't have holes in them," Mike chimed in, sticking one foot out from under the table where he sat doing his homework.

Guilt dropped over Marie like a shroud. She'd spent hours making sure inmates got decent socks, but hadn't done the same for her own sons.

She realized she was "maxed out."[6] She lay awake most of that night, agonizing over what to do. She had never felt as fulfilled as she did with her work on behalf of inmates. But she dearly loved her sons and husband and felt they needed her more. By morning, she knew what she had to do.

As soon as she got to the VAC office, Marie went to talk with Ann.

"Sounds like you need a 'prison break,'" Ann said, getting right to the heart of the matter as usual. Marie blinked back tears, as she smiled at Ann's pun.

"Do whatever you need to do. Your family and your own health must come first."

Marie went to her desk and sat quietly looking out the window for a while. Then she sighed and rolled two sheets of typing paper with a carbon sheet between them into her typewriter.

Gentlemen:

This letter is to inform you that I am taking a short vacation from my volunteer work after a period of five years, three of which involved visiting each Thursday in Houser Hall. Because of the honest sharing I received and the many friends I've made there, a deep dedication to prison visitation and alternatives to prison has been instilled in me. I want you to know that I will miss the visits very much and I intend to be back as soon as I take care of some immediate family responsibilities.

Marie stopped typing for a minute. She thought about all they'd accomplished through the volunteer visits at Rockview. They'd learned so much and come so far. The volunteers were a dedicated bunch and Marie was confident they'd continue to serve the B Block inmates very well without her involvement. The jail program wasn't as well-established or stable, but she knew Rose Cologne would keep it going and their BVS volunteer, Gary, would help.

She needed to get home and start addressing those immediate family responsibilities, so she wrapped up the letter.

> I hope that our visits continue for a long time and I will continue to work toward that end as long as possible. Please know that you are important and that people do care—indeed, some have made a lifetime dedication to working for and with you. My sincerest good wishes to you all.
>
> Your friend, Marie Hamilton,
> Coordinator, Volunteers in Prison[7]

She made a few notes for Gary, tidied up her desk, and stuck her head into Ann's office to say goodbye.

"You've made miraculous things happen, Marie," Ann said as she hugged Marie tightly. "We'll keep it all going. And you know where to find us any time you want to come back."

Marie nodded, unable to speak. She hugged Ann again, and then left quickly.

AT HOME, MARIE turned her attention to the boys, Joe, and the house. Steve was in eleventh grade and had a part-time job in a restaurant where he worked evenings and weekends. Mike, a freshman, was on the school wrestling team and spent his spare time fishing. Marie soaked in every moment her boys spent with her.

During the day, when they were at school, she poured herself back into cleaning, decorating the house, baking, and preparing gourmet meals. Joe was moving up the career ladder with A&P. During the week, he stayed wherever a new store was opening, and came home only on the weekends. Marie asked Joe if they could move someplace where she and the boys could be with him during the week.

"There's no one place that would make sense to move to," Joe told her. "I travel from New Jersey to Williamsport to Altoona. I want to keep this house. So you just stay here and take care of it."

Every couple of days, Ann or Rose or Gary called Marie, asking for her advice about how to handle a situation with an inmate, or where to find certain documents, or what to do about a conflict with the prison staff. They always apologized profusely for interrupting her at home, but the truth was, they weren't really interrupting much of anything. Once she'd gotten caught up on the housecleaning and laundry, Marie found that the days at home alone seemed long and lonely. She was always glad to hear a little news about what was happening back at the VAC.

A month into her prison break, Ann stopped by the house one afternoon and handed Marie a letter. "I thought you should see this."

Marie recognized Rocky's handwriting immediately.

> Dear Mrs. Cook,
> Hello, and how are you? I had the opportunity of meeting you once and it was a pleasure. . . . I am a former resident of BBN Pre-Release Program here at SCI Rockview. I want to bring it to your attention about the wonderful job the volunteers are doing. They have shown and given me the love I had so long ago lost. I have been in prison for over 8 years and I had no desire to love, care, or share anything with anyone. Then one day I met Marie Hamilton and the other volunteers and they gave me something that I need for so long. They told me I can be successful and shown me how to reach my goals,

that I was afraid to face. They told me I was not an animal but a real being capable of loving and be loved. . . . Marie Hamilton has been a big help to me. She showed me that if you give love you will be loved in return. . . . We all mis Marie and is praying that you can talk her into coming back. . . . Thank you. With love.

Sincerely, Rocky[8]

Marie realized she missed Rocky, too. In fact, she missed all of the men, and the volunteers, even the guards and staff. She looked up from Rocky's letter to see Ann watching her, with eyebrows raised in an unspoken question.

Marie nodded.

Ann smiled.

5
Common Ground

*With the pounding of each step . . . their goal became clearer
. . . . By the end of the day . . . they had accomplished the
unthinkable. . . . A hardened judge and bitter inmates found
a common ground.*

—Jerry[1]

Lawrence

Lawrence[2] wanted to run. He'd been thinking about it for almost a year as he sat in his concrete cell at Rockview. He had convinced dozens of other inmates to run with him. He'd even discussed it with a few prison guards who didn't see a problem with it. Lawrence wanted to hold a marathon in the prison yard to raise money for children's charities.

When Lawrence found out that a friend's six-year-old son back home in Philadelphia had leukemia, he had felt helpless to do anything for the family. By the time he'd gotten permission from the guards to call his friend to ask how he could help, his friend's little boy had died. Lawrence was heartbroken. He felt he had to do something so other children wouldn't suffer the same terrible fate. He had heard that the United Nations had declared 1979 the "International Year of the Child." It seemed the perfect time to help sick children by raising money for research.

He took his idea for a charity marathon to Dr. Mazurkiewicz. The gruff superintendent was supportive, but told Lawrence that an organization outside the prison would have to sponsor the event. So Lawrence wrote to local churches and agencies, including the Voluntary Action Center, looking for a sponsor.

"Some say we just exist from day to day and don't have any human empathy," the thirty-four-year-old wrote. "But we conscientious inmates know better and we are willing to give of ourselves completely to show that we do care.

We here at Rockview run the yard every day; please help us run with a greater purpose. If we can help in saving just one child from these dreaded diseases, we feel it will be worth the sweat, breath, and money."[3]

B ack at the VAC office after her short "prison break," Marie read Lawrence's letter, then leaned back in her chair, looking out the window. She knew the effort to pull off what Lawrence was proposing would be huge. But she had also seen the miracles that happened when people from the community were willing to volunteer to help inmates. Now, here was a group of inmates willing to volunteer to help children in the community. There seemed to be only one right response.

She wrote to Lawrence and said that the VAC might be able to help and that she'd visit him at Rockview the following Thursday afternoon to discuss it. The next week, after her visit to B Block, Marie went to the visiting room and asked to see Lawrence. When he arrived in the visiting room, he greeted Marie enthusiastically. They found a couple of empty seats in the crowded room and sat down. Lawrence leaned forward, his dark brown eyes sparkling, as he described what he envisioned for the inmates' charity marathon. Marie could picture it—inmates, guards, maybe even some of the volunteers, all running side by side, raising money for a common cause. Local community leaders handing out water and snacks to runners. Another opportunity to break down walls of fear between inmates, corrections staff, and the community.

She had just one requirement before she'd commit the Voluntary Action Center as the sponsor: Rockview staff and administration had to be fully on board with the idea. After her conversation with Lawrence, Marie went to see Mike Condo, the activities director at Rockview.

"A real marathon?" Condo laughed. "No way! None of these inmates could go that kind of distance."

"Oh." Marie frowned. "Lawrence told me many of them run laps every day in the yard."

"Well, sure, some of them run a few laps, couple of 'em might even run four or five. But, a marathon is 26.2 miles, Marie."

"Really? Twenty-six miles? I had no idea. . . ."

"The perimeter of the yard isn't quite a mile. They'd have to run thirty laps, maybe more to qualify as a real marathon. There isn't a single inmate here who could do it. It's out of the question."

"Well, what if we didn't call it a marathon then? Maybe just a . . . a 'run-athon'?"

"I don't know. . . ." Condo replied dubiously.

"We'll call it the 'Rockview Runathon.' Has a nice ring to it, doesn't it?" Marie flashed a smile at Condo.

"Hmmm. . . ."

"We could even get 'Rockview Runathon' T-shirts printed up."

Condo held up a hand. "Hang on a minute, Marie. It would take a huge effort to pull something like that off. Prison staff couldn't work on it. It would have to be you and your volunteers."

"And the inmates," Marie added. "Lawrence has a group all organized. They're really committed to doing this. What do you say, Mike?"

Condo exhaled loudly, then shrugged. Marie smiled.

OVER THE WEEKS that followed, messages from Lawrence and his runathon committee were waiting for Marie every time she went into the prison.

The inmates designed a logo for runathon T-shirts. They designed pledge forms and hammered out procedures for registering runners, tallying pledges, and measuring distances run. The men gathered information on sickle cell anemia and children's cancer research centers and discussed the merits of each organization as a possible recipient of their donations.

Marie found the men's enthusiasm and desire to help children absolutely contagious. She formed a runathon committee at the Voluntary Action Center.[4] They made lists of community leaders and organizations to approach for support, drafted a pledge letter, designed posters and advertising brochures for the event, and discussed how to secure donations of food and drinks for the event, as well as certificates, patches, plaques, and T-shirts for the runners.

Then, one afternoon Marie got a phone call from the prison. It was Lawrence, calling from the phone in the prison dental clinic where he had a job as a dental assistant.

"Marie, you're not gonna believe this! They're telling us we can't do it! They're saying *no* runathon!" Lawrence told her, his voice shaking.

"What? Why not?" Marie asked. "Who did you talk to and what exactly did they say?"

"Dr. Mazurkiewicz decided. Condo told us. He said they thought we'd never get this thing together. They didn't think we were serious. They said they never would have approved it if they thought we were really gonna do it. But, Marie, we inmates already decided—we're *doing* this runathon. We put in too much time, *you* put in too much time. To hell with them! Everybody's signed up and ready to run. We're *doing* it!" he repeated.

Marie drew in a deep breath as she thought of all the hours the inmates had put into the runathon, as well as the hours the VAC staff and volunteers had committed. The tightrope she and the volunteers always walked between prison staff and inmates suddenly seemed more tenuous than ever. If Lawrence and the other inmates tried to run and staff tried to stop them, there could be a riot. And the VAC would be connected to it.

"Lawrence," she said. "I'm coming in to see you. You cannot do this."

Marie made a quick phone call to Mike Condo, who confirmed what Lawrence had told her. She had learned when to question decisions made in the prison, and when to bite her tongue. Condo made it clear—this one wasn't negotiable.

She had to use her Prison Society Official Visitor card to get in to see Lawrence. The gate guard seemed surprised to see her there on a day other than Thursday, but he completed the required security checks and let her in. She waited in the visiting room for nearly half an hour before Lawrence arrived. He glanced at Marie, then looked away as he folded his muscular six-foot frame onto the bench next to her.

Marie shifted so she could face him. "Lawrence, you know that the Voluntary Action Center can't support the runathon if it isn't approved by the administration."

Lawrence scowled. "Well, we're running anyway. We worked too hard on this. We're not gonna let them shut us down. You and the VAC worked too hard and we're not gonna let them shut *you* down either, Marie."

Marie glanced over at the security guard, then spoke quietly. "Lawrence, listen to me. You must tell the men that the VAC cannot support this without the approval of the administration. If you want to do something for me, you need to go to the inmates and tell them *not* to run. If the administration is saying you can't do a runathon, you absolutely should not do it."

He dropped his head into his hands, his fingers twisting through his long Afro. He tapped his size-thirteen feet rapidly, saying nothing for a few minutes. Finally, he looked up at her, one last desperate plea in his eyes.

She shook her head. "I'm so very sorry, Lawrence. I know how much it would have meant to you and the men."

Lawrence got up and shuffled out of the visiting room, his head hung low, shoulders slumped.

Marie sat motionless as she watched him go. *So much work . . . so much excitement . . . so much potential . . . gone,* she thought.

As she left the prison, she nodded briefly to the guard, avoiding their usual friendly banter. Back at the VAC office, she gathered the staff and delivered the news. Stunned, they all stood speechless while Marie went into her office and closed the door. She knew that if she hesitated she'd break down. She pulled out her contact list and, one by one, called each runathon committee member to tell them that there would be no runathon. Between calls, she prayed that Lawrence and the other inmates wouldn't try to rebel.

SEVERAL DAYS LATER, Marie got another call from Rockview, this time from Mike Condo.

"Marie, the inmates have agreed to your request that they not run," Condo started.

Marie let out a relieved sigh. "Well, I told them that the VAC couldn't sponsor the runathon if the administration wouldn't approve it."

"I know. Actually, that's why I'm calling. I just talked with Dr. Mazurkiewicz. I told him you advised the inmates not to defy the administration and that they agreed out of respect for you."

"I'm glad to know they made the right decision," Marie said.

"Well, here's the thing. After I told Dr. Mazurkiewicz all of this, he thought about it some more . . . and, Marie, he was so impressed with the way you handled things with the inmates that he said he'll allow the runathon after all. He asked me to call and tell you."

Marie sat in stunned silence.

"I guess you and your volunteers and the inmates better get busy," Condo said before hanging up.

The tears that Marie hadn't allowed to flow when the runathon had been shut down now streamed down her cheeks. Her mind whirled with the dozens of details still left to arrange. But first she had a phone call to make. She called the prison dental clinic and pleaded with the dentist to let her talk with Lawrence, though it was against prison policy.

When the dentist put Lawrence on the phone, she said, "Lawrence, I'm coming in to see you again." When she hung up the phone this time, she was smiling.

THE REASSEMBLED INMATE runathon committee dubbed themselves "The Prisoners Who Care" and named Lawrence their chairman. Marie got on Lawrence's visiting list and met with him regularly. Prison activities staff even got involved, helping the inmates plan the details—dignitaries to invite, approvals and clearances to obtain, and categories of awards to give to runners.

Marie asked Mike Condo to relay an offer from her to all of the participating inmates. "Tell them I'll personally award a special T-shirt to anyone who runs the distance of a full marathon. Oh, and Mike, that's 26.2 miles, in case anyone besides me didn't know that."

Condo laughed.

The inmates renamed the event: Rockview Runathon—Phase 1. Lawrence explained to Marie that the men were so excited about the first runathon that they hoped it would become an annual event. The men wrote letters to the American Cancer Society and to various children's medical research centers, explaining the purpose of the runathon and offering to donate the proceeds to their research efforts. The American Cancer Society replied that they'd be pleased to accept a donation. Only one research center responded. The Children's Hospital of Pittsburgh wrote to say that they'd love to be one of the recipients of the funds raised.

Over four hundred inmates pledged to sponsor their fellow runners, donating their prison wages.[5] Many donated an entire week's wages or more. Even former inmates who were now out of prison made pledges out of gratitude for what the pre-release program and the volunteers had done for them.

One former B Block resident, who had been released from prison months earlier, wrote:

Dear Friends:

You all have my best wishes in regards to the campaign you're having, it's a very worthy cause. . . . As for myself, I'm working hard to make ends meet, something like 10 hrs. a day but I don't mind. . . . I feel really good about being back in society, after so many years of being away. I also want all of the Volunteers to know that I deeply appreciate the time and understanding they gave me. . . . I just can't find the right word to express what they've given me.

Sincerely, Michael[6]

He enclosed a money order for $7.50 to support the runathon.

Meanwhile, Marie and the VAC runathon committee regrouped, picking up where they'd left off—securing community pledges, contacting newspapers, TV, and radio stations for publicity, and assembling the small army of volunteers required to staff the event. Marie's parents, both in their sixties, offered to help register runners and tally laps.

Marie approached several respected community leaders to ask them to publicly support the event. She secured donations from the local Kiwanis, Lions, and Rotary clubs to underwrite all of the printing, telephone, and other expenses so one hundred percent of all pledges for the runners would go directly to the selected charities. Dave Stickell, a Rockview volunteer, accepted the bookkeeping responsibility for all the monies collected and set up a Rockview runathon bank account.

As word spread about the unique event, support materialized in many forms. A group of former marathon runners from the Nittany Valley Track Club volunteered to coach the inmate runners before the event and to officiate. Baseball great Willie Stargell, of the Pittsburgh Pirates, sent word of his support for the inmates' effort. State

Representative Gregg Cunningham, who counted the inmates among his constituents, secured pledges from Pennsylvania's Governor Dick Thornburgh and Lieutenant Governor William W. Scranton, III. Cunningham personally committed to run alongside the inmates.

Every detail had to be planned, written, and submitted to the administration for approval, including extensive security and clearance procedures for every person and item entering and leaving the prison on the day of the runathon. The administration established policies dictating what volunteers, members of the press, and others from "outside the wall" would and would not be permitted to do while at the runathon.

Guards agreed to temporary changes in daily procedures, including count times[7] and meal routines. Inmates who weren't running would be permitted to watch and support the runners. Runners could trade in their browns[8] for shorts and T-shirts, if they owned any.

Staff and inmates hammered out rules for a preliminary qualifying five-mile run to be held one week before the runathon. The prison physician agreed to give each runner a complete physical to clear them for participation in the event.

Over one hundred inmates participated in the qualifying run. Sixty-six of them finished the five-mile course, qualifying to participate in the June 16 event.

By then, Marie was running on adrenaline, exhausted from the emotional roller coaster of the past six months: the marathon meetings, the thousands of minute details to be worked out, and the worrying and praying that nothing would go wrong on the day of the event. She knew only too well that the slightest infraction of rules, the mildest concern about security, or the tiniest misstep on the part of a volunteer or inmate would shut the runathon down instantly. And she was experiencing real doubts about whether a runathon behind prison walls would really make much of a difference to anyone on the outside.

THE MORNING OF the runathon dawned sunny and hot. Marie, her parents, and their army of volunteers arrived at Rockview and were cleared through security. Lawrence was one of the first people to greet Marie inside the prison yard. His eyes sparkled as he talked with her and the volunteers about the day ahead.

Marie introduced Lawrence to her parents. "He's the gentleman who came up with the idea for the runathon."

Lawrence ducked his head shyly as he shook hands with Virginia and Robert Fortney. Then he joined the other sixty-five inmates warming up for the run.

The early morning hours passed quickly with a flurry of registration and setup activities as the temperature rose. At 9 a.m., the runners lined up for the official start, as onlookers cheered. After the brief command—"Ready, Set, Go!"—the runners started making laps around the dirt track. The volunteers organized their paperwork and prepared to tally every lap.

Marie collapsed into a chair, fanning herself with the last-minute to-do list she'd scribbled in the middle of the night, while she had lain awake praying that nothing would go wrong. The exhaustion and doubts that had been building over the weeks leading up to the runathon finally claimed her. At the beginning, she'd gotten caught up in the inmates' enthusiasm. They hoped to raise a few hundred dollars for children's medical research. It seemed like a lot to them, but Marie knew it would be a tiny drop in the vast ocean of multimillion-dollar medical research projects. When she thought about the hundreds of hours VAC staff and volunteers had committed to this project, it hardly seemed worth it. She looked around for a scrap of shade to sit in, but found none. She pulled her straw hat down to shade her face and stared blankly at the track.

She overheard her parents chatting with inmates on the sidelines nearby, asking about their families, their homes, and their dreams for the future. She had to smile as she watched the inmates in earnest conversation with her mother and father. *There are no two better people in the whole world for the inmates to talk with,* she thought.

Marie's jaw dropped as Jim Newkirk, a *Harrisburg Patriot News* reporter sent to cover the event, asked a spectator standing next to him to hold his camera, then jogged onto the track and joined a group of inmates doing laps.

District Attorney Charles Brown ran past, side by side with an inmate he'd helped to prosecute six months earlier.

District Attorney Charles Brown runs in the first Rockview runathon (June 16, 1979).
Photo courtesy of CentrePeace, Inc.

Some of the guards sat near Marie on the bleachers and watched as the inmates ran. She noticed that the officers had loosened their usual stern, straight-postured demeanor, though she was sure they were on high alert for any sign of trouble. The inmates seemed happy to be under surveillance while doing something good.

Even Dr. Mazurkiewicz stopped by briefly. Though she'd talked with him on the phone several times over the past few years, Marie had seen him only one other time, after the very first orientation for volunteers at Rockview nearly four years earlier. He looked just as stern and intimidating as he had back then, but Marie approached him and reintroduced herself.

"I remember you," he said, as he watched the runners intently. "My staff thought I was crazy for allowing this runathon thing," he said gruffly.

Marie nodded, sensing both begrudging approval and a warning in his words. She mouthed another quick prayer that the day would go smoothly.

"Then again, they thought I was crazy four years ago for allowing volunteers to go into the cellblock. Now they wouldn't want to be without you." He turned toward Marie and gave her a wry smile.

It was the most he'd ever said to her about the Volunteers in Prison program, but those few words were like gold. "Thank you, Dr. Mazurkiewicz. I'm committed to making sure our volunteers continue to serve the needs of the men here, as well as the staff, and I'll do whatever it takes. . . ."

The superintendent waved impatiently. "I know you will, Marie." Then, seeming uncomfortable either with the heat or their heartfelt exchange, Mazurkiewicz turned and walked away. Marie laughed for the first time that day.

As the runathon continued through the sweltering afternoon, one inmate's brown prison-issued boots came apart. He went to Marie.

"I don't want to quit running yet. What should I do?" he asked.

Marie looked around. "Does anybody here wear size eleven shoes?"

"I do," a volunteer responded. "He could have my sneakers."

Marie asked Mike Condo if that would be allowed and Condo nodded.

The men quickly traded shoes and the inmate returned to the track to run several more miles in the volunteer's brand-name track shoes while the volunteer slipped his feet into the inmate's worn-out boots and continued counting laps.

By the time the afternoon sun had drifted to the other side of the prison yard, Marie saw the runathon in a new light.

Runners at the first Rockview runathon (June 16, 1979). Photo courtesy of *Centre Daily Times* (State College, Pennsylvania).

AT 3 P.M., MIKE CONDO raised his hands to signal the end of the runathon. Spectators cheered the last few runners as they slowed to a walk. Volunteers tallied the final laps while the exhausted men wiped sweat from their foreheads and stretched aching muscles. Sixty-six inmates had run a total of 785 miles, an average of nearly twelve miles per person.

The newspaper reporter, Jim Newkirk, had accompanied the men around the track for several hours. State Representative Gregg Cunningham had logged eleven miles with the inmates. And District Attorney Brown had run and talked with many of the men throughout the day.

"All of the inmates I was running with knew I was a DA," Brown said, "but none of them said anything to me other than 'thank you very much for being here—for doing this with us.' Because the inmates were willing to do something like this to reach out and help kids, I thought I should support that. And I thought maybe by participating in the runathon myself, I could show that I didn't forget about the people I had helped to send to prison." Then, with a laugh, he added, "Of course, I never let them see me walk. It was a *runathon*—so I *ran!*"

A MONTH LATER, all of the runners were recognized at an awards ceremony in Rockview's auditorium. When Marie announced the final tally of collected pledges, the inmates cheered wildly. They had raised $2,396.

Representatives from the American Cancer Society attended the awards ceremony and commended the runners. They told the men how important their contribution would be to children with cancer.

The top ten runners received special awards, including four men who ran at least the official marathon distance of 26.2 miles. As promised, Marie awarded each of them a special T-shirt to recognize their accomplishment.

Every runner received a certificate of commendation for his participation in the runathon. But it was the patch they received that read "I helped save a life" that meant more to the men than anything else.

At the end of the awards ceremony, Lawrence came to the podium. He bent down to the microphone. "Marie, we have something we'd like to give *you*." He motioned for Marie to come forward.

"Sometimes it's hard to find hope behind the walls of a prison," Lawrence told her. "But you had faith in us. You gave us hope. Thank you."

Everyone was quiet as Lawrence reached into a bag beside the podium. He pulled out a pale blue T-shirt. On the front were printed the words: "June 16, 1979—Rockview Runathon—PHASE 1."

IN THE DAYS and weeks that followed, the men were euphoric about their success. They immediately began to plan another runathon for the following summer. Representatives from seven different inmate organizations pledged their help. The Athletic Department, Brothers of Islam, Holy Name Society, Lifers Association, New Breed Jaycees, Nittany Gavel Club, and Protestant Church inmate groups planned and led the Rockview runathon, phase two, on June 7, 1980.

Together, the men ran a total of 586 miles and raised another $2,358.10 to donate to sickle cell anemia and cancer research. Two inmates ran the distance of a full marathon. This time reporter Jim Newkirk came prepared to run. He ran shoulder to shoulder with the other top runner, a twenty-five-year-old inmate from Philadelphia who had been in prison for three and a half years. The inmate was inspired to run to help other children when his own daughter got sick. Newkirk was inspired to run by the dedication he'd seen from the inmates the previous year. Each of the two men logged twenty-eight miles.

This time, Lawrence was allowed to personally present the donations to the Pittsburgh Children's Hospital administrator, Glenn Lanier, for their sickle cell anemia clinic and to Dr. Edwin Gaffney, a cell biologist who conducted cancer research at the hospital.

Word of the Rockview runathons spread across Pennsylvania and beyond. One of New York's state prisons contacted Marie seeking advice about how to organize and coordinate a runathon for their inmates. JT, who had been moved from Rockview to the state prison in Pittsburgh the previous year, was talking with people there about

Marie (standing, wearing hat) with her father, Robert (seated, wearing Rockview runathon T-shirt), and mother, Virginia (seated, wearing white hat), counting laps for runners at the second Rockview runathon (June 7, 1980). Photo courtesy of CentrePeace, Inc.

organizing a runathon at the Western Penitentiary. Inmates all over Pennsylvania wrote to Marie, asking her to bring the runathon to their prisons.

Marie remembered Ronald Marks' long-ago invitation to let him know if he could ever do anything to help advance her prison efforts. Marks had just been named commissioner of Pennsylvania's Bureau of Correction, with responsibility for all nine state prisons. It seemed like the perfect time to take him up on his offer.

6
COMMITTED

When that cell door slams and it's just you, with yourself, you can't hide any more. You come to understand the Russian roulette you've played with your life. You meant to be a good son, a good husband, a good father . . . but you've been a speed racer on the road to hell with all your good intentions. Then along comes the Runathon, giving you an opportunity to give back, to finally do something truly good, and you latch onto that opportunity for dear life.

—Yusef[1]

Marie wrote a letter to Commissioner Marks, congratulating him on his promotion. She told him of the success of the first two Rockview runathons and reminded him of their conversation about continuing to promote alternatives to incarceration.

"An exciting thought has been nagging me," she wrote. "It is the possibility of all institutions running at the same time next year—having all pledges and contributions going to alternative programs. I find the idea easy to sell to the inmates; and placing the money in worthy community programs would [raise] the awareness we need to get alternatives moving in other parts of our state. . . . Please advise me if you would support such a venture."[2]

She received a prompt reply from Marks, who promised to discuss her idea at the next statewide superintendents' meeting. "I hope we may be of some service to you in your 'nagging thought,'" Marks wrote.[3]

While waiting to hear from him, Marie turned her attention back to the "Alternatives to Violence" training that she and the other Rockview volunteers had taken with the Quakers. She wrote a proposal to John McCullough to incorporate the course into their B Block programs, and McCullough approved but stipulated that volunteers, not inmates, teach it. Marie asked the Quakers to adapt the training to fit Rockview's requirements and the "Creative Nonviolent Conflict Resolution" course was launched.

The curriculum included communications and problem-solving exercises; activities to explore and share feelings, especially anger; role plays to help participants practice dealing with conflicts; games designed to build trust; and affirmations to acknowledge positive qualities in each participant, improve their self-esteem, and foster acceptance of others.

Marie and volunteers Warren Smith, Betty Bergstein, and Dave Stickell mapped out a plan to team-teach the course. When they'd taken the course themselves, the volunteers had discovered that laughing together during the games, called "Light and Livelys," led to greater openness in group discussion.

"The sharing is as deep as the laughter is loud," Marie had observed.

The affirmations throughout the program had established a powerful bond between the volunteers as they had practiced acknowledging their own and others' positive qualities. They thought the affirmations and Light and Livelys would be even more powerful for the inmates, for whom both laughter and affirmation were rare.

The first group of twelve curious, if somewhat skeptical, men signed up for the course. During their first session, after introducing the program, Marie paired the men up and asked them to tell each other something positive about themselves.

"Listen carefully to each other," she said, "because you will then introduce your partner to the rest of the group by sharing those positive things about him."

A few of the men laughed nervously. One muttered, "Are you kidding me, man?" They were an eclectic group, including men who were serving time for murder, drug dealing, rape, armed robbery, and assault. B Block's "pull up" system was based on watching for and confronting failings in others. Finding something good to say seemed to unnerve them. Marie, Warren, Betty, and Dave offered encouragement and, when necessary, ideas. Then, hesitantly and awkwardly, the men introduced each other.

After this unusual beginning, Betty led a values exercise. "I'm going to read some values statements. If you agree with the statement, go to the right side of the room. If you disagree, go to the left. If you're undecided or neutral, stand in the middle."

"The man should be the head of the household. . . . The woman should be the head of the household. . . . Children should be seen and not heard."

The men laughed and jostled to get to their desired spot in the room as she read each statement. Then things got more personal.

"The death penalty is fair. . . . Marijuana should be legalized. . . . The answer to crime is to build more prisons. . . . I would shoot to kill if my life were in danger. . . . Walking away from a fight can be the mature thing to do."

These statements led to a lively discussion. Betty explained that values are neither right nor wrong, but are influenced by education, upbringing, religious beliefs, and life experiences.

"Differing values can also result in conflict," she added.

Then Marie led the first Light and Lively, an old summer camp game called "Zip, Zap, Boing." The men stood self-consciously in a circle. Marie explained the rules and encouraged them to relax and have fun with it. Within a few minutes, they were laughing loudly, ribbing each other as they struggled to get the hang of it.

Suddenly, several guards were at the door, wanting to know what was going on. In prison, laughter was suspect, evidence that something shady might be going on. But the volunteers had agreed that bringing laughter into the prison was one of the most important things they could do. After reassuring the guards that everything was under control, Dave took over the discussion.

"Think about who you most admire and what you admire about them. Perhaps you admire a friend or family member, maybe someone famous. Tell us who you chose and why." On the small blackboard in the corner, Dave wrote, "Characteristics we admire." As the men talked, Dave listed the attributes they mentioned, translating as they went, from "won't BS you" to *honest*, "don't take crap from nobody" to *respects himself*, "takes care of his own" to *stands by his friends*.

"These characteristics that we admire in others can be ours with practice," Dave explained.

A few of the men looked surprised. Others looked skeptical.

"We'll talk more about that in future sessions," Dave added.

Their time was almost up for the day, so Marie wrapped up. "Next week we'll discuss listening skills, and we'll continue working on affirmations—that is, saying positive things about ourselves and others."

Several men groaned, while others laughed.

"Don't worry—it gets easier with practice."

After the class, Marie, Warren, Betty, and Dave went to Betty's house to debrief and plan the following week's session, a routine they would follow for years.

Marie hoped the conflict resolution skills would help the men both while they were in prison and after their release. While many inmates couldn't wait for their release, some feared it. Rocky was one of the latter, and he wrote to Marie asking for help.

> I am trying to prepare myself for the outside life but how do I do that when I don't even know what it is or how to expect it. . . . Believe it or not I don't know if I want to come out there. Right now I am thinking about turning down parole. . . . Everyone has fears and this one of mines now. If I had someone I could talk to maybe I would feel differently. . . . I can't talk to my parents cause they wouldn't understand and might think that it is something they did or said. How can I tell them how I feel without hurting them. I hope you can help me.
>
> Love, Rocky[4]

Marie went to Rockview to encourage her dear friend. "Just think of all the ways you've changed, Rocky, and how hard you've worked to become a better man. You're going to do just fine. I know it."

Rocky smiled nervously. "I hope so," he said, tapping his bony fingers on his seat.

"Can you believe it's been nearly four years that we've known each other, Rocky?"

He shook his head and sat quietly for a minute. Then, he blurted, "Marie, when I get out of here, I'm going to find a girl just like you to marry. What makes you so different anyway?"

"I know you don't like religious people, Rocky, but I have to tell you—it's because I'm a Christian."

"No!" Rocky objected. "No, no, no. That can't be. Not like all those people who come here from different churches, telling me one Sunday that I'm going to hell, then the next Sunday saying I'm forgiven and I'll be saved. Those people can't even make up their minds."

Marie rarely discussed religion with inmates, since she knew many of them had been turned off the way Rocky had. But she told him, "It has to do with *love*. God is love, and there's something of God in each of us. God's love is in me, and his love is in you, too, Rocky. Our hearts have recognized that love in each other."

They sat quietly together for a long time, neither wanting to say goodbye. Marie wanted more than anything to give her dear friend a hug. Instead, she simply clasped his hand and said, "Please stay in touch, Rocky. If you ever need anything, you know where to find me."

A few weeks later, Marie received her last letter from Rocky.

> You know what a big help to me you have been and thanks to you I was able to do this time without it really getting to me. There were times when I thought that it was over and I would stop and think about you and how I would hurt you if I did anything that was stupit. I can get you a list of names that would tell you the same thing. You have helped too many people to stop what you are doing now. . . . If I don't see you again before I leave you remember that I LOVE YOU.
>
> Always & forever, Rocky[6]

Marie prayed daily that he'd make it on the outside. Though she was happy for him, Rocky's release left an empty ache and Marie missed visiting him. But for now, she had a new project to keep her busy.

She had finally received a letter from Ronald Marks. Six prison superintendents were interested in holding runathons the following year, and they had appointed their activities directors to work with the Voluntary Action Center to coordinate the event. Marie reassembled the large group of volunteers that had helped organize the first two Rockview runathons to figure out how to coordinate a six-prison event. She wrote to the activities directors at Rockview, Dallas, Graterford, Mercer, Greensburg, and Muncy, the state's only women's prison, asking to meet with representatives of their inmate organizations to start planning. She emphasized the importance of allowing inmates to *own* the runathon, as it would give them an opportunity to take responsibility, make decisions, and get credit for their positive efforts. She knew that none of it could happen without staff approval, but she prayed they'd also be open to letting the inmates take the lead.

Marie and VAC board member Bob Goerder drove together to the Muncy women's prison for their first runathon planning meeting. It was the first time they'd been to the scenic campus in the heart of the Susquehanna Valley. The stone cottages and rolling, landscaped grounds looked more like a college campus than a prison. As Marie and Bob approached the administration building, chimes rang in the steeple of the prison chapel.

"It sure doesn't feel like a prison, does it?" Marie commented. Bob shook his head. They were shown to a meeting room, where they were to meet with inmates, staff, and people from the local community. When they arrived, several beautiful, well-dressed women were already in the room. Marie and Bob introduced themselves.

"And who are you with?" Bob asked the women.

"We're with the PLA," one answered.

As they made small talk, waiting for others to arrive, Marie admired the women's sleek hairstyles, makeup, and manicures.

"So, what does your organization do?" Marie asked.

"It's the Pennsylvania Lifers Association," another woman answered. "We're all lifers here at Muncy."

Marie could barely disguise her shock. They certainly didn't look like inmates, let alone lifers. When the rest of the meeting participants arrived, the women from the PLA took charge. A petite, older woman named Lois[6] was their chairwoman. She was clearly well-respected by both staff and inmates, who seemed to regard her as a mother figure. The women were passionate about raising money to help children and shared poignant stories about their own children and how much they missed them. The PLA agreed to pledge a penny per mile for every runner at Muncy, and the women had set a goal of having the highest participation of both staff and inmates in the state. Lois and the other inmates conducted one of the most professional, well-run meetings Marie had ever attended.

As soon as she and Bob got into the car to drive back to State College, Bob blurted, "Those women can't possibly be lifers. That would mean they killed someone."

Marie shook her head. "I know. I can't believe it!"

"Lois, especially, seemed like such a wonderful person. I don't care what she's accused of, she's innocent in my eyes!"

"She reminded me of my mother," Marie added.

When she was with incarcerated men, Marie often thought about their mothers and the anguish mothers must feel at having a son in prison. But in her meeting with the women at Muncy, Marie found herself thinking about their children. She couldn't fathom the heartache of separation for both the mothers and their children. She could already see that working with incarcerated women would be a whole new part of her education.

A week later, Marie made her first three-hour drive to the Graterford prison to meet with the inmates on their runathon committee. Graterford was, by far, the largest of the participating prisons and it had a tough reputation, with the nickname "Pennsylvania's Attica." As she crossed Perkiomen Creek and followed a winding country road past farm fields, Graterford's thirty-foot-high, nine-sided concrete wall and nine guard towers dominated the landscape. As she entered the prison through the formidable gate, she felt more intimidated than she ever had at Rockview, even during her first visit to B Block.

She was escorted to a meeting room, where committee members were already gathered. Their designated chairman was Yusef,[7] a twenty-nine-year-old former Black Panther affiliate. Yusef was treasurer of Degrees of Captivity, an organization that offered support services to children and families of inmates. He was one of Graterford's most active and respected inmates. At 6'1" tall, with a large Afro and startling gray-green eyes, Yusef had a commanding presence. Representatives from Graterford's Lifers, Jaycees, Holy Name Society, and other inmate groups attended the meeting. Marie had sent a runathon information packet in advance, and all of the men had read through it and were prepared.

"One of the most important decisions you'll need to make, gentlemen, is where you want to donate the pledges you raise here at Graterford," Marie told them. "This is your event, your opportunity to give something back to the community. The men at Rockview have been talking about giving their money to programs for at-risk youth, programs that help kids stay out of jail."

The Graterford committee had selected three organizations—two youth mentoring programs and Degrees of Captivity. Representatives of each organization were at the meeting. A Philadelphia woman named Mattie Humphrey served as president of Degrees of Captivity. Humphrey was well-known to the Graterford inmates, as she had been visiting the prison twice a week for many years and was a leader of the local prison reform movement.

Marie supplied applications for each organization to receive runathon proceeds and reviewed other details of the runathon. Then she headed back to State College. A week later, she received the application for Degrees of Captivity, signed by Yusef. In order to be eligible for runathon proceeds, organizations had to be registered with the Pennsylvania Commission on Charitable Organizations, and had to have a board of directors. Degrees of Captivity, however, didn't meet either requirement.

Marie notified Cliff Parris, Graterford's activities director, and Parris asked Marie to return to Graterford to explain the situation directly to the inmates. Marie made another trip to Graterford and explained the eligibility requirements for organizations they chose to receive donations. She told them that one of the organizations they'd chosen didn't qualify, but they could donate their proceeds to the other two. After the meeting, Marie pulled Yusef aside to tell him the registration number he had listed on the application for Degrees of Captivity wasn't valid. Yusef said he'd follow up with Humphrey, who had supplied the information. A few days later, Yusef called Marie and said that

Humphrey had given him the number of an organization that provided office space for Degrees, since Degrees wasn't a registered charity.

"I told Mattie that was completely unacceptable and that she's damaged my integrity," Yusef said.

Fortunately, the runathon planning meetings at the other prisons were going smoothly and excitement mounted for the first statewide runathon.

Design for the plaque that was awarded to the top three runners in each prison after the runathon went statewide (circa 1981). Photo courtesy of CentrePeace, Inc.

On Saturday, May 9, 1981, a total of 740 inmates at Rockview, Graterford, Dallas, Mercer, Greensburg, and Muncy ran for their chosen charities. They logged a combined 5,795 miles and raised over $3,000. Marie sat in the sunshine at Rockview, counting laps for the runners and cheering them on, glad to have all the months of planning behind her. Little did she know that two hundred miles away, at Graterford, Mattie Humphrey was walking around the prison yard, carrying a bullhorn and asking inmates not to participate. The inmates kept running.

Later that summer, Marie traveled to each of the six prisons to attend their awards ceremony. Graterford's ceremony was held in the prison chapel, and Marie sat among the inmates in a pew. One inmate leaned over and told Marie that Mattie Humphrey had tried to get a judge to agree that Degrees of Captivity should be able to receive runathon donations without being a registered charity.

"The judge told Mattie she didn't have a leg to stand on," the inmate reported.

Yusef told Marie he had resigned from Degrees of Captivity.

At Muncy, seventy-five women had run a total of 605 miles. Many staff members had run with the inmates and all were honored at an awards banquet. Several of the women spoke movingly of how they thought of their own children while they were running and how it had motivated them to keep running to help other children. They donated the money they raised to Big Sisters of Philadelphia.

Though it had been a tremendous amount of work, Marie wanted to be sure there would be a second statewide runathon. She nominated the Pennsylvania Bureau of Correction for an award from the National Association on Volunteers in Criminal Justice (NAVCJ) for supporting the Pennsylvania Prison Runathon. When she was notified that the bureau had won the award and would be honored at the annual

Marie presents a plaque to Rockview Superintendent Dr. Joseph Mazurkiewicz after the runathon goes statewide, recognizing Rockview as the place where it all started (circa 1981). (Left to right) Deputy Superintendent Jeffrey Beard; Superintendent Mazurkiewicz; Marie Hamilton; inmate chairman of the Rockview runathon committee; and Rockview Activities Director Donald Stine. Photo courtesy of CentrePeace, Inc.

NAVCJ conference, Marie asked Commissioner Ronald Marks to attend to accept the award. Marks told Marie he was grateful to her for casting the bureau in such a positive light and for bringing national attention to the runathon. He couldn't attend the conference, but designated William Jordan, pardons case specialist for the bureau, to attend and accept the award.

Marie went to the conference with Jordan and was tickled to see him so energized about prison volunteerism after meeting and talking with prison volunteers from all over the country. She hoped his enthusiasm would open up new opportunities for volunteers in the Pennsylvania prison system.

The first statewide runathon had also lit a fire in the inmates. One inmate named David[8] wrote to Marie to express what the runathon had meant to him.

> Dear Marie:
>
> I grew up as an only child. At about age 10 I had reached the point where I could no longer relate to my parents. I took to the streets! At age 13 I went to my first reform school! I learned how to lie and steal. At age 15 I went to another reform school. I learned to blame everyone for my problems except me. At age 16 I went to Camp Hill for 2 years. I learned how to become a complete loser. At age 19 a judge sentenced me to Life Imprisonment. I'm now almost 37 and still serving the Life Sentence. I was thankful for the opportunity to coordinate the Runathon. . . . I realize how important the cause was. Alternatives to Imprisonment for Youth is a wonderful project. I don't know if an alternative in my day would have saved me . . . and others like me. But we never got the chance. We went from the street corners to the Juvenile Institutions and on to the penitentiary. A wasteful lifestyle! Being able to help with the Runathon was a special part of my life. The kids are our future society. Imprisonment destroys kids. And through imprisoning kids, society helps to destroy itself. . . . The sentiments I express are not

> unique to me. There are many imprisoned men with similar experiences and who feel the same about the Runathon. Thanks again for the opportunity to help.
>
> David[9]

SOON AFTER THE RUNATHON, Marie's son, Steve, graduated from high school. He would start college at Penn State in the fall. He had already worked his way up the management ladder in a local restaurant and was a serious go-getter like his father. Mike was doing well at school, had a steady girlfriend, and went fishing at every opportunity. Marie couldn't believe they'd grown up so quickly. She was glad Mike had a few more years of high school before he'd be off to college.

Joe still traveled a lot with A&P, but he was a good provider for her and the boys. They had lived longer in State College than they'd lived anywhere else. When Joe wasn't traveling, he and the boys went hunting, fishing, and camping regularly. Marie knew that Joe loved being a father to his boys as much as she loved being their mother. She felt like a very lucky woman.

Her pastor, mentor, and friend, Mike Scrogin, was leaving University Baptist and Brethren Church to take a pastoral position in Massachusetts. He was one of the best listeners Marie had ever known and she would miss their regular conversations about the prison work. With Mike's support, both CACJ and Volunteers in Prison had become solid, well-run organizations. Mike had arranged for CACJ to use donated space in the third floor of the church and had advocated for ongoing financial support for Volunteers in Prison from the Middle Pennsylvania District of the Church of the Brethren.

Marie went to see him one last time before he left. "You know, Mike, for seven years I've been coming to you for advice—and never once have you told me what I should do."

"Seems to me you've found your own answers, Marie," Scrogin replied. "You make things happen with your energy and commitment. You've opened doors and accomplished things that no one else could have. I can't wait to hear what parts of the criminal justice system you'll decide to take on next. They won't know what hit them."

Marie laughed as she gave him a farewell hug. "Blessings to you, Mike."

"Godspeed, Marie!"

MARIE CONTINUED TEACHING the conflict resolution course on B Block at Rockview, while the other volunteers moved on to leading other discussion groups. She'd start one ten-week session as soon as the previous one ended and, as word spread about the course, the sessions filled quickly.

Each group of men came in awkward and skeptical at first, then grew more confident week by week as they learned how to give and receive affirmations, how to listen to each other, how to use "I-messages" to communicate their feelings, and how to brainstorm solutions to problems. Sometimes they remembered to put these skills to use in daily life in the cellblock, but at other times old behaviors and patterns of thinking returned.

During one class, Marie could tell something was seriously wrong among the men and called a time-out.

"I'm sensing some tension here today," she said. "Is there a problem that you'd like to talk about?"

A few of the guys shifted uncomfortably in their seats and looked around at each other. Then one of them spoke up. "Yeah. We're having a big problem with one of the COs."

"I see," Marie replied quietly. "Is it something you'd like to talk about?"

"Oh, we already got it figured out," another inmate said. "We just gonna take him out, that's all."

The men's expressions told Marie they were serious. "Would you want to say a little more about what the problem is?" she asked.

"He's been threatening a lot of us, giving write-ups, just looking for a way to trip us up," one man explained.

Marie knew that write-ups, especially on the pre-release unit, were among the inmates' greatest fears, as they sometimes resulted in time being added to an inmate's sentence. She thought through the techniques and exercises that were part of the conflict resolution course. They'd covered brainstorming and problem solving a few weeks earlier, so she decided to help the men apply the techniques they'd learned.

"Let's use this as a problem-solving exercise and see if we can come up with a solution." She wrote on the blackboard, "How to handle problem with CO."

"Let's brainstorm. Share whatever ideas you can think of," she said, "and I'll write them on the board."

The men came up with a long list. The last one was their final solution. Marie took a deep breath and wrote, "Kill him" on the blackboard with all the other ideas. She prayed none of the staff would stop by the classroom as they sometimes did.

Following the problem-solving process she'd taught the men, she had them consider each option and decide whether to keep or eliminate it. They went through the whole list, and as the men eliminated each option, Marie's stomach was in knots. When they got to the last idea, *Kill him*, no one thought it should be eliminated. She didn't know what to say next.

This one's for you, God, she whispered.

"Okay," she said, stalling for time, "well . . . let's . . . let's go ahead and kill him. . . . But let's do it *my way*, if you'll trust me to do that. Do you trust me?"

"Yes," a few men replied. Others nodded.

"What do you know about this CO? Does he have any pets?" she asked.

"Oh yeah, he has a dog," one man said, rubbing his hands together evilly.

"Okay, good, be sure to ask him about his dog—what kind of dog is it, what's the dog's name, how long has he had it. Who will talk with him about his dog?"

The men looked at each other, then at Marie, confused. Then one man tentatively offered, "Uh, I'll do that."

"Good, thank you," Marie said. "What about his hobbies? Does anyone know what his interests are outside of work?"

One man snorted. "Why should we care about this joker's hobbies?"

"I just want you to find out. See what he's interested in—sports, maybe? He might have some kind of interesting collection or know how to do photography or woodworking. Who will find out what he's interested in for us?"

Another hand went up.

"Perfect," Marie continued. "Now, he has to dress neatly because he's a sergeant, right? So, let's use our affirmations. During the next week, each of you should find a way to tell him he looks sharp. Say something positive about how he's dressed, in any way, using your own words. Everyone needs to be sure to do this one. Can you do that?"

She looked at each man, one at a time.

"Yeah."

"Okay."

"I guess."

"Each of you will need to report back next week on your conversations. In the meantime, no one should do *anything else* with this CO, except to have these conversations that we've talked about. Then, next week, we'll take care of this. Is everybody in agreement?"

Marie made sure each man agreed, though a few still looked confused.

Their time was up. Marie dismissed the class, then quickly erased the men's list of options for dealing with the CO from the blackboard. As she wiped away the evidence of their final idea, she prayed they wouldn't decide to try it.

7

A RAY OF SUNSHINE

If we could read the secret history of our enemies, we should find in each man's life sorrow and suffering enough to disarm all hostility.

—Henry Wadsworth Longfellow (1807–1882)

During the following week, Marie read the newspaper every morning and watched the evening news, praying there would be nothing about a disturbance at Rockview. She knew she had taken a huge risk and had violated prison rules. The volunteers were obligated to report any threats from inmates against staff or other inmates, or threats to harm themselves. If anything happened between the men and the CO, Marie knew she'd be culpable.

As she arrived in the B Block classroom that Thursday, Marie felt an overwhelming sense of dread. The men filed in and sat down. When everyone was situated, Marie took a deep breath and exhaled before asking, "Well, what happened?"

The men looked at her, confused.

"Whaddya mean?" one asked.

"The problem with the CO—what happened?"

"Oh, him," another man answered, shrugging casually.

"He thinks he's the greatest thing walking, now that we all told him what a sharp dresser he is."

"Too bad he got such a ugly little dog though. He showed me pictures of that thing. We're talkin' UG-LY!"

"Least his kids are cute."

Marie interrupted their banter. "So, there's no problem between you gentlemen and the CO?"

"Only problem he got now is a swelled head!" one inmate quipped. The men laughed.

The tension Marie had felt all week eased out of her neck and shoulders. She struggled to refocus on the day's agenda. "Well . . . let's get started, then. Today we'll be talking about decision making."

THE MONTHS PASSED quickly and it was soon time to start planning the second statewide runathon. Inmates had offered numerous ideas for making the next runathon bigger and better. David, the inmate who had written so movingly about his first runathon experience, was so energized that he sent two pages of ambitious suggestions to Marie.

> The inmates love to help kids. . . . Where there's a will, there's a way. . . . If we do it again, then let's do it as big as possible. The Voluntary Action Center has started the ball rolling. But Marie Hamilton and company shouldn't have to do all the work. Let's get the public involved . . . we (can) raise at least 1/2 million dollars for the youth of this state. . . . Perhaps it seems I'm thinking on too large a scale. But for kids and for such a good cause nothing is too great.[1]

David suggested seeking celebrity endorsements for the runathon, including heavyweight boxing champions Joe Frazier and Larry Holmes, and Dr. J.

Marie wrote back to David: "The celebrity names are good. How do we reach Joe Frazier and Larry Holmes? Who is Dr. J? Do you mean Dr. Joe Mazurkiewicz?"

David wrote back immediately: "Dr J is with the 76ers."

That evening, over dinner, Marie told her sons about David's ideas for the runathon.

"Do either of you boys know what '76ers' are?" she asked.

"Mom! You seriously don't know who the 76ers are? The Philadelphia 76ers?" Steve started laughing.

"They're a famous professional basketball team, Mom," Mike said.

"Oh," Marie replied. "I never heard of them. Well, then who is Dr. J?"

Both boys doubled over laughing. Marie wasn't sure what was so funny.

When the boys finally got their laughter under control, Mike explained. "Dr. J is Julius Erving—one of the greatest basketball players ever. He's the star of the Philadelphia 76ers."

"He's a legend, Mom," Steve added. "A huge sports celebrity!"

"Hmmmm. . . . I wonder if he'd endorse the runathon."

Mike and Steve laughed the rest of the way through dinner.

Marie started noticing newspaper articles about the 76ers. She researched and found their address and wrote a letter to Julius Erving.

Dear Mr. Erving,

I am writing to you hoping that you can help with a project being organized by our committee. It is unlikely that you are familiar with the Pennsylvania Prison Runathon. It can best be described as a 'unique charitable event' . . . [where] the State's correctional institutions allow their inmates to run within the walls and have money pledged on a per-mile basis. . . . [The] proceeds are then given to organizations of the inmates' own choosing, which are alternatives to incarceration of youth. . . . It is our understanding that you have been involved with youth programs. Since the Runathon benefits youth programs, it was felt that you might want to be part of this event in some way.[2]

Marie suggested several options for Erving and the 76ers to get involved, including making a public statement of support of the runathon, sponsoring runners, or participating as celebrity runners.

Marie told David that she had written to Erving, but realized that if he was as big a star as her sons had said, getting his support would be a long shot. She turned her attention to the hundreds of other runathon details yet to be arranged.

Problems arose again at Graterford, when another group of inmates wanted Degrees of Captivity to receive runathon proceeds. However, Degrees still wasn't a registered charity. Graterford's volunteer coordinator, Joan Gauker, arranged a meeting between Marie and the inmates.

Three inmates sat at a desk in the middle of the meeting room and others sat along the walls. Marie and Joan sat down on the opposite side of the desk. Yusef sat nearby. One inmate demanded to know why Degrees of Captivity had been excluded from receiving runathon proceeds the previous year. Marie explained the eligibility requirements and said that Degrees hadn't qualified.

"The Voluntary Action Center would be closed down if we raise money for an organization that isn't registered with the Pennsylvania Commission on Charitable Organizations," she told them.

"You're just saying that because you're part of the United Way, and everyone knows the United Way is racist!" one inmate shouted from across the room.

"Yeah, they're working for South African interests!" another added.

Marie was almost too stunned to reply. *Where had this come from?* she wondered. She knew nothing about the South African interests they were talking about, but decided to just stick with the facts. "The runathon is not a United Way event. Runathon proceeds can only go to registered charitable organizations that have a board of directors."

"Isn't the United Way on your letterhead?" someone asked.

"The Voluntary Action Center is a member of the United Way, but the United Way has nothing to do with the runathon."

"Your group is sponsored by people who oppose the divestiture movement!"[3]

"If you weren't such a racist, you'd see that the money went to Degrees of Captivity!"

Marie looked at the angry faces that surrounded her. She'd never been accused of being a racist. It stung. Not knowing what else to say, she repeated, "We can only give the money to organizations that are registered charities and that have a board of directors. Degrees of Captivity isn't registered and doesn't have a board."

"What percentage of our money are you going to be taking out for your own racist organization?" another inmate shouted.

"We don't take anything out for expenses," Marie replied patiently. "We have a very generous donor who covers all of the expenses. So, one hundred percent of the money you raise will go to the charities you choose—but they have to be registered and they have to have a board of directors."

Objections continued from various inmates and Marie simply repeated the two criteria over and over until the inmates seemed to run out of arguments and the room fell silent. Finally, shaken and exhausted, Marie excused herself and left the meeting.

Joan Gauker walked out with her, whispering, "That was brave. I don't know how you did it."

Marie didn't know either. She was relieved to get back on the road to State College.

Yusef

Back inside the Graterford meeting room, as soon as Marie and Joan left, the inmates rushed toward the door. Yusef got there first and turned and blocked the door with his broad-shouldered frame.

"Everyone, sit down!" he ordered. "The real meeting is just beginning!"

Yusef roared and cursed, accusing the men of using the race card to curry favor with Mattie Humphrey.

"Let me tell you what Mattie did. She submitted the ID number for another organization since Degrees of Captivity isn't registered. That's clearly an act of fraud!"

He looked around the room. Everyone was silent.

"Degrees can't get the money. They don't qualify. So get over it. You're missing the whole point. The runathon is about us, pulling together to do something good for a change, something beyond self-interest, an accomplishment we can finally take pride in. That's what Mrs. Hamilton is trying to give us, and you just ran that good woman out of here with stupid, baseless accusations of racism, trying to use the South African divestiture movement as cover. Something not a single one of you know anything about—not one! Be real men for once. Stand for what's right and principled. If you don't, don't you ask me for anything—ever!"

Yusef sat down, looking at each man one by one, challenging them with his eyes to argue. No one did.

SOON AFTER THE Graterford meeting, Marie got a phone call from a staffer in U.S. Senator John Heinz's office, asking what the runathon was and how the charities were chosen. Marie explained the requirements. The staffer said that Degrees of Captivity had contacted their office to file a complaint of racism in distribution of runathon proceeds.

"We know Mattie Humphrey and always check out her complaints. But you're right that her organization shouldn't receive donations if they aren't a registered nonprofit," the staffer told Marie.

A few days later, Marie heard from Senator Arlen Specter's office, asking the same questions and saying they'd also received a complaint from Mattie Humphrey. Marie rubbed her temples as she repeated the same answers. She considered herself a very patient person, but this was sorely testing her.

She finally heard from Graterford's runathon committee. The men had been impressed with how Marie had handled the confrontation and agreed that only properly registered organizations should receive their donations. The men had decided to give their runathon proceeds to Big Sisters of Philadelphia and Second Mile, a foster home and mentoring program for boys.

Marie still couldn't understand what had set Mattie Humphrey so firmly against her. She hated being in an unresolved conflict, but felt she had at least tried to resolve it peacefully. Though she didn't like to admit it, she hoped it was the last she'd ever have to hear of Mattie Humphrey.

After the frustrations at Graterford, the planning meetings at the other prisons seemed easy. Muncy's runathon committee was one of the most enthusiastic and set new goals for that year. Lois chaired their committee again. As Marie had gotten to know Lois, through their meetings and correspondence, she'd become very fond of the fifty-six-year-old lifer.

Volunteer Helen Magnuson, Marie, and Muncy runathon chairwoman Lois (far right) award T-shirts, certificates, and trophies to runners at an awards ceremony at the Muncy women's prison (undated). Photo courtesy of CentrePeace, Inc.

On May 15, 1982, 921 inmates from all eight of the state's prisons logged over 8,000 miles and raised over $7,400. At the awards ceremonies later that summer, Marie awarded special marathon T-shirts to the nineteen inmates who had run at least twenty-six miles, including two women from Muncy. The Muncy women had reached their goals of raising the most money for their chosen charity and having the largest percentage of inmate and staff participation. The Muncy runners had also averaged more miles per runner than the men at Graterford and Dallas. Muncy's deputy superintendent and the activities director ran side by side with the women, along with William Jordan, the state's pardons case specialist.

When Marie arrived at the Graterford prison chapel for their awards ceremony, the inmates cheered and shouted.

"Marie! Do we ever have a surprise for you!" one told her.

The inmates stood up on their chairs and stomped and yelled. Marie couldn't imagine what was happening. Four unbelievably tall men walked into the room and onto the stage. The inmates sat down and a hushed silence fell over the room.

One of the men leaned down to the microphone at the pulpit and said, "I'm not sure why they want me to speak first."

The room erupted in loud chants. "Dr. J! Dr. J! Dr. J!" Marie laughed and clapped her hands. So, this was the famous Dr. J. The awards ceremony lasted for hours, punctuated by regular bursts of cheering.

After all of the certificates and T-shirts had been distributed, the inmates asked Marie if she'd like to have her picture taken with the 76ers. A group of men escorted her to the front of the room where Sixers Bobby Jones, Mike Bantom, Doug Collins, and Dr. J were waiting with the Graterford photographer. Marie was astonished at their height and had to tip her head way back to look up at each one. She introduced herself without mentioning that she'd never heard of them until recently.

Marie didn't say anything to her sons about the Graterford event until she received the developed photo of herself with the 76ers a few weeks later. At dinner, she laid the photo on the table without saying a word.

Steve grabbed it and stared. "No *way*! You got to *meet* Dr. J?"

Marie and top runner at Graterford prison with (back row, left to right) Philadelphia 76ers Bobby Jones, Mike Bantom, Julius Erving, and Doug Collins (June 1982). Photo courtesy of Marie Hamilton.

"This is completely unfair, Mom! You didn't even know who he was!" Mike complained.

"Unbelievable!"

"That's not right at all!"

"Don't you boys want to hear about my afternoon with the 76ers?" Marie asked sweetly.

"No!"

"Absolutely not!"

It was the most fun Marie had ever had with the runathon.

As SUMMER TURNED to autumn and the leaves on Bald Eagle Mountain started to turn gold and russet, Marie was already thinking ahead to Christmas. Every December since the volunteers had started their weekly visits on B Block, they'd had a holiday social with the men on the block. Though the socials had always been festive, lifting the men's spirits, Marie knew that holidays were incredibly painful times for prison inmates. This year, she was determined to see if something could be done to lift the holiday gloom throughout Rockview. She did some brainstorming with the volunteers and they created a long list of possibilities. Then Marie called Dr. Mazurkiewicz.

"The B Block volunteers were wondering if we could do something special for *all* of the Rockview inmates around the holidays this year. Maybe put on a Christmas play for all of them?"

"Too complicated," Mazurkiewicz replied brusquely.

"What about holiday music, then? I know some wonderful choral groups in the community who could perform."

"We can't do extra security clearances for outsiders," said Mazurkiewicz.

"How about a holiday social for the whole prison instead of just B Block?"

"Not with our budget."

Though Marie had expected the gruff superintendent to say no to some of their ideas, she was caught off guard by his unwavering vetoes.

When she got to the last idea and he'd said no, again, she twirled her pencil, trying to come up with just one more. She hated the thought of the men facing another bleak holiday season. She started talking, not sure where the words were coming from.

"How about if we just send Christmas cards to the men then? Maybe cards from children in the community . . . children could draw pictures and write a little message, and we could deliver them to the men."

"You couldn't put children's names on them. We can't have inmates knowing names of children in the community," Dr. Mazurkiewicz said.

"Okay, we could just put the child's first name," Marie countered. "Oh—and their age," she added.

"They couldn't be in envelopes—it would be too many for the staff to open."[4]

"Just cards, then—no envelopes," she agreed quickly.

"And the cards would all have to be a standard size. We couldn't have different sizes or styles of cards going to different inmates."

"That's no problem."

"Marie, I'm just afraid you'll never be able to get enough cards together. And you can't give cards to some inmates and not others," Mazurkiewicz warned.

"Well, if I can get enough cards so there's one for every inmate, and we don't put them in envelopes, and they're all exactly the same size, and if I personally screen every card to be sure there's nothing that would uniquely identify any child, just first names, no last names . . . if we do *all* of that, can we go forward with this, Dr. Mazurkiewicz?"

The superintendent let out a long sigh. "If you think you can get enough cards and do all of that before Christmas, you let me know."

That was all Marie needed. She and the volunteers just had to figure out how to get 1,500 cards manufactured, distributed to children's groups, decorated, returned to the VAC, and inspected in a little less than three months.

They decided to have each child draw a picture on the front of the card and write their first name and age inside. Inside each card, they would include the name and address of Volunteers in Prison, and a preprinted message saying, "This is a card decorated by a child expressly for a prison inmate."

But Marie wanted another message inside the cards too—something to offer hope to inmates, and something children could understand and feel good about saying to them. She looked at other Christmas cards for ideas, but none of their messages seemed appropriate for people who would be stuck inside a prison for the holidays.

One morning as she watched a favorite TV show, the Robert Schuller Hour from the Crystal Cathedral, the television camera zoomed in on a Christmas ornament they were offering to anyone who made a donation. Marie read its engraved message: *Christmas means you are loved.* "That's it!" she shouted. She grabbed a scrap of paper and wrote it down. First thing on Monday morning, Marie discussed it with the volunteers. They thought it was perfect.

They had a few thousand cards printed and crafted a letter to send out with them, explaining the project, and providing instructions and a deadline for returning finished cards. They asked churches, scout troops, and youth groups to participate. The response was tremendous. Soon packets of blank cards were being mailed out from the VAC office to organizations all over Centre County.

Within a few weeks, decorated cards came pouring back in. Marie and the volunteers were overwhelmed by the beauty of the children's artwork, and the sincerity and compassion of the messages children had included for the inmates. From pictures of Christmas trees with brightly colored lights to manger scenes to drawings of poinsettias, wreaths, stars, and other symbols of the season, each card was painstakingly drawn and colored. Children from ages five to eighteen had created cards.

Some were humorous, like one showing a chubby baby Jesus peeking out of a manger with the caption, "It's a BOY!" Some were finely detailed and artistic. Others were simply drawn by a young child's hand.

The volunteers examined every card carefully to be sure children hadn't included any personal identifying details. They also screened the messages for anything that might create a problem at Rockview. One child had written, "The next time—be smart!" Though the child had probably meant well, Marie knew they couldn't take the chance that the message might offend someone or be taken the wrong way. That card and a few others had to be excluded from the stack that would be sent to Rockview.

Finally, the cards were ready, nearly 1,500 in all, and Marie took them to the prison. Guards delivered the cards to each inmate along with a small bag of goodies, handing them through the bars, laying them on inmates' cots if they were out of the cell, and even sliding them through the small opening in the thick steel doors to inmates in "the Hole."[5]

Back at the VAC office, Marie and the volunteers sighed with relief as they organized the notes, lists, and phone numbers they had used to pull this off. Then each of them headed home to spend the holidays with their families.

In early January, when they returned to the VAC office, their mailbox was stuffed full again—this time with letters from the inmates.

To whom it may concern,

I received a Christmas card on Christmas Eve . . . a true gift. The card was hand made by a ten year old child named Leon, which is my own name in reverse. I found it a pleasant coincidence and it touched me in a special kind of way. I do not have children of my own and my parents have passed away since I've been in prison. There are a lot of reasons why I have not felt in a Christmas kind of way over the years but I will not get into that. My point is that, I wanted to thank you and a ten year old boy named Leon for softening my heart and reminding me what it felt like to see Christmas through the eyes of a child, when things were simpler and hopes and dreams were so vivid. . . . Thank you. Happy New Year. May it be prosperous and peaceful for you and yours.

Sincerely, Noel[6]

I had to write concerning the Christmas card I received. . . . The card was wonderfully done by an 11 year-old named Christian. But even if it was merely scribbled it would have been appreciated just the same. My teenage son has not contacted me for a long time and the love I have for him can't be put into words. We became so close when his mother and my wife of 22 years left us and moved out. But I broke down and he was again abandoned by a parent, not voluntarily. You don't need that story. What I want to express is how the card from Christian filled a void and drained a few tears from my eyes and to tell someone how much it meant to me. In return, I'm enclosing a copy of a Christmas poem I wrote for family and friends. It's not much but it's all I have right now . . . if someone could tell Christian how much his card meant to someone else, a stranger he'll never know or need to know, maybe I can transfer the warm feeling I got back to him to let him know the value of giving.

Thank you. Thomas[7]

To Matt, age 12,

I write to extend thanks from the heart to all who participated in the very humanizing act of giving, sharing from the best part of us. I am inspired by the art work of young Matt. The artwork brought back memories of childhood, when at school in art class, I found the most peace and feelings of being. Having been abandoned as a child, such an experience is for me a dear memory. . . . I am not a Christmas person but who could deny the beautiful spirit of it all when efforts such as yours have brought real and positive emotion/thoughts to this beastial place and a wretch like me. . . . God bless you!

Sincerely, Nathaniel[8]

My little buddy, Dear Cool Brent,

First things first, I would like to thank you for the nice card you sent me. It really touch my heart, in fact that was the only card I received from anyone. And I'll always treasure that card, it will go home with me. . . . Cool Brent, check this out, although you is only eight, in time you will be at the age wheres though you might want to start hanging out. Well let me tell you something now. Being cool is okay to a extent, but the more you try to show your coolness, the more you'll have to prove yourself to hang with the crowd and by doing so, that's where the trouble will begin. Trouble is the easiest thing in the world to get in but believe me, it's definitely the hardest thing to get out of. So always do the right things in life and you should never have those problems! Take care of yourself, always listen to your parents, stay in school and try not to be too cool!! God bless you always.

Your friend, Phil[9]

Hello and a Merry Xmas to you Stanley,

I just got back from working in the kitchen and I came to my cell and to my surprise there on my bed was a Christmas card and I said who put this card on my bed? But no one said a word so I open it up and started to read it. Stanley I just don't know what to say. You sure made me feel a lot better . . . I'll always keep this card and put it out at Xmas time. Stanley let me tell you a little bit about me. I am a Anonymous and I use drugs and this is why I'm in jail. I'm 47 and trying to get better and with God help I will. And Stanley I can't read or write to good eather so I hope you can read my letter. Stanley I wanted to tell you a little bit about me so you won't every try drugs or alcohol because they are no good for you. And Stanley you tell your friends ok no drugs they kill you. So Stanley I hope you get everything you pray for. Good luck and stay in church Stanley. O and don't forget to listen to your Mom and Dad they know what better for you. I will be thinking of you this Xmas. Be good I know you will. And thank you for the Xmas card Stanley.

Love, Michael[10]

Thank you for remembering that even though inmates committed a crime we are still human and have feelings. . . . I generally don't celebrate holidays, even on the streets, but the card from Alex (age 8) lifted my spirits. For that, please give him a special thanks if you can. It reminds me of my own children. May the almighty bless you in all you do.

Sincerely, Wes[11]

I want to thank Christine for the hand-drawn card. I myself and most of the other guys thoroughly deserve to be in jail. But some of the guys come from a background almost guaranteed to produce the cynical anti-social attitude that leads to criminal acts and jail terms. So by demonstrating that at least some people have kindness and regard for others, as you people have done, you provide a model for the guys. It may be just enough to make the difference. . . .

Thanks again. Frank[12]

Dear Jessica,
    Your card was a little ray of sunshine in a place of cold steel and concrete. . . .

From Douglas[13]

Some of the inmates' letters were written in fine, flowing script, some in chunky block letters, others in painstakingly tiny print. A few inmates enclosed poems they'd written, some shared Bible verses or other inspirational writings, and many included their own artwork. One was handwritten on the prison's "General Purpose Request Form":

NAME: Any Inmate
BLOCK: All
CELL: All
COMMUNICATION TO: OTHER (Please specify): God

I want to request that God grant a special blessing to all the people who took part in Volunteers in Prison program. . . . My gratitude and thanks to all the children who spent their time and effort to bring happiness and joy to an otherwise bleak time behind bars. The Christmas cards that we received that were decorated by the children were the highlight. . . . There were guys everywhere showing off their cards, telling others with excitement and pride the little information that we had about the particular child artist—their first name and their age. Everyone's card was the best to him. No others could have been better. . . . The card I received is worth more than any masterpiece hanging in any art gallery anywhere.

Greatfully, Any Inmate

THE NEXT TIME the volunteers went to Rockview, they saw the children's cards everywhere—taped on the walls above inmates' bunks, propped up on small stacks of books, laid reverently on top of prison-issued pillows. For weeks, letters from inmates continued to pour into the VAC office. For months, the men on B Block talked about the children who had drawn their cards and how they were praying that those children would grow up well and stay out of trouble.

Christmas means you are loved. It seemed like such a simple message, but many of the inmates told Marie and the other volunteers that it was the first time they'd ever been told that, that they'd grown up without ever hearing anyone say I love you.

Marie's mother had always told her: "Whatever the question, love is the answer." Marie had hoped the actions of the volunteers and their weekly visits were enough to convey to the men that someone cared about them, that they were loved. After seeing how the men responded to the message in the Christmas cards, she wanted them to hear that message more than just at Christmas. Marie started using the word "love" regularly when she talked with inmates. And though she knew there was a risk that, someday, someone might misconstrue her meaning, she started to tell the men that she loved them.

The Christmas Cards for Inmates program continues today. Thousands of inmates receive a card like this one at Christmas. The artwork on the front is an original, created by a child expressly for a prison inmate. Courtesy of CentrePeace, Inc.

8
LOVE IN PRISON

There is no fear in love, but perfect love casts out fear.
                                                    −1 John 4:18[1]

While Marie pondered how she and the volunteers could demonstrate love for inmates more clearly, halfway across the country Keith J. Leenhouts, a former judge and director of Volunteers in Prevention, Probation and Prisons, Inc. (VIP),[2] was planning a national think tank on the topic of love and its role in the criminal justice system. VIP had started as a small volunteer program in a Michigan district court and had grown into a division of the National Council on Crime and Delinquency, with a high-powered board that included U.S. Supreme Court justices, university presidents, and corrections administrators from several states. Leenhouts invited professionals and volunteers from all over the country to exchange ideas and information on successful love-based programs for rehabilitation of offenders. His invitation to Marie was all the affirmation she needed that she and the volunteers were on the right track. She accepted with enthusiasm.

Marie's love for those in prison earned her the prestigious 1982-83 Benjamin Rush Award[3] from the Centre County Medical Society. Letters recommending Marie for the award had flooded into the award chairman's office from Judge Charles Brown, Department of Corrections Commissioner Ronald Marks, John McCullough, Dr. Mazurkiewicz, her former pastor, Mike Scrogin, and George Etzweiler of the Middle

Pennsylvania District of the Church of the Brethren. Among the many letters was a tribute from Butch, who had been on B Block North years earlier. Butch was now at the Huntingdon prison, where Marie visited him often.

In his three-page recommendation, Butch wrote:

> To truly be concerned about the welfare of another requires a sweet gift of 'expression.' A divine gift, because sometimes just caring isn't quite enough. Marie Hamilton, with every word, gesture, and deed, expressed it. Sweetly. Her profound and honest interest in our feelings, our misfortunes, and our few triumphs demanded much of her time, energy and understanding—yet she always could find a moment to hear us out. She would share a few secrets, carry a few burdens, and, occasionally, enjoy a few of our dreams. . . . She was like an ear for the silent screams of men who, for most of their lives, felt ignored, and a voice for many who had never been heard. . . . The eagerness in which she displayed her willingness to be involved in our causes, our ideas, our very lives, made her an important part of our everyday endeavors, and kept her close to our hearts.[4]

After reading his tribute, Marie wrote:

My dear Butch . . . The reading of your letter brought tears. You captured what I would like to be. . . . If per chance I should be chosen to receive the award, it would be anticlimactic to my reading of your letter. I will cherish the letter—as I do our friendship.

Always, Marie[5]

She wished every letter was as beautiful to read and as easy to respond to as the one from Butch. The volume of letters from inmates requesting help with parole plans, legal cases, counseling, employment, financial issues, and numerous other serious concerns continued to escalate. Marie responded to every letter, but the work involved had grown nearly unmanageable. It was time to rethink the process.

At a symposium on alternatives to incarceration, she talked with Angus Love, an attorney who worked on prison issues. She told Angus about the volume of letters she received every month and about the lists of support services she'd compiled.

"I've been thinking that if I could get all of this information printed in some type of directory, I could just send each inmate a copy of the directory and they could find what they need," she said.

Angus told her that a man named Sam Milkes from Central Pennsylvania Legal Services had created a directory of legal services for inmates. He suggested they join forces with Milkes and offered to provide financial backing if Marie would be willing to put it all together. It was a deal Marie couldn't refuse.

Angus introduced Marie to Milkes and they agreed that the VAC would compile the directory and update it every two years. Marie gathered information from organizations across Pennsylvania and, with the help of student interns from Penn State, published the first "Prison Advocacy and Support Directory."

Marie hoped it would be as easy to get support for another major project she had in mind. After the first two successful statewide runathons, prison administrators in several other states had written to her, asking for advice on how to organize their own runathons. At national conferences she attended, people had asked for information about the runathon and how it worked. She was invited to meet with staff and inmates in a prison in Rahway, New Jersey, to help them start a runathon. All this consultation gave Marie another nagging thought.

She approached Anthony P. Travisono, executive director of the American Correctional Association, and proposed that they take the runathon national. Travisono was intrigued by the idea and asked Marie to draft a proposal. He thought many states would be interested if someone else coordinated it, and he promised to contact corrections commissioners across the country to propose it.

With the promise of support from a major national organization, Marie brought the idea back to the Voluntary Action Center board. Using a strategy she'd learned from her mentors, Rose and Ann, she met with each VAC board member individually and sought their input before presenting the idea to the whole board. At their next board meeting, Marie received unanimous approval to pursue it. She created cost estimates and job descriptions for the coordination effort, then started the search for funding and potential organizations to coordinate it. Pennsylvania's runathon had consumed a tremendous amount of VAC time and resources. A national runathon would demand dedicated staff in an organization large enough to manage a project of that magnitude. Marie approached churches, civic groups, and every other organization she could think of, asking for funding and organizational support.

Travisono sent letters endorsing the idea to corrections officials around the country. Officials in Alabama, Connecticut, New York, and New Jersey expressed interest. Marie convened a meeting of interested parties at the 1982 National Workshop on Voluntarism. William Jordan, Pennsylvania's pardons case specialist, gave the runathon a glowing endorsement and told of his experience running alongside female inmates at Muncy. The meeting attendees generated ideas for funding and coordination and Marie pursued every possibility they suggested. After months of phone calls, letters, and speaking engagements, she couldn't find anyone willing to commit to funding or coordinating a national event.

Finally, Marie went to Dan Katkin, head of Penn State's Administration of Justice program, to see if the university would be willing to coordinate a national runathon and help secure funding for it. She was thrilled when Katkin agreed to pursue it. He asked Marie to work with Professor Thomas Bernard, whom Katkin assigned to write grant proposals for the project. As Marie talked with Dr. Bernard, she felt the first glimmer of hope that it might become a reality.

Dr. Bernard submitted grant proposals to over ninety foundations. But when Marie read the university's proposals, she had serious concerns. They included a research component to assess the impact of the runathon, which Marie knew wouldn't sit well with prison administrators. She was shocked at the university's high cost estimates for staffing and expenses, something she hadn't included in her calculations since she was used to working with volunteers and securing donations to cover major expenses. But what she found most disappointing was that she couldn't be involved if the national runathon became a project of the university as all of the job descriptions they'd written for the project required people with college degrees.

The project had suddenly become awkward and embarrassing. Marie went to Ann and Rose. They weren't comfortable with the university's proposal either, but suggested that Marie talk with John Ferguson, a vice president at Penn State. John's wife, Eleanor, had been a long-time prison volunteer with the VAC and Marie knew the Fergusons well. John listened carefully as Marie explained her concerns.

"Marie, you can't expect Penn State to be a human service agency. It's a university—our focus is research and education," Ferguson explained.

He suggested that Marie ask Dan Katkin to relinquish the project back to the VAC. Marie talked with Dr. Bernard first to explain the VAC's concerns, then wrote a brief letter to Katkin. The project was stalled, again.

Meanwhile, plans were underway for Pennsylvania's third runathon. Marie loved reconnecting with men and women on the planning committees at each prison. Butch was the activities director for Community First Step at the Huntingdon prison and chaired their runathon committee. Lois chaired the Muncy runathon for the third year in a row and she greeted Marie like a cherished friend at each meeting.

Governor Dick Thornburgh proclaimed May 21, 1983, the date of the runathon, "Run for Youth Day." U.S. Senator Arlen Specter wrote letters of commendation for the members of the inmate planning committees at each of the participating prisons. Senator John Heinz pledged a penny per mile for the total miles run in the 1983 runathon. Nearly seven hundred inmates from seven prisons logged 8,755 miles and raised over $8,000.

Each year, the event became bigger and better, and the inmates became more committed to the runathon. The women at Muncy raised more money through inmate and staff pledges than any other prison, and had the highest percentage of inmate and staff participation in the state.

One inmate named James[6] summed up the feelings of many when he wrote, "I would have run until I died if it meant I could save one kid."[7] James had run twenty-eight miles in his prison-issued, high-top leather boots, stopping only when his ankles hurt so badly that he couldn't take another step.

After that year's runathon, Marie's youngest son, Mike, graduated from high school. Mike had always had a great sense of humor, but Marie thought he sometimes seemed withdrawn and unhappy. Right after graduation, he started taking summer classes at Penn State. Marie hoped that starting college would bring back her fun-loving son.

With another runathon and Mike's graduation behind her, Marie needed to spend some time on her responsibilities as criminal justice reform representative with the Middle Pennsylvania District of the Church of the Brethren. She wanted to engage Brethren congregations in death penalty abolition work, prison visitation, reentry mentoring, and conflict resolution training. She recommended that the district survey their congregations to assess interests, attitudes, and current involvement in these areas. She also asked that Volunteers in Prison be made an official Brethren Volunteer Service project so that BVS volunteers could be assigned on a regular basis.

In a letter to Bob Gross, a fellow Brethren who was associate director of the National Coalition Against the Death Penalty, Marie wrote, "Although the response to criminal justice concerns has not been popular in our churches in the past, I believe we can get to this."[8]

The prison programs were growing so rapidly that Marie had to continually recruit additional volunteers. Thankfully, several dedicated Rockview volunteers like Dave Stickell, Betty Bergstein, Cynthia Schein, Eleanor Ferguson, and Bob Olsen had been with the program for years and provided continuity for the weekly visitation program.

The pre-release program at Rockview had undergone extensive changes. After their block sergeant died, the pre-release inmates had moved out of B Block North into modular units. A new team of corrections officers and treatment staff was running the program. John McCullough was no longer involved on a day-to-day basis. Marie missed his wise counsel. However, she and the volunteers continued visiting, leading discussion groups, and teaching conflict resolution classes to the pre-release inmates every week. Marie felt the conflict resolution course was one of the most powerful programs they had ever implemented. But in the summer of 1983 she found something even more powerful.

Community Alternatives in Criminal Justice had hired Barb Seibel to develop their alternatives to incarceration programs. Barb was also a trained mediator. She proposed that CACJ offer mediation services and the CACJ board enthusiastically agreed. Twenty people, including Marie, became trained mediators and they set up a community mediation center. They educated district judges about the benefits of mediation and asked them to offer mediation to disputing parties as an alternative to having the judge decide their fate. A local agency that worked with teens and families began referring clients to CACJ's mediation center. As local residents began to hear about mediation, community interest in mediation grew.

Marie co-mediated one of her first cases with CACJ's director, Bonnie Millmore. A drunk university student had trespassed into the home of a local Mennonite family in the middle of the night. The student was arrested, charged, and sentenced. His sentence would have prevented him from continuing his studies toward a medical degree, which the homeowners felt was too harsh. They requested mediation with the student. The student apologized for his actions and reassured the couple that he had meant them no harm. As they talked, it became clear that the student had a drinking problem and the couple talked with him about it. As part of the agreement they crafted, the couple asked the young man to stay in contact with them so they would know he was working on his drinking problem. The couple then asked the court to drop the charges, but their request was denied. Despite that, the young man stopped drinking and stayed in contact with the couple. Marie invited the couple to go with her to speak at churches and civic groups about their experience and the word spread about the power of mediation. Marie began to see mediation as the best possible alternative to the court system and incarceration.

Then she encountered a conflict even mediation wouldn't resolve. Her husband, Joe, was having an affair. When Marie confronted him, Joe didn't deny it. Marie was devastated. She adored Joe and had tried so hard to be a perfect wife. It hadn't been enough. His work travel had kept him away from home for long periods of time and they had grown apart.

Marie prayed about her marriage, but for the first time in her life she felt that God didn't hear her. She threw herself into her prison work and dreaded going home each night. Though Steve and Mike were both living at home while they attended Penn State, they had lives of their own. Steve had a demanding work and school schedule and was rarely at home. When Mike wasn't in classes, he spent most of his time in his room or off fishing by himself. Marie was alone.

An incident at the annual VAC picnic highlighted the growing differences between Marie and Joe. The VAC always invited Rockview and Centre County Jail inmates to join the VAC staff and volunteers for a day of games, socializing, and a cookout. Though she had intentionally kept religion out of her prison work, Marie also wanted to have sunset vespers at the picnic, like the ones she'd loved so as a teen at Camp Harmony. She hoped the experience of quietly singing hymns as they watched the sun go down would give the inmates a sense of peacefulness before they had to return to the chaos and din of prison life. As the sun started to go down, everyone hiked up the highest hill in Spring Creek Park in silence. At the top, Marie handed out song booklets and led the group in singing several favorite hymns.

Suddenly, in the midst of a song, gunshots cracked loudly from a neighboring hill. The inmates jumped and looked around nervously. More gunshots echoed. In the tense silence, someone observed that it was probably hunters. Marie knew immediately it must be Joe, Mike, and Steve, dove hunting. The boys had mentioned their plans that morning. She had always hated Joe's guns, but this was the ultimate irony. *While I'm trying to offer something peaceful to the inmates, my husband and sons are shooting the symbol of peace.*

Though her marriage continued to disintegrate, her prison work blossomed.

THE DATE FOR Judge Leenhouts' national think tank finally arrived. Marie went to Canada for the event, titled: "Love: The Greatest Therapeutic Force in Our War Against Crime."

"Why are your programs effective?" Leenhouts asked the attendees. "I only invited people who are running effective programs for offenders. What makes them work?"

After several days of dialogue, the attendees concluded that it wasn't flashy brochures or big budgets or nice facilities that made programs effective. The programs that worked were those whose staff and volunteers showed genuine love for offenders.

Leenhouts later formulated their conclusions this way: "Treating the offender when s/he first comes in contact with the justice system with an intensive program of rehabilitative services motivated by firm, realistic, demanding, affectionate and caring love is the true solution to the problem."[9]

Marie returned from Canada with renewed confidence in the importance of what she and the volunteers were trying to do for and with inmates. Their programs were growing so rapidly that she constantly had to scramble to secure enough funding to support it all. Twice as many inmates participated in the 1984 runathon as had run the year before, which meant twice as many T-shirts, sports drinks, and certificates, and extensive travel to all of the planning meetings and awards ceremonies. Children in over one hundred churches and schools made more than 5,500 Christmas cards for inmates that year, which meant added printing and postage costs. While she was thrilled that they were reaching so many additional inmates, she was also exhausted at times.

When the VAC's part-time director resigned the following spring, the board asked Marie to add the VAC directorship to her half-time coordinator role for Volunteers in Prison, giving her an official full-time position. It would mean turning some of the prison work over to others to focus on day-to-day operations of the VAC, but Marie felt maybe it was time for a change. Trying to get a national runathon off the ground, keeping up with the prison programs, and the rift in her marriage had taken a major toll on her, physically and emotionally.

Marie continued to pray about her marriage, but Joe's affair continued. One night, she sat alone on the sofa, staring into space as night fell. Near midnight, her son, Mike, came out of his room and sat down next to Marie in the dark. After sitting silently for a few minutes, Mike confessed that he was extremely depressed.

"I've been thinking about suicide," he told her.

Marie snapped out of her daze and turned on the lamp to look at him. It was obvious that he was serious. Mike revealed that he'd gone through long periods of intense sadness. Marie put her arms around him, thinking about all the time he'd spent alone. She should have seen the signs.

"My life is going to be miserable. I just know it is," he concluded.

"I'll help you through this, Mike," Marie promised. "There will be better days. I promise."

They sat and talked for hours. Finally, Mike went to bed. The next day, Marie took him to a mental health agency for an evaluation. They referred him to a psychiatrist, who recommended that he check into a hospital for treatment. Marie and Joe set aside their differences to focus on Mike and spent long hours by his side at the hospital.

When Mike was discharged, Marie spent as much time as she could with him, while trying to keep the prison work going. Joe continued to travel extensively, but when he was at home he spent as much time as possible with Mike. Both Marie and Joe desperately wanted their son back.

Marie with her parents, Robert and Virginia Fortney, and her sons, Steve and Mike (undated). Photo courtesy of Marie Hamilton.

Marie asked for help with her VAC work and two VAC volunteers, Madhu Sidhu and Virginia Dimeling, stepped in to take over much of the administrative work. In June 1985, more help arrived in the form of a BVS volunteer named Birgit Maier, from Germany. Birgit enthusiastically jumped into the prison work, helping to keep all of the programs going and preparing for the Fifth Annual Pennsylvania Prison Runathon.

The Volunteers in Prison programs gained national recognition as Marie spoke at conferences and conducted conflict resolution workshops around the country. The National Association on Volunteers in Criminal Justice invited her to serve on their board of directors. Though she was glad for the national visibility, Marie thought more could be done within Pennsylvania to raise the visibility and acceptance of prison volunteers. She had been invited to lead a workshop on "Volunteers in Corrections" at the Pennsylvania Association of Volunteers conference. There, she partnered with Harvey Bell, the Department of Corrections' pardons case specialist, and sparked interest in volunteerism among other organizations around the state.

Marie and CACJ were expanding volunteerism in another way. In the first four years of CACJ's Community Service alternative sentencing program, judges had sentenced five hundred offenders to community service. Those "volunteers" had provided over ten thousand hours of service to fifty Centre County agencies. Inmates from the county jail had even been allowed to earn "good-time credit" for volunteer work conducted through a work-release option.

The Voluntary Action Center welcomed offenders as volunteers and put them to work sorting, cleaning, and pricing donated toys, clothing, furniture, and household goods for the VAC's frequent yard sale fundraisers. They often told Marie that the chance to make a positive contribution and demonstrate their worth by volunteering meant as much to them as earning time off of their sentence. Offenders frequently returned to volunteer for VAC even after their release from jail, and Marie took many of them with her to speak to church and civic groups to promote the prison programs.

One inmate named Robert[10] told Marie, "If you give me some tools, I could fix some of the donated appliances and furniture and you could sell them for a lot more money at your yard sales." Robert's suggestion gave Marie another idea, for an even bigger inmate volunteer program that would teach inmates furniture and appliance repair skills. But for now, she had all the work she could handle.

She was planning a special event during National Volunteer Week to honor the dozens of volunteers who helped with all of the Volunteers in Prison programs. The event would also have to raise money to continue those programs. She tracked down several former Rockview inmates who had demonstrated their musical talents at the B Block North socials over the years and invited them to provide entertainment for a "Serenade to Volunteers" concert and fundraiser.

Marie mentioned the idea to Harvey Bell at the DOC.

"We should recognize *all* of the prison volunteers statewide," Bell suggested. Since speaking at the Pennsylvania Association of Volunteers conference, Bell had become a real advocate for volunteers within the DOC. Marie offered to make the Serenade a statewide volunteer recognition event and invited DOC Commissioner Glen Jeffes to be the keynote speaker. Jeffes accepted and Marie invited Dr. Mazurkiewicz to introduce him.

Suddenly, the work to plan the event mushroomed. Fortunately, Marie had Birgit, her energetic BVS volunteer, and OJ,[11] a former inmate who had become a full-time VAC volunteer, to help. The trio threw themselves into writing letters to prison superintendents and chaplains, volunteer organizations, and civic groups across Pennsylvania, inviting all to participate in the First Annual Serenade to Volunteers in Corrections. They expanded the entertainment to include two inmate groups, the Rockview Glee Club and the Muncy Womens' Ensemble.

As Marie calculated the projected cost of the event and compared it to the ticket price they'd agreed to charge each attendee, she realized the event would lose money, not make money. She went to Ann Cook for advice.

"How much is the shortfall?" Ann asked.

Marie threw out a rough figure.

"I'll cover it," Ann said.

When Marie started to object, Ann stopped her with a wave of her delicate hand. "When my brother died, he left me a good bit of money. I want to put it to good use. This is one of the most worthy causes I can imagine."

The gala event took place at the Elks Country Club in Boalsburg, on April 20, 1986. Marie couldn't stop smiling as she watched religious and community leaders, inmates and former inmates, prison staff and volunteers sitting together, talking, and laughing.

"The Department of Corrections strongly supports a positive volunteer program," Jeffes told the three hundred attendees. "Volunteers provide an added dimension to the program area and provide inmates with successful role models from the community." That evening, Jeffes recognized over one hundred volunteers for their contributions.

The DOC was making a concerted effort to welcome more prison volunteers across the state. Jeffes had charged Bell with creating a standardized DOC volunteer orientation packet containing a welcome letter from Jeffes, guidelines for volunteers, an overview of DOC rules, and a volunteer application form. Volunteers in each prison would also receive a welcome letter from that prison's superintendent and a profile of that prison. When Bell sent a sample packet to Marie for her input, she had to laugh, thinking about the crash course she and the Rockview volunteers had gotten in their first orientation with Jeff Beard and John McCullough.

Soon after the Serenade, JT visited Marie at the VAC office, happily reporting his newfound success on the outside. He had a job, a home, and a steady girlfriend.

"I'm afraid I'm turning into a square, Marie," JT told her, laughing.

"It's not so terrible, you know," Marie replied.

"Well, as much as it pains me to admit it, I've concluded that squares make it in this world."

Marie laughed and threw her arms around JT. "Welcome to the club!" she told him. They'd all come a long way in ten years.

Though John McCullough was no longer involved in the day-to-day operation of Rockview's pre-release program, he invited Marie and the volunteers to a celebration he and the inmates had organized to recognize the volunteers' decade of service. Over 120 pre-release inmates and members of the Rockview staff honored Marie and volunteers Dave Stickell, Eleanor Ferguson, Bob Olsen, Birgit Maier, Eileen Penn, Connie Tinkleman, and Margaret Moerschbacher.

"Ten years ago, bringing outsiders into the prison, especially right into a cellblock, was very unusual," McCullough said. "Dr. Mazurkiewicz had the vision, and the VAC had dedicated volunteers who could make it work."

"And you've always been supportive of the program, John," Marie replied. "You've always been honest and straightforward in your dealings with us as volunteers."

"You've all shown the men here that there are people out there who care about them without expecting anything in return," McCullough observed. "You've demonstrated that goodness exists by itself, without any religious or other agenda. People in corrections don't trust goodness. And in the inmate world, kindness equates with weakness. But you've shown the men something different. You brought humanity to Rockview. And you've been able to get through to the men in seemingly miraculous ways." McCullough paused. "How was that possible, Marie?"

Marie smiled and shrugged. "That's the power of love, John."

The celebration was also a farewell. The pre-release program was changing and would no longer accommodate weekly visits from volunteers. The volunteers and the men said emotional goodbyes, with promises to stay in touch.

Then the volunteers turned their attention to their new assignment—weekly visits with the seventy-five new residents of B Block North, which had been converted to a special treatment needs unit for inmates with a range of mental health concerns. Dr. Greg Gaertner, Rockview's staff psychologist, asked Marie if she'd teach the conflict resolution program to these inmates. Marie was hesitant.

"How would I know if I was getting through to them?" she asked Gaertner.

"I guarantee you'll see an even greater impact from your program on these men."

Marie wasn't sure, but was willing to try it. She learned all she could about different types of mental health issues and treatments. She started to recognize common traits and behaviors associated with depression, paranoia, and schizophrenia. Her own experience with depression and Mike's diagnosed bipolar disorder helped her to better understand the men. She learned about the effects of medication and the results when the men's medications weren't well-regulated. Though these men were different in some ways than those who had been in the pre-release program, she saw that they, too, craved love and compassion. She was happy to offer it. Unlike the pre-release inmates, most of the men now on B Block wouldn't be released from prison for many years, if ever.

OCCASIONALLY, FORMER INMATES who had been released from prison visited Marie at the VAC office to let her know how they were doing on the outside. One afternoon, a man she didn't recognize appeared in her office doorway.

"Marie Hamilton?" he asked.

"Yes, I'm Marie."

"Then this is your day," he said, suddenly glaring at her. "Because of *you*, I had to spend five extra years in prison." He moved toward her. "I wrote letter after letter to you, asking for your help, but you ignored me."

A hot flush went through Marie's body. She realized he must be the inmate whose bizarre letters she'd stopped answering years earlier. John McCullough had predicted that if he ever got out of prison, he'd kill again.

Hatred blazed in his eyes.

Marie's mind and voice were frozen. Her heart pounded. *Help me, God.*

"I shoulda been out a long time ago," he said loudly.

She thought about her training in nonviolence.

He took another step toward her.

She slowly pushed her chair back from the desk. She breathed.

He stopped moving.

She swallowed. "That is terrible," she said quietly. "You sat in that prison for five extra years." She slowly stood up. "And here I sit in this nice office." She took a step toward him. "How awful." She took another step. "How terrible."

He stared at her.

"That's awful that you were in prison for five long years." She slowly walked toward him. "Just terrible . . . awful." One word with each step. She reached him. Put her arms around him.

He tensed in her embrace.

"Five extra years," Marie said quietly. She turned, kept her arm around his shoulder, and pointed toward her desk. "And there she sat in that chair."

She turned to look at him with as much love as she could muster.

The man looked confused. He jerked away. He turned and ran out of her office, down the stairs, and out the front door.

As soon as she heard the door slam behind him, Marie collapsed into the nearest chair.

Birgit rushed into Marie's office. "Marie! Are you okay?"

"Did you hear that?" Marie asked, dazed.

"Yes, I heard it all. I was trying to figure out what to do." Birgit peered out into the hallway. "Thank goodness he's gone. . . . Oh! Where's my duffel bag? It was right there in the hall."

Marie stood up to see where Birgit was pointing. "I wonder if he grabbed it when he ran out. Was anything valuable in it?"

"Just my workout clothes." Birgit shrugged. "Nothing worth worrying about."

"He was so angry, he probably felt like he had to *take* something. I think he intended to take my life."

"I'm so glad you're okay, Marie."

Marie hugged the beautiful young woman she'd grown so fond of. She would miss Birgit terribly when her year of BVS service was over in June.

Marie and Birgit agreed not to say anything to the other staff about what had happened. They didn't want to alarm anyone. They just got back to business.

A few days later, Snooky's wife called again. Marie had known Snooky was back in prison—Rockview this time.

"He had a stroke at the prison a few days ago and they took him to the hospital," Snooky's wife told Marie. "He's so depressed. I'm afraid he'll get suicidal again. Would you go see him at the hospital?"

"Of course," Marie replied, writing down his room number.

She went to the hospital that afternoon. Guards were posted outside Snooky's hospital room. They recognized Marie and allowed her into his room. Sitting on the edge of the vinyl visitor's chair next to Snooky's bed, Marie covered his curled-up hand with hers.

"How are you doing, Snooky?" she asked gently.

He struggled to get a few slurred words out. "I . . . I guess . . . okay."

"Your wife says you've been having a pretty rough time," Marie said. "I wanted to come and see you, and ask if there's anything I can do for you."

Snooky blinked slowly a few times as he tried to get his breath. "Uh . . . uh yeah. . . . Will you . . . pray for me?"

"Yes, I sure will," Marie answered, giving his limp hand a squeeze.

"Rose too . . . ask Rose to pray . . . and Ann Cook."

"I know they both will pray for you, Snooky. I'll be sure to ask them."

"And Eleanor? . . . And David?"

"Absolutely."

"Bob and Margaret, too? Ask them to pray for me, too," Snooky said, finally out of breath.

"Yes, of course, we'll all be happy to pray for you," Marie answered. "But, I'm curious about something, Snooky. In all the years I've known you, this is the first I've ever heard you mention anything religious. Why this interest all of a sudden in praying?"

Snooky's breathing became more labored. A few glistening tears rolled down his dark cheeks.

"Because I don't . . . know how," he admitted. "To pray, I mean. And I'm afraid, Marie. . . . I'm afraid I'm going to die."

Marie took Snooky's hand between both of hers and just held it for a while. Prayer was such a natural, everyday part of her life. It had never occurred to her that there were people who didn't know how to pray.

She talked with Snooky for a little while longer, then headed home with his poignant request on her mind.

That Sunday she was the guest speaker at Dunnings Creek Church of the Brethren and she had her message planned. But as she started speaking, Snooky's request was on her mind. So she set her notes aside and shared his story with the congregation.

As she concluded, she said, "You know, I think there may be many more inmates like Snooky who would be so grateful to have someone out here in the community who would be willing to pray especially for them—someone who would be a sort of 'prayer partner' for them."

She paused, looking around the room, then added, "Who knows? In return, maybe the inmate would be willing to pray for you, too."

There was a long, awkward silence. As Marie looked out at the people in the congregation, she suddenly realized the audacity of - suggesting that prison inmates—murderers, thieves, rapists, drug addicts—might pray for members of a church congregation—community leaders, business owners, teachers, doctors, and nurses. Embarrassed, she offered a brief closing prayer and sat down. When the service ended, Marie left Dunnings Creek quickly and didn't mention the prayer partners idea again.

9

No Chicken Tonight

*Life is a series of experiences, each of which makes us bigger,
even though it is hard to realize this. For the world was built
to develop character, and we must learn that the setbacks and
grieves which we endure help us in our marching onward.*

—Henry Ford (1863–1947)

A few weeks after her embarrassment at the Dunnings Creek
church, Marie received a letter from them.

"Dear Marie, Thank you for sharing Snooky's story with us. Here
is a check to help cover the costs of starting a prayer exchange program with the inmates. We have also included a list of people from
our congregation who would like to be matched with an inmate as
prayer partners."

Marie leaned back in her chair and laughed. *I should have trusted
you to make it happen, God,* she prayed. *Forgive me for doubting.* Then
she got to work. She had learned when proposing anything new at the
prison to anticipate all possible concerns and figure out in advance
how to address them. She wrote to several inmates to ask what they
thought of the prayer exchange idea and to seek advice on how to get
the word out to inmates who might want to participate. She talked
with Chaplain Bigelow and Father Crouse at Rockview, and with Father Menei, chief chaplain for the Department of Corrections.

Father Menei mentioned the risk that some inmates might want a
more personal relationship than their prayer partner was comfortable

with, or that some might ask their prayer partners for money, favors, or gifts. To avoid this, they decided that the program should be conducted on a first-name only basis, with no direct contact between inmates and community members. All correspondence would be routed through the VAC office. As they did with the Christmas cards, VAC staff would screen letters between inmates and community members to be sure they didn't include last names, addresses, or other personal information.

Marie told Father Menei that, while she was sure community members would be willing to pray for inmates, she wasn't sure whether community members would ask inmates to pray for them.

"In some ways, Marie, those of us on the outside may need the prayers even more," Father Menei observed. "We don't talk about our problems because we worry about what people would think of us if they knew. I think the anonymity will help both parties open up and share deeply. It's going to be a beautiful program," he concluded. "Simple, but powerful."

With Father Menei's blessing, Marie took the idea, which she started calling "PrayerMates," to the VAC board for approval. She knew the perfect people to coordinate it. OJ had been a long-time VAC volunteer as well as a former prison inmate and understood both community and prison perspectives. As a well-known gospel singer, OJ also had connections with many churches where they could recruit prayer partners. Another VAC volunteer, Martie Musso, had terrific organizational skills. Marie knew Martie would also be diligent about protecting the anonymity of both inmates and community participants.

Marie's initial letters to a few inmates about the program quickly resulted in requests from over one hundred inmates, both men and women, asking to be matched with a prayer partner.

"I feel so lonely in this world," one wrote. "I tell myself that I don't need no one, but I'm only fooling myself. . . . Please pray for me."[1]

"I, like King David, feel cut off from God . . . like a spiritual leper,"[2] wrote another.

Another wrote, "I do not request prayer for myself, but I would be most grateful if prayers would be said for my daughter who has gone astray."[3]

In a brochure they created for the program, OJ and Martie wrote, "Many of us have erroneous ideas about those who are incarcerated. To mention the words 'prisoner' or 'convict' might conjure thoughts of someone to fear, someone who is totally void of feeling and without hope or redemption. In reality, they are men and women (sometimes boys and girls) who by wrong decisions have committed crimes against fellow citizens and society. Prison is their punishment; humanity is still their birthright. All people share basic needs and concerns . . . whether our walls are within (self) or concrete (prison)."[4]

They met with dozens of church and civic groups to recruit community participants. They expected it to be an easy sell, as the program required little of participants other than a few moments of daily prayer. So they were caught off guard by how few people in the community were willing to have an inmate as a prayer partner. Fortunately, the Dunnings Creek church members got things started and many of the regular VAC volunteers offered to participate too.

As inmates began to experience the power of having someone pray for them and of praying for someone else, they told others about the program. The waiting list of inmates who wanted PrayerMates mushroomed, while the list of willing community participants lagged far behind. Marie, OJ, and Martie formed a PrayerMates committee to brainstorm ways to promote the program. They scheduled community prayer breakfasts, posted flyers, and sent letters and brochures to numerous organizations. Gradually the list of willing community participants grew, but never quickly enough.

In the meantime, Snooky had recovered from his stroke and was nearing the end of his sentence at the county jail. Marie visited him just before his scheduled release and told him about the PrayerMates program.

"Just think what your simple request for prayer inspired, Snooky," she told him. Snooky grinned. "You'd be an ideal person to serve on the PrayerMates committee," she added. Snooky agreed, and, upon his release, became one of the most active and committed supporters of the program.

Successes like Snooky's gave Marie hope. She struggled to understand when some of the men and women for whom she had high hopes ended up back in prison. For some, prison culture became a poison that seeped into their attitudes and mindset. She had been visiting Butch regularly since he'd started serving a new sentence at the Huntingdon prison, two years after his release from Rockview. Butch had become like family. Marie had attended picnics and socials at Huntingdon as his guest and met his mother and siblings. She could tell Butch was struggling to rise above the ugliness of prison life and knew his connections with people on the outside were critical. But a new DOC policy prohibited anyone who was on an inmate's visiting list from also being a prison volunteer. Marie was forced to make a painful decision. She had so many volunteer obligations in prisons across the state that she couldn't abandon. So she broke the news to Butch that she would have to stop visiting him. As she anticipated, he was hurt and angry. She prayed daily for Butch, hoping that bitterness wouldn't overtake her dear friend.

Marie believed completely in the power of prayer. She wrote a letter to all of the Brethren congregations in the Middle Pennsylvania District requesting prayers for the Volunteers in Prison programs. She reminded them of the denomination's 1975 Annual Conference statement:

The imprisoned are perhaps the most neglected and abused group in our society. Ironically, when these offenders are neglected and abused, not only they, but society as well is victimized.

The New Testament symbol of the towel impels Brethren to reach out to those who have been made outcasts and scapegoats. Whenever this effort is fruitful, society itself becomes healthier and more secure.

Her letter concluded: "As Brethren, we are uniquely called to heal the brokenness wherever we find it. We must consistently and constantly enable the power of Love within us to be released. We are seeing many opportunities to have a powerful ministry, not only in our prisons but in the lives of all who are searching for justice and wholeness."[5]

She made arrangements for a group of Brethren to visit Rockview's B Block North to get a glimpse into the realities of prison life. One of the most urgent issues Marie hoped her fellow Brethren would take up, not just through prayer but through action, was abolition of the death penalty. Pennsylvania's execution chamber was housed at the Rockview prison. She and the volunteers were chilled by the prospect of executions taking place in their community. The inmates were even more disturbed by it. Several men at Rockview had told Marie that, periodically, all of the lights dimmed and flickered at the prison. The inmates believed it meant the administration was testing the electric chair to be sure it still worked.

The death penalty had been reinstated in Pennsylvania in late 1978, after eight years of wrangling in the courts over the constitutionality of the state's sentencing procedures. Soon after his January 1987 inauguration, Marie wrote a letter to Pennsylvania's new governor, Robert Casey.

I do not know you and I am not a politician. I will probably never bother you again (except to support the Pennsylvania Prison Runathon!). I plead with you to stop the terrible play with death row inmates and thousands of us who are aware of the horrible effects of the Death Penalty. Along with other citizen volunteers, I have for eleven years visited weekly in the cell blocks of Rock-view. We shudder when it is announced that an execution is awaiting your stay. . . ."[6]

In her letter to Casey, Marie enclosed an article from the National Coalition Against the Death Penalty about Governor Toney Anaya's commutation of the sentences of all death row inmates in New Mexico. Anaya's actions were, Marie wrote, "an example of how a governor can exercise what truly must be the highest calling of his office—to enable his state to rise above vengeance and that which breeds vengeance: To proclaim that his state Will Not Lower Itself To Kill People to teach other people that killing is wrong." Before Anaya's commutation, New Mexico had five death row inmates. Pennsylvania had eighty-seven.

Keith Zettlemoyer was one of them. Zettlemoyer was scheduled to be executed on February 24, 1987. Marie, OJ, several Rockview volunteers, and members of the local Prison Society branch had formed Centre County Citizens for the Abolition of the Death Penalty and planned a protest vigil at Rockview for the date of Zettlemoyer's scheduled execution. Zettlemoyer's death warrant had been signed by Casey's predecessor, Dick Thornburgh.

On February 19, Casey stayed the execution.

During his eight-year term, Thornburgh had enacted mandatory sentencing legislation for violent offenders that was considered to be among the toughest in the United States. At both the state and national level, Marie had seen a shift in attitudes and philosophy away from treatment and rehabilitation of offenders, toward a greater focus on punishment.

When Casey took office, he vowed to improve the state's prisons and appointed a cabinet-level task force to review the prison system. The recommendations of that task force made Marie feel hopeful once again. The task force recommended expanding basic education, vocational, and job training programs; providing better employment and follow-up support for the approximately five thousand inmates released from Pennsylvania prisons each year; improving drug, alcohol, and mental health treatment programs; increasing visitation rights for inmates and families from one hour per week to at least five hours per week; and reducing prison overcrowding through community-based corrections, intensive parole programs, and "earned time" credits for good behavior that would reduce the amount of time an inmate had to serve before being eligible for parole. At the time, Pennsylvania was one of only two states in the nation without an earned time credit program.

Casey's newly appointed commissioner for the Department of Corrections, David Owens, welcomed the task force report as a road map to the future. Marie had established a good working relationship with the outgoing commissioner, Glen Jeffes, in the four years he'd been in office. She hoped to do the same with Owens.

Just before departing as commissioner, Jeffes had issued an official Department of Corrections commendation for Marie, recognizing her for her "many contributions to improving the quality of inmate life in prison." Jeffes cited the runathon as one example, quoting an inmate participant who said, "The runathon is important, not only for the sake of the children, but also for the sake of the inmates who need the opportunity to express their self-worth and their humanity." Jeffes' citation read, "Plans are now being formulated for other states to participate in this worthy cause with hopes for a national prison runathon some day."[7]

Marie wished she felt Jeffes' optimism. She had thought 1987 would finally be the year when they'd be able to get a national runathon off the ground. She had placed ads in various national prison-related publications asking for support and had heard from prisons as far away as Nevada asking how they could get involved. Despite over four years of letter writing, phone calls, and speaking engagements to drum up financial support for a national runathon, Marie hadn't been able to get the necessary funding. She thought sadly of all the time and effort that had been put into it. It felt like one of the biggest failures of her career.

At least the strained relationship with Dan Katkin at Penn State had healed after their conflict over the university's national runathon proposal. And now Marie's former BVS assistant, Birgit, was engaged to Dan. They were to be married in September.

It was bittersweet for Marie to hear Birgit talk excitedly about her wedding plans. Marie and Joe had finally decided to separate. As devastated as she was about the end of her marriage, her priority was her son, Mike, and helping him cope with bipolar disorder. Some days he stared vacantly for hours, not noticing anything or anyone around him. On other days, his face twisted in torment, with tears flowing down his cheeks, though he seemed unaware of it. Those days scared Marie far more than the days when he ranted and stormed, full of rage. She hated being away from him when he was having an especially rough day, but knew she needed her work to help keep her own sanity.

Birgit told Marie that her family would be coming from Germany for her wedding. Marie wanted to do something special to celebrate with Birgit and Dan, so she offered to take them and their families to The Pines in Belleville for an authentic Amish chicken and waffle dinner. Marie thought Birgit's family would enjoy meeting the Amish family who ran the place, and she knew the food would be excellent.

Birgit happily agreed and Marie made their dinner reservation. But when the day arrived, Mike was in especially bad shape mentally. It had been one of those days where he sat and stared vacantly all day, looking right through Marie without seeing her. She had tried talking to him, but couldn't connect with him. She was terrified about leaving him at home alone that evening, but didn't want to spoil the occasion for Birgit and Dan and their families. Marie had never told Birgit about Mike's illness and certainly didn't want to bring it up now. So she kept her dinner plans and prayed that Mike would be okay.

Their party of ten traveled to The Pines in two cars. Marie drove distractedly, oblivious to the lively conversation in the car. When they arrived, they waited on the porch for their reserved seating time. After a few minutes, the hostess came to the door and asked, "Is Mrs. Hamilton here?"

Marie looked up and nodded.

"I'm afraid I have dreadful news. Would you come with me please?"

Marie gasped and stood up quickly. She followed her on shaky legs, bracing herself to hear that something awful had happened to Mike. By the time they got inside, she could scarcely breathe.

The hostess led Marie to a quiet corner, then turned to her and said, "Mrs. Hamilton, I am so very sorry to have to tell you this."

Marie grabbed the arm of a chair to steady herself, blinking back the flood of tears that had been building through Mike's long depression.

"Mrs. Hamilton . . ."

"Yes," Marie replied weakly.

"I am so sorry, but . . . the ovens have gone out. And there will be no chicken tonight. I am truly sorry."

Tears streamed down Marie's cheeks as she eased into the chair. "No chicken?" she asked. "There will be no *chicken*?" She stared up at the hostess, confused. "There will be . . . no . . . *chicken* tonight?"

"No, Mrs. Hamilton. I am truly sorry."

Marie started to laugh. "Oh, no—it's *fine. Really!* That's *wonderful* news! There will be *no chicken tonight!*" She stood up suddenly and hugged the baffled hostess, then returned to Dan and Birgit and their families and delivered the news about the chicken. No one knew why Marie was so buoyant about it, and they laughed and teased her about taking them to a special chicken and waffle dinner with *no chicken*.

Marie was still anxious to get home to Mike, but was able to enjoy the evening with Birgit, Dan, and their families. When she arrived home, Mike was safe and doing a bit better. She knew there would be other rough days, but for the moment she was immensely grateful that the worst thing that had happened that night was that there had been no chicken.

MARIE'S WORK HAD become a refuge from the stresses at home. She wanted to expand the Volunteers in Prison programs, but knew she'd have to obtain more funding. Harvey Bell suggested she start with the new DOC commissioner. She wrote to David Owens introducing herself and describing the services she'd been providing in Pennsylvania's state prisons for twelve years.

"Recently, the request for my involvement in the state prisons has become more than I am able to facilitate on a volunteer basis," she wrote. She asked Owens to consider "an avenue for the Department to contract my services to take programs into the institutions."[8]

Owens agreed to meet with Marie, but said that fiscal constraints made it impossible for the DOC to pay her for her programs. She'd have to look elsewhere for funding.

That Christmas was lonely for Marie. Her days were brightened by cards and letters she received from many of the men and women she'd worked with over the years, including JT, who seemed to be succeeding on the outside.

"Marie: Miss you much," he wrote. "Will visit after the New Year. *Squares make it!* Much love, JT."

Yusef and his wife sent a beautiful, hand-drawn card full of news of their lives and future plans. Lois sent a loving letter full of comfort and wisdom that brought tears to Marie's eyes.

One of the B Block inmates also helped Marie put her own challenges in perspective.

"I've been in prison for five years," he told Marie. "Each Christmas, I've received a card from a child. I have saved every card and I pray for each child, every day. Since coming to prison, I haven't received anything else from anyone—no letters, no cards, no packages—nothing. Not from my family or friends or anyone. But those cards from the children—they've saved me."

The VAC had collected enough decorated cards that year to send to the women at the Muncy prison. The women's letters of gratitude touched Marie deeply.

It's hard being away from my seven year old daughter. . . . I miss my daughter so much. Please tell Alicia, age 8, thank you so much for the beautiful Christmas card.

Freda[9]

Thank you for the Christmas card. . . . I first came here on December 9 and it was very scary. I originally thought it was a cold and impersonal place. I literally felt like a number without a face. I know that there is a lot more to me than the fact that I committed a crime. But it didn't seem like anyone else was interested in that. Since then, I have seen evidence that there really are people who care. . . . Thank you again.

Amy[10]

To Dear Nicole
Thanks for your lovely Christmas card . . . and for the words of care and Christian love you sent in every line. The holiday time is a difficult one for prisoners and especially for me because it is my first Christmas away from my own family and my daughter (your same age). . . . I will pray for you, Nicole, and I will always remember your kindness. . . .

God bless you . . . Judith[11]

The Christmas card that Jenny, age 10, drew and sent me really touched my heart. . . . I am far from home and those I love. Thank you so much for sharing the true meaning of Christmas with me. . . .

Gaye[12]

Even though the holidays are usually rough times for those incarcerated, your gift of sharing has brightened up a lot of hearts. Thank you for taking the time and consideration to think about those who are far away from children and family. May God richly bless you and continue to keep you safe in his arms.

Sincerely, Eleanor[13]

Marie couldn't imagine the pain of being in prison, away from family and children. It was especially devastating for those sentenced to life in prison. In Pennsylvania, a life sentence had become a virtual death sentence, as the number of commutations for lifers continued to shrink every year. Meanwhile the number of inmates serving life sentences in Pennsylvania's prisons had grown to over 1,500 men and women.

Some of those lifers asked Marie for letters of recommendation to support their appeals for commutation. When Lois asked for such a letter, Marie was happy to write on behalf of her dear friend.

"There have been several occasions previous to this that I have recommended commutation for an inmate; however, this recommendation for Lois is one which I support stronger than any," Marie wrote in her letter to Harvey Bell. "She has become a friend . . . [and] she is someone I would welcome into the community, into my office or into my home. To me, she is a Mother figure, warmly welcomed by all. . . ."[14]

After reading Marie's recommendation, Lois wrote, "I was touched and humbled. I really appreciate it." But, she added, "I am under no illusions," regarding the likelihood of a pardon.

The pain of being separated from their children was devastating to the women in prison. Many carried photos of their children during the runathons to remind themselves why they ran (undated). Photo courtesy of CentrePeace, Inc.

Marie hoped things would improve under the new DOC commissioner, David S. Owens. She was encouraged by his speech at the Third Annual Serenade to Volunteers in Corrections in April 1988.

"The goal of corrections is to make people better and we cannot succeed without volunteers," Owens told the audience. He told them that the Pennsylvania prisons were at 34 percent over capacity. "It's evident that these people did not have the life skills necessary to be successful in society. We must educate them, teach them, show them the way to a crime-free life. We must not lock people up behind a forty-foot wall and think that's rehabilitation. It's not."[15]

Owens reiterated the DOC's commitment to volunteers in a letter to Marie later that year when the Pennsylvania Prison Runathon was one of seventy volunteer programs from across the country to be recognized by President Reagan's Volunteer Action Awards.

"Volunteers are an essential component of a prison's entire rehabilitative program," Owens wrote. "Volunteers serve to remind inmates that society is indeed interested in their well-being and eventual reentry into the community. Volunteers are also welcome because they choose to channel their time and energy into a prison setting, and their enthusiasm eventually spreads throughout the institution. . . . The commonwealth and this department deeply appreciate the time and effort your program has devoted to corrections."[16]

Despite the recognition for the volunteer programs, Marie realized there was so much more to be done. The most pressing need was for support programs for men and women coming out of prison. She had seen inmates come out of prison and make real contributions. Snooky was one of them. In addition to his involvement in the PrayerMates committee, he also worked with CACJ, providing an ex-offender perspective as they worked to expand their programs. One of their biggest efforts was developing a full-fledged community reentry program, including a halfway house and a self-help group for parolees, modeled on Alcoholics Anonymous. Snooky helped to write a proposal and suggested the name "A Chance" for the program.

They approached Pennsylvania Probation and Parole for funding of the halfway house, but were told that programs in Philadelphia and Pittsburgh took priority for funding. However, they told the CACJ group, "If you set up a halfway house yourselves, we'll help fill it."

A local group offered to donate an old church building, but the neighbors fought vigorously against having a halfway house in their neighborhood. After months of battling the community objections, the CACJ group decided to put the halfway house project on hold.

For Marie, it felt like another in a long string of setbacks.

Lois had written, saying her petition for commutation of her life sentence had been denied. Despite Owens' message at the Serenade, it seemed prisons were increasingly focused on punishment, with fewer rehabilitation programs available to inmates with each passing year.

OF ALL THE prison programs Marie and the volunteers had started, she thought the conflict resolution course had the greatest rehabilitative potential for inmates. She had discovered that inmates often struggled with the concept of nonviolence, which was the foundation of the whole conflict resolution course.

In early 1989, Marie taught the course to twenty inmates at the Camp Hill prison, where the men engaged her in a lively discussion about nonviolence. Marie especially wanted that group to have a firm grasp on principles of nonviolence, since the Camp Hill administration had approved a plan for those twenty inmates to teach the course to other inmates.

The men she trained at Camp Hill were part of the New Values therapeutic community, an intensive eighteen-month drug and alcohol treatment program. They lived in Mod 8, a housing unit separated from the rest of the prison population. There, they received counseling and treatment from a team of specially trained corrections officers and counselors. The program focused on helping the men overcome their addictions, change their attitudes, think before they acted, make wise decisions, and turn their lives around. Because of the structure of the New Values program, the men were generally more mature and responsible than inmates in the general population at Camp Hill. But in Marie's class, they struggled with the idea that, even when confronted with violence, it was best to respond nonviolently.

Marie read to them from one of the class handouts:

People say you have to fight fire with fire, not so! You fight fire with water. The objective is to quench the adversary's anger by being cool, offering to help him in some way, showing you bear good will toward him and that he has nothing to fear. – Lawrence Apsey[17]

Some of the men in the class looked dubious.

Marie extended her hands, palms outward, and drew an imaginary wall across the front of her body. "Violence stops here," she told them. "It's an attitude you have to adopt that says, 'There isn't anything anyone can say or do to me to make me want to hurt them.'"

"But what if someone's coming after you?" Douglas[18] asked. "Planning to hurt you? You'd defend yourself then, right?"

"Not with violence," Marie insisted.

"Hmmph," another inmate said. "If you'd ever see some of the characters we see in here, and they was coming after you, you'd do what you had to to survive."

"Well, I can tell you what I would do, because it's happened to me," Marie said.

The men stared at her, looking surprised.

"I was in my office one afternoon not too long ago, and a man I didn't know appeared at my door. He looked at me with such rage and said, 'Because of you, I had to spend five extra years in prison. Well, today is your day.' Then he moved toward me. I knew immediately that he was there to kill me."

She paused and took a sip of water. The men in the class sat stock-still, all eyes on Marie.

"At first, I couldn't move, I couldn't think. I whispered a little prayer as he took another step toward me." Marie paused again to take a deep breath. Telling the story still made her heart pound.

"I knew I needed to acknowledge how angry he was, this terrible injustice he felt had been done to him. So I said, 'Oh, how terrible. You sat in prison for five extra years and here I sat in this nice office.' I got up out of my chair very, very slowly. I looked at him with all of the love I could muster and just kept saying, 'How awful, how terrible,' as I slowly walked toward him."

"You walked *toward* that joker?" Douglas asked. "Man, you need to be getting *away*!"

"Well, he was between me and the door. And my moving slowly toward him probably wasn't at all what he expected. He might have expected me to jump up and try to run, or to scream, or to yell at him to get out of my office. So, what I was doing—moving slowly, speaking quietly, acknowledging his feelings—was completely disarming to him. And when I got to where he was standing, I gently put my arms around him."

"Say, *what*? No way!"

"Yes, that's what I did."

"You coulda been dead right there. That's when he coulda got you with a knife, gun, whatever."

"But he didn't," Marie said.

"What *did* he do?"

"He was so confused, I think he didn't know what to do. So he turned and ran out the door, down the stairs, and out of our building. I never saw him again."

Several of the men sank back into their seats, looking relieved. One let out a long, loud breath. A few of them shook their heads in disbelief.

"But he was going to *kill* you!" said Douglas.

"Perhaps," Marie said. "But I believe that the power of nonviolence I showed to him was stronger than his violent intentions. Before we finish for today, I'd like to read to you one more thing that Lawrence Apsey wrote:

While acting non-violently may be dangerous, it is no more dangerous than acting violently. Violence evokes violence from the adversary and he may be stronger, a better fighter, or more skillful with weapons than you. Violence is no guarantee of safety. Even if you win, the other party will be on the lookout to get you the next time. Also, the law may get you.[19]

"There are many reasons to choose nonviolence. If I had responded differently in my situation, I probably wouldn't be here today telling you this story. And he would probably have ended up in prison for the rest of his life. It wasn't easy, but I'm convinced that choosing the path of nonviolence saved my life. That's why I believe it's so important to adopt the attitude that nothing anyone could say or do would ever make you want to hurt them." Marie held her hands out in front of her body again, and moved them in a gentle arc. "Remember, gentlemen, violence stops here."

Letters from several of the men after the class confirmed for Marie the power of what they had learned.

> I want to again extend my appreciation to you for intro-
> ducing me to Conflict Resolution and for teaching me what I
> think is something very important to me. . . . I want to learn
> all I can about Conflict Resolution before my release. I feel
> that it will be very helpful in my future with dealing with
> others. God bless you, Marie.
>
> Douglas[20]

The enthusiasm of the men at Camp Hill for the conflict resolution program inspired Marie to propose that the prison staff take the training as well. She sent a proposal and materials to Camp Hill's Training Department and offered her services to train the staff.

She received a response from the training coordinator a few weeks later.

> I have reviewed your material with key staff at the institution and we
> decided that there is presently no need for this training at SCIC. Our
> staff are well versed in conflict resolution, as these skills are prac-
> ticed daily with their interactions with inmates.[21]

It was rare for a group to refuse free training. But she had plenty of other teaching engagements to keep her busy. The most exciting for Marie was the training she offered to two hundred people at the conference of the U.S. Association for Victim-Offender Mediation in Minnesota. She had been hearing about victim offender mediation and was hungry to learn more. The conference brought her into contact with mediators from all over the country. Victim offender mediation had originated in Canada in 1976 and was first tried in the United States through a project in Elkhart, Indiana, in 1978.[22] It was based on restorative justice, principles that really resonated with Marie.[23] She had seen such a need for those who had committed crimes to redeem themselves. She'd seen so many victims of crime who continued to suffer for years after a crime, unable to move on with their lives. And she'd seen how ineffective the court system could be. The courts were sentencing more and more people to longer and longer prison terms. The country's "war on drugs" had led to an exploding prison population.

Commissioner David Owens addressed the issue in his keynote address at the 1989 Serenade to Volunteers in Corrections. Owens told the audience that it cost taxpayers between $50,000 and $100,000 to build a single prison cell, and about $17,000 to incarcerate one person for one year.

"If we are to incarcerate in greater numbers, then we must be prepared to pay for it," Owens said. "There is no free lunch. It is costly to imprison people, and we cannot incarcerate individuals in substandard living conditions. First of all, it is dangerous for staff to work in institutions where the standard of living is inhumane. Secondly, it is dangerous for the inmates who are forced to live in such conditions. Lastly, prisons that lack the resources to operate properly are counterproductive to rehabilitation and treatment. Indeed, they return to society individuals who are more dangerous than when they entered the system."[24]

No one in that audience could have imagined how accurate Owens' warning would prove to be.

10

VIOLENCE STOPS HERE

While acting non-violently may be dangerous, it is no more dangerous than acting violently. Violence evokes violence . . . .
—Lawrence Apsey (1902–1997)

At approximately 3 p.m. on Wednesday, October 25, 1989, a riot broke out at the Camp Hill State Correctional Institution near Harrisburg, Pennsylvania. In the two days that followed, the Camp Hill riot would become one of the worst prison riots in U.S. history.

George

The sounds of hammers and saws filled the carpentry shop. Fine sawdust swirled in the beams of late autumn sunlight streaming in through the tall, barred windows. George Snavely looked at his watch and calculated how much more he and the inmates who were his students could get done in the last hour of the carpentry class. He walked around the shop, stopping to check on the progress of each team of men assigned to work on the new storage room they were building.

"Nice workmanship, Curt.[1] Great job, Jamal.[2] That's looking real good," he said to the men who were painstakingly measuring and cutting lengths of lumber to frame the walls.

"Bill,[3] you okay with those joists?" he asked another.

"Yes, sir," Bill replied. "Thomas[4] is helping me. We got it under control."

"Mr. Snavely!" Khalid[5] shouted from the outside work area. "Something's going down over at E-Gate!"

George rushed to the window and looked out. His throat tightened.

"Khalid, get the men in here! We need to lock down, now!" he shouted.

George looked up to the second floor deck where Bear[6] was working with a group of new students.

"Bear, bring your guys down here right away!"

George locked himself and the men inside the carpentry shop. He went back to the window. Hundreds of inmates, their faces covered with bandannas, stormed the gate. Some carried two-by-fours. Others wielded lengths of steel pipe. They flooded Unit II of the prison complex in waves. Corrections officers sprinted toward the control center. Inmates swung at everything and everyone in their paths. Several people were knocked to the ground and beaten. George looked away, his heart pounding. He met the eyes of one of his students and saw the same raw fear he felt—that they might all die there.

"Let's get the tool room secured," George ordered. The men scrambled to gather up the hammers, saws, screwdrivers, and other tools scattered around the shop and put them on the wide closet shelves. George pulled the closet key from the large ring on his belt and locked the door. He checked the handle twice to make sure it was locked.

George grabbed the phone and called Mr. Fleagle, the instructor in the machine shop.

"There's a riot in the yard," he warned his fellow teacher. "I'm locked down here with my students."

"I heard," Fleagle replied. "I'm taking the women to the storage area at the west end. They should be safe there."

George hung up and went to double-check the exterior locks on the shop door, praying they'd hold. His students stared out at the chaos. Some stood silently, visibly flinching at the attacks they witnessed—inmate against CO, CO against inmate. Others paced back and forth along the row of windows. A few whispered prayers, others cursed under their breath.

"Yeah," one student shouted, pumping his fist in the air. "Get those pigs!"

Another grabbed at the steel bars across the shop windows and rattled them. "Go! Go! Go!" he yelled. "Kill the white-hats!"[7]

George was chilled by the sudden change in some of the men he knew as his students. He never allowed himself to forget that they were inmates, but inside his classroom he had worked to establish an air of mutual respect, treating the men as human beings worthy of his time and concern. George's own

Brethren upbringing had made him a lifelong pacifist, opposed to violence of any kind. Hearing a few of his students talk this way and seeing what was going on outside made him feel nauseous. Suddenly, he wondered about a couple of the men who hadn't shown up for class today. Were they part of this? He didn't want to even consider the possibility.

He heard the sound of breaking glass, then a loud crash next to the shop. George rushed to the door to look out. Inmates had broken into the commissary next door and were taking everything they could grab. Within minutes, flames shot high into the air from fires set by the rioting inmates. Thick smoke began to filter into the shop.

"Everyone cover your mouth and nose," George shouted. "Get down on the floor!"

George and the men lay on the floor, listening to the pandemonium outside. George squeezed his eyes shut. He wished he could close his ears as well to the shouts, screams, and the heavy thuds of bodies. Amid the human sounds were the noises of breaking glass, the crash of steel against wood, steel against steel, steel against concrete.

Curt crawled across the shop floor to George's side.

"Listen, Mr. Snavely, if it looks like they're gonna get in here, I'll give you my browns," Curt said. "You're a little taller than me, but they should fit. You just take 'em and put 'em on so they think you're one of us."

"Yeah, you gotta do it, Mr. Snavely," Bill urged. "Otherwise, you ain't gonna make it out of here alive."

"I hope it won't come to that," George quietly told his students. "But I thank you."

Some of the students began coughing as the smoke drifted down to the floor where they were crouched. George was short of breath. He strained to hear from which direction the sounds were coming. It sounded like the rioting inmates had moved out of the commissary.

"I think we need to move," George told the men quietly. "We'll try to get to the machine shop. I want everyone to stay together and stay low. We don't know what we're going to find out there."

George and his students crept down the hallway to the machine shop, where they joined several other instructors and their students. For the next two and a half hours, George, his fellow instructors, and about 125 of their inmate students were trapped in the education building.

Finally, heavily armed state police officers arrived to escort them out of the building, taking the inmates to a lockdown area and delivering the instructors to the administration debriefing room. George and the other instructors remained there for another five hours, answering questions about everything they'd witnessed, which inmates they recognized as participants, and which inmates had been with them.

"They [inmates] had the opportunity to take any of us [instructors], but they chose not to act accordingly," George reported.[8]

By 11 p.m., the instructors were finally given permission to go home for the night. Badly shaken by the day's events, George called his sons and asked them to pick him up. He reached home around midnight. Though physically and mentally exhausted, images of the brutality and destruction he had witnessed made sleeping nearly impossible.

Bear

Bear shivered in the cold night air as sirens pierced the dark. Hours earlier, police had escorted him and the other student inmates out of the education building, past a lineup of officers armed with long, wooden riot clubs. They'd been taken to an outdoor recreation yard, locked in and left there, while chaos raged around them. Smoke rose above the cellblocks and the air smelled scorched.

Though he was only twenty-nine, Bear was already an old-timer. He'd been sentenced to life in prison at seventeen for serving as a lookout while his cousin attempted a robbery. His cousin had ended up killing a woman and Bear had suddenly found himself charged as an accomplice to homicide.

When he'd come here as a terrified teenager, he'd quickly learned that prison could be an unforgiving, violent place. But this riot was on a completely different scale from anything he'd experienced in the past twelve years. The brutality he'd witnessed that afternoon chilled him.

Bear was especially worried about the new female employee at the commissary and prayed that the rioters hadn't captured her. Since her first day on the job, she'd made frequent disparaging remarks about prison inmates and had treated the men rudely. Bear knew that if the rioters found her, they'd take revenge.

As he stared at the stars winking overhead, he prayed that Mr. Snavely would get out safely, too. Mr. Snavely had become a cherished teacher and mentor to Bear over the past two years. The carpentry class was a haven where Bear always felt respected, like he had something important to contribute. Mr. Snavely had even asked Bear to help train some of the new students.

Bear wondered about the condition of their carpentry shop and all of the projects they'd been working on. With all of the wood in there, it would be like a tinderbox if the rioters got to it. Bear had been looking forward to the next day's class, as Mr. Snavely was going to let the guys work on their own projects, using materials they had paid for themselves. Bear had saved up for months to buy the dark walnut wood and other materials he'd use to build a corner cabinet for his friend Nataly. He planned to make raised panel doors for the bottom and glass doors for the top. To distract himself from the surrounding chaos, Bear tried to concentrate on what he needed to do the next day to start on his project.

A little after 1 a.m., guards returned to the recreation yard, unlocked the gate, and started escorting small groups of men to their housing units. Bear hung back, wanting to be among the last to go inside. He hadn't spent time outside at night since tenth grade, before he'd been sent to prison. Despite the surreal events of the day and the destruction surrounding him, Bear wanted to savor a few extra moments under the vast openness of the starlit sky.

When the officers came to escort Bear and the few remaining inmates back to their cells, Bear could feel the tension radiating from the guards. They passed furniture that had been dragged out of the administration offices, smashed and burned. They passed a golf cart used by staff to get around the fifty-two-acre campus. It had been flipped on its side and torched.

Bear was relieved to get to his cell and be locked in, alone. He sat down at the small wooden desk in his cell. He pulled out his pen and tablet and wrote down everything he had seen, heard, and felt through that long disturbing afternoon and night, struggling to comprehend the violence he had witnessed.

All around him men stood at the bars of their cells, talking in low voices, telling and retelling stories of the day's insanity, as though the telling might make sense of it all. Bear wrote page after page, into the deep hours of the night, before finally falling asleep just before dawn. A few hours later, he was awakened by an officer who reached through the bars with a small brown paper bag containing two hard-boiled eggs and two pieces of white bread—breakfast. Feeling unsettled and exhausted, Bear prayed fervently for calm in the hours and days ahead, but feared the worst.

George

After a restless night, George reported back to work at Camp Hill by 8 a.m. Thursday. As he went through the main gate, two things became eerily apparent. Not a single inmate was in sight; though that was to be expected, it gave the place an unnatural silence. But George didn't see a single state police trooper, either. He remembered the scores of officers who had patrolled the Camp Hill complex for days after the 1983 riots. Now, their absence after the previous night's riot troubled George deeply.

He picked up his keys at the control desk and went to the education building to inspect his carpentry shop. Fortunately, the rioting inmates hadn't broken in, and no tools were missing. The shop had suffered only smoke damage.

George was asked to work in maintenance for the day, helping repair the damaged lock systems throughout the cellblocks. However, by midmorning the administration had concluded that photos of the damage should be taken first and the repair work on the locks was put on hold. George was reassigned to repair an inside fence around the stockade field that had been damaged in the rioting.

Throughout the long afternoon, the prison loudspeakers crackled periodically with announcements about the lockdown. George tried to stay focused on the work at hand, but couldn't shake the deep uneasiness he'd felt since walking through the gate that morning.

As George worked on the fence, a CO he knew patrolled the outside. When the CO saw George, he came over.

"Snavely, you've got to get out of here," the CO warned.

"What do you mean?" George asked.

"Man, I'd just leave as soon as you can."

George finished up, and by 4 p.m. he was on his way home. A few hours later, riots broke out again at Camp Hill.

Douglas

The men in the New Values Mod 8 housing unit were hunkered down inside with one of their COs while other inmates stormed their building and tried to set it on fire. One of the men trapped inside was Douglas, who had been in Marie's conflict resolution class the previous year. He and the other men tried to hold off the rioters by putting lockers in front of the windows. Several of the men grabbed fire extinguishers to put the fires out, while others watered down the entire Mod 8 unit to keep it from burning.

"We're going to kill you," the rioting inmates outside their door screamed. The men knew that if the rioters broke in, their CO would be attacked first. They insisted that the CO put on one of the men's prison browns to disguise himself. When the rioters finally broke in, Douglas and the others formed a protective circle around their CO, and then ran for the front gate. The rioters beat, punched, and kicked Douglas and the others, shouting at them, "Traitors!" Finally, the men from Mod 8 and their CO reached the front gate and were escorted to a safe place away from the riots.[9]

BY FRIDAY MORNING, October 27, the Camp Hill prison campus lay in ruins. More than 140 staff and inmates had been injured. It had taken hundreds of corrections officers, state police, and others to put a halt to the riots. Eighty percent of the buildings on the fifty-two-acre campus were damaged. Six of the prison's ten cellblocks were destroyed by fire. George Snavely's carpentry shop in the education building had been torched and everything inside was destroyed. In all, damages due to the riots were estimated at over $17 million. Mod 8 was one of only two housing units still standing amid the smoking rubble, thanks to the efforts of Douglas and the other men from New Values.

A FEW WEEKS after the Camp Hill riots, Marie received a letter from one of the inmates from the New Values group who had completed her conflict resolution training.

> Dear Marie,
>
> We are witnessing history in the making. . . . My efforts to defuse a potentially explosive situation placed me in the eye of the storm, and on the front line as a soldier of peace. I feel that it is very necessary that the success of your Conflict Resolution techniques be made known . . . your methods work.
>
> Nathan[10]

Marie saw another of the New Values inmates later that month. She asked him about the riots, saying she had been told that his group had not participated in the violence.

"It was no big deal," he told Marie. "We just refused to get involved. We didn't play into the anger and the harassment that was going on. Besides, Marie, remember what you taught us?" he added, drawing an imaginary wall across the front of his body with his hands. "Violence stops here."

Marie wrote a letter to the men of the New Values group and sent it to their director, Robert Morck, to disseminate, as many of the Camp Hill inmates had been shipped out to other state and federal prisons after the riots.

> It was you gentlemen who took the Creative Non-Violent Conflict Resolution course who saved the day from complete destruction . . . you did shine brilliantly amidst the conflict and violence. Truly if there has ever been a test put upon people to see if conflict resolution skills make a difference, it was tested and proved with you. . . . Although few will know of your contribution, I personally will never forget. . . . Continue to rise above. Continue to be an example for others.
>
> Sincerely, Marie[11]

Deeply disturbed by the violence at Camp Hill and increasing tensions and overcrowding in many other prisons, Marie also wrote an open letter to all inmates and staff across the Pennsylvania prison system.

> You are all in prison: the staff and inmates. Those of us who care for you are also involved . . . [and] the safety of the staff and the inmates is heavy on our hearts. . . . We have given the staff an impossible task. We have asked the inmates to accept an impossible situation. . . . The only successful demonstrations in prisons have been non-violent. Once violence starts, all rules are lost—all listening stops—and all

regret later. If we are to resolve our conflicts, we must listen to each other. We must have respect for each other's values. We must recognize that anger and hatred destroy those who harbor it and forgiveness frees the forgiver. We can use mediation. We can create a justice system based on wholeness rather than vengeance. It can start in our prisons. . . . This is an opportunity for us to work together. My concern and blessings to each and every one of you.

Most sincerely and respectfully, Marie Hamilton[12]

At the time of the riots, the Camp Hill prison had 1,414 single cells, and a rated capacity of 1,825 beds. The actual population of the prison was 2,656 inmates. A governor's commission appointed to investigate the riots reported that inmates were "frustrated by overcrowding, food quality, inoperative and overcrowded showers, inadequate educational and vocational opportunities because of understaffing, and limited law library privileges."[13] Sudden policy changes related to family visitation and inmates' access to medical care in the weeks prior to the riots also were cited as contributing factors. Commissioner David Owens' words at the Serenade to Volunteers in Corrections the previous spring suddenly seemed prophetic. Within a few months after the riots, Owens resigned as head of Pennsylvania's Department of Corrections.

He was soon replaced by Joseph Lehman, whose prescriptions for the state's burgeoning prison population included construction of seven new prisons in a two-year period, along with legislative changes that would allow the use of alternatives for nonviolent offenders, including work release, house arrest, and electronic monitoring. Lehman also opposed mandatory sentencing and life sentences without the possibility of parole, and he urged lawmakers to reevaluate these policies.

While Marie was glad to hear that Lehman supported alternatives to incarceration, she had also seen that much more needed to be done to improve conditions in the existing prisons. She wondered how much more of the violence at Camp Hill could have been averted if more inmates and staff had completed the conflict resolution training. She and other VAC volunteers had already trained over one thousand people in the program across the state and nationally.

But Marie wanted to train even more people. She was offered a unique opportunity at the Huntingdon prison to train inmates and corrections staff together. The combined training was the brainchild of Bill Love, Huntingdon's superintendent. Love believed that putting inmates and COs together for the training would foster greater levels of understanding and respect between them. Sixteen inmates and two COs signed up.

Partway through the morning of the first day of class, one inmate who had been staring at the two COs all morning blurted, "Now I recognize you. You two were at Camp Hill during the riots, weren't you?" Marie held her breath. She knew that tensions between inmates and guards who had been at Camp Hill during the previous year's riots were still dangerously high.

"Yeah," another inmate chimed in. "I remember seeing you there, too!"

The COs shifted uncomfortably in their seats. Every inmate in the room turned to look at the two COs.

Finally, one CO spoke. "Yes, we were at Camp Hill."

In an instant, the inmates' expressions darkened. The COs sat straight-shouldered, as though daring the inmates to respond.

The atmosphere was heavy and electric, like the air before a thunderstorm. Marie sent up a quick, desperate prayer. *This one's for you, God.* She knew it would be impossible to refocus on the course until the volatile feelings between the inmates and guards were addressed. Not knowing what else to do, she suggested they take a break. She went to the activities manager's office and asked whether they could break early for lunch. He consented. The inmates were sent back to their cells until their lunchtime, and Marie and the volunteers went to the staff dining room. There, Marie approached the COs from the class.

"I'd like to do a role play after lunch," she said. "Do you think one of you could act out the role of an inmate?"

One of the men frowned. The other said, "Yes, I can do that."

"Wonderful. Now, we'll need a sample situation to use. What kinds of situations come up between COs and inmates?"

The COs laughed.

"Where do you want us to start?" one said.

"Lots of stuff comes up at mealtimes—the inmates are always trying to get away with something in the chow line," said the other.

"Great, we'll do something with that. I'm going to also ask one of the inmates to play the role of a CO."

"That should be pretty funny, but okay," one CO replied.

Marie went to one of the inmates she knew was a leader within the group. "I want to do a role play after lunch. Do you think one of the inmates could act the part of a CO?"

"Oh, yeah, that'll be no problem," the inmate replied, laughing.

"Thank you," Marie said, silently praying that her crazy plan would work.

When the group reassembled after lunch, Marie had the actors sit across from each other at a table, with the CO playing the role of an inmate and the inmate playing the role of a CO. In their conflict scenario, the "inmate" had gotten in the chow line a second time, which was against the rules.

"Go sit down!" the "CO" ordered.

"But Sarge, all I want is another piece of chicken—I'm a growing boy. C'mon," the "inmate" whined.

"Do you want me to give you a write-up for disobeying a direct order?"

"Why is it such a big deal? One more little piece of chicken isn't gonna hurt anybody."

"The DOC rulebook, page forty-four, section forty-two, says, 'If an officer gives a direct order and an inmate doesn't obey, he may issue a write-up as stated in section three.'"

The audience howled with laughter, as each actor's depiction of the other party struck chords of truth.

After a few minutes, Marie stopped the role play and asked the CO playing the part of the inmate how he felt about the way the "CO" treated him.

He blurted, "Well, it wasn't so much what he said to me, it was the way he said it." Then, his face registered sheepish recognition that the way the inmate had role-played the "CO" reflected his own attitudes.

"And how are you feeling right now, Mr. CO?" Marie asked the inmate.

"He was just mouthing off, not following the rules and not giving me respect," the inmate replied. "Kinda like what we inmates do sometimes," he added with an embarrassed chuckle, breaking the thick cloud of tension in the room.

"Seems like it's about respect and communication," another inmate observed. "A lot of us are really the same no matter what type of uniform we have on."

"That's right," Marie said. "We're going to pretend for a minute that we don't have any COs in this room and I'm going to tell you a little inside story about them."

The inmates laughed. The COs smiled nervously.

"Not too long ago some COs told me they were so sorry that their position does not allow them to really be helpers to inmates. Their role dictates that they be security- and discipline-minded, but they wished it could be different. I've had COs tell me that they love the annual runathon because it is the only time they get to really cheer on and encourage inmates in a positive way."

Throughout the rest of the course, Marie noticed changed attitudes among both the inmates and the COs. During their closing circle, one

CO said, "I've learned so much. You will definitely see a different person in me."

Corrections officers loved the runathon because it was the only time they got to really cheer on the inmates in a positive way (undated). Photo courtesy of CentrePeace, Inc.

After that class, Marie was invited to teach another mixed group at Huntingdon. A few weeks after the second course ended, Huntingdon's superintendent, Bill Love, called Marie into his office.

"We were going to fire some of the guards you taught in these classes, Marie. They weren't getting along with other staff or with the inmates. We saw such a change in the guards who attended the first class, but we thought it was a fluke. That's why we wanted you to teach a second class. But again, the staff changed so much that I am recommending to the Department of Corrections that you teach this to more staff and inmates together."

Marie clapped her hands together and smiled. "Whenever and wherever you want me to teach this again, Bill, you just let me know."

Her happiness about the successes with the conflict resolution training was dampened by only one thing: the conflict with her husband that she'd never been able to resolve. After five years of separation, they were finally getting a divorce. Ann Cook drove Marie to court the day the divorce was finalized. Marie was left with the house, but no car.

With her trademark generosity, Ann said, "Marie, you know my brother left me a good bit of money and he wanted me to put it to good use. Please allow me to use some of it to help you buy a new car. You'd be doing me a favor, by helping me to carry out my brother's wishes." Marie couldn't refuse.

With her new wheels and newly found independence, Marie quickly learned to navigate on her own, in a way she had never done while she was married. She felt a sense of freedom she had never known.

11
HEALING BROKENNESS

Energy and persistence conquer all things.
                                    –Benjamin Franklin (1706–1790)

Jerry

Jerry[1] woke at 5 a.m. It took him a minute to get his bearings. Rockview. He'd been here only a few months, after having been moved from the Camp Hill prison.

Christmas morning, 1991. The realization pierced him just as painfully as it had each of the previous four Christmases. Despite being surrounded by hundreds of other men, twenty-four hours a day, loneliness was a constant ache. Holidays were the worst. There was no escaping it, though he'd seen plenty of other men try, with drugs, booze, sex, or just shutting down emotionally. Jerry prayed he'd never get like that, no matter what happened to him in here. At least he had the prison-issued Christmas package to open this morning.

Guards had come around the night before to deliver one small package to each inmate. The other men on the block had opened theirs immediately. Jerry had asked his cellmate not to show him what was in the package. Waiting until Christmas morning to open gifts was a tradition Jerry clung to, despite being in prison. It was the only gift he had received from anyone.

He got out of bed, dressed quickly in his prison-issued browns, and washed up at the sink in his cell. He pulled the thin cotton sheets and heavy white blanket up over his bunk and smoothed them. He switched on the small lamp on his desk, picked up his Bible, and thumbed the whisper-thin pages until he reached Luke 2. Then he silently read the story of the birth of Christ, seeking comfort in the ancient, familiar words. *Be not afraid.* He swallowed, trying to ease the tightness in his throat. When the shepherds had returned to their flocks, Jerry closed his Bible and ran his hand over the worn cloth cover. Then he carefully laid it back on the desk and picked up his Christmas package.

No bows, ribbons, or colorful holiday designs. Just a nondescript brown paper bag, no bigger than a lunch sack, folded over and stapled once at the top. Its plainness made him ache at the memory of Christmases past with his two young children and his beautiful wife, nestled comfortably in the home he had built for them beside a lake. Christmases before his wife had filed for divorce, before his brother's unexpected death, before his mother's suicide, before losing the business he'd built from the ground up—all in rapid succession. Before his life had disintegrated. He squeezed his eyes shut and shook his head to clear away those thoughts. He was here now, and would be for a very long time. *Deal with it,* he told himself.

He held the paper bag on his lap for a few minutes, wanting and yet not wanting to open it. Finally, he gently pried the staple out of the top of the bag and unfolded the flap. Item by item, he removed the contents—a pair of socks, a pocket-sized address book, a packet of instant soup, a strip of beef jerky, a bag of potato chips and one of pretzels, a granola bar, a few pieces of hard candy, and a small package of fudge. He laid everything out on the bed and started to flatten the bag. Then he felt something stiff along the side of the bag. He reached in again and pulled out a Christmas card.

A crayoned Christmas tree adorned the front of the card, with brightly colored ornaments drawn among the branches, and tiny square packages drawn beneath. Below that, a carefully printed *"Merry Christmas."* Jerry opened the card.

At the top, he read: *"This is a card decorated by a child expressly for a prison inmate. Sent by Volunteers in Prison, Inc., State College, PA".*

And below that: *"Christmas means you are loved . . . From Melissa, Age 9".*

Nine. Nine. His own daughter had been nine the last time he'd seen her. Skinny and tall for her age, his blonde, blue-eyed little girl had looked just like him.

He still vividly remembered the night she was born, February 2, 1978, at 12:20 a.m. She'd been so tiny, red-cheeked. Five pounds, twelve ounces. From the first moment he'd held her, Jerry hadn't wanted to put her down. She was Daddy's little girl.

He wondered what she looked like now. She'd be thirteen already. He couldn't imagine it—his little girl a teenager. What was she doing this morning? Did she get the presents he had sent to her through the Angel Tree[2] program?

Would she like them? Had her mother even given them to her? His ex-wife had severed all ties between Jerry and his children, arguing that they needed to focus on their relationship with their new stepfather. Jerry wondered whether his daughter or his son ever thought about him, remembered anything about him. His son had been so little when Jerry had been sent to prison.

He pushed the ache over losing his children back into the carefully constructed place in his heart where he'd had to keep it, or risk breaking down completely.

Jerry ran his fingers over the message in the card. *Thank you, Melissa, whoever you are,* he whispered. Bowing his head, he said a long prayer for Melissa and for his own two children. Then, opening his eyes to the dim reality of his surroundings, he carefully placed the card on his desk next to his Bible. Finally, he gathered up the other items from the Christmas bag and put them in the cardboard storage box under his bunk.

Throughout the long, bleak Christmas day, he kept thinking about the card, about the nine-year-old girl who had made it, and about his own daughter and son. Though it was bittersweet, getting that card had helped him reconnect with precious memories of his own children. It had given him something to hold on to. Who were these "Volunteers in Prison"? Whoever they were, he wanted to tell them what a priceless gift the Christmas card from that little girl had been. Before going to bed that night, he picked up the tablet and pen from his desk.

Dear Volunteers in Prison . . .

Marie clutched the letter to her heart, scarcely able to breathe. She sat like that for a long time, praying for the man who had written it and for his children. She didn't remember ever meeting a Jerry at Rockview. She wondered who he was. His experience put her own loneliness on this first Christmas as a divorced woman into sharp relief.

Letters like Jerry's were the best Christmas gift she could have hoped for. Thousands of children like Melissa, from more than two hundred children's groups across the state, had participated in making 15,000 cards for inmates.

Though questions had been raised over the years about whether it was appropriate to send the cards to non-Christian inmates, letters from Jewish and Muslim inmates like Victor and Yasin reassured Marie.

> Though I am Jewish I can still appreciate the beauty in your message. It is always good to know that "I am loved." It is hard to accurately express the full impact of your organization's efforts on behalf of prison. May the GOD of Abraham—your GOD and mine—bless you all tenfold for your selfless acts of human kindness and compassion.
>
> Warmly, Victor[3]

> Dear V.I.P,
> I want to thank you for making it possible for the inmates to receive holiday cards. Even though I'm Muslim, I was very touched with your *charity* which really is the true spirit that I pray to (God) will become contagious in our daily lives. Your intentions probably rehabilitate more inmates than the prison system. May (God) bless you. Happy New Year.
>
> Yasin[4]

Each year, the program had spread a little more love to incarcerated men and women across the whole state. Marie found hope in knowing that so many children were learning that there were real human beings behind bars, who needed love and concern just as much as everyone. She prayed that, when those children grew up, they'd help make much-needed changes in the criminal justice system.

She had hoped more adults would also begin to see the incarcerated as people with real needs and concerns. The PrayerMates program offered a simple way to transcend prison bars, but people in the community were still reluctant to participate. Martie Musso, OJ, and the rest of the PrayerMates committee organized another prayer breakfast, hoping to recruit new community participants. Marge Holland, chaplain from the Muncy women's prison, and Rev. Harry Strong, from State College Presbyterian Church, spoke about the power of prayer. Willie,[5] a former inmate and VAC volunteer, spoke movingly of his prison experience and how prayer had saved him. OJ sang and offered his own testimony to the power and importance of prayer for people who are incarcerated. Several attendees agreed to become PrayerMates, but the VAC still had a long list of inmates awaiting prayer partners.

Marie and the volunteers turned their attention to the 1992 runathon. With fifteen prisons now involved, Marie was in constant recruiting mode to get enough volunteers to manage it all.

She saw her good friend Ed Hall at a meeting. Ed already served on the board of Volunteers in Prison, visited B Block weekly and led discussion groups there, and occasionally taught conflict resolution courses at other prisons with Marie.

"You're such a terrific listener, Ed," Marie told him. "What an asset you'd be on the runathon committee." She flashed a smile.

Ed agreed to add the runathon to his other volunteer duties. It was hard to say no to Marie.

In the twelve years since the runathon had gone statewide, Marie had visited every prison in the state and had met and gotten to know hundreds of inmates. Twenty-four inmates served on Rockview's runathon committee that year, including Hawk,[6] one of Marie's favorite guys from B Block, and Bear[7] and Victor, two leaders of the lifers group. The months of planning and preparation flew by, and suddenly it was summer.

At the Rockview runathon, a tall, broad-shouldered, white-haired man approached Marie tentatively.

"Mind if I sit down here?" he asked.

"Please do. I'm Marie."

"I know. I'm Jerry," he said, holding out his hand.

Jerry, Marie thought. *That beautiful Christmas letter.* Looking at his tanned face and deep blue eyes, she now recognized him. He had been at a few of the runathon planning committee meetings, but he had been reserved, quiet.

"I see you and the other volunteers coming in every week," he said. "I have a good friend who lives on B Block, Brother Harry.[8] He's told me about your visits."

"Brother Harry is a dear soul," Marie replied with a smile.

"Your visits mean a lot to him and the other guys over there. My mother used to work with people with mental health issues before she died, so I know how important you are to those guys."

As the runathon got underway, Jerry and Marie sat side by side and counted laps for the runners. He asked about her other prison projects.

The struggles with the PrayerMates program were weighing heavily on her mind. She explained the program and the challenges. "There are still so many negative attitudes and stereotypes among people in the community about people who are in prison. Will you pray for the program, Jerry? Pray that more hearts will open up to the idea of reaching out to inmates by becoming a PrayerMate."

Jerry nodded solemnly. "I will, Marie."

The 1992 runathon was another record-breaker. Over 1,700 runners in fifteen prisons raised more than $16,000 for Big Brothers Big Sisters.

LATER THAT SUMMER, Marie was invited to speak at the On Earth Peace luncheon at the Church of the Brethren Annual Conference. She titled her speech, "When Lions and Lambs Meet."

"We peacemakers think we are the lambs, but there are times when the lions show us the way," she told her audience. "Lambs and lions can meet when we listen to each other. When the transforming power of love allows the lion to teach the lamb how to be the peacemaker. When the lamb learns that there is that of God in each of us: the murderer, the victim, the manipulator, the lover, the priest, the child."[9]

Even after seventeen years working in the prisons, she was still learning continually from the men and women she served. In her conflict resolution classes, at runathon awards ceremonies, lifers' picnics, and other gatherings, she had often told inmates that they were the ones who had taught her, not the other way around.

The men on B Block at Rockview taught her too. When B Block had been a pre-release unit, the volunteers regularly said goodbye to men who were being released and welcomed new men into the block. Now that it was a Special Needs Unit, there were few changes in the group of eighty men who lived on the block. Some were lifers, many others had long sentences, and few were ever released. As a result, Marie and the volunteers developed much deeper relationships with these men.

Hawk greeted Marie every week with the latest photo of his children or the latest letter from a family member. Unlike many inmates, Hawk had a devoted family that kept in close touch with him.

"They can't wait for me to get back home," Hawk told Marie each week.

Marie thought often about inmates' families. *This is someone's son, someone's husband or father,* she thought as she talked with each man. *And somewhere out there, his mother, his wife, his child is grieving.* She could barely fathom such heartache.

Many inmates were estranged from their families. Edward[10] was one of them. He hadn't seen his parents since he'd come to prison. Edward filled his days by participating in every educational program available to him. Every week, he showed Marie his papers from whatever course he was taking at the moment.

"My parents always said I was retarded," he told Marie. "I believed them until I came to prison and started taking classes here. I'm not retarded. I can learn. I write good and I'm good in math. Look at this paper right here—I got an 87! And they said I was dumb!"

Many inmates with mental health issues also had a spark of genius in them. Marie enjoyed having them in her conflict resolution classes. She taught the ten-week course over and over on B Block, with a week off between each class to give a new group of inmates time to sign up. An inmate named Joseph[11] signed up soon after moving to B Block.

When Marie taught the segment on listening skills, Joseph replied, "Nobody listens to me, why should I listen to them?"

When she explained how to use "I-messages" to express feelings, he said, "I don't talk about my feelings and if I ever did, I sure wouldn't say it like that."

"A waste of time," he said when she covered problem-solving methods.

"So what?" was his reply to class discussions on stereotyping and values.

Week after week, Joseph challenged, questioned, and dismissed every conflict resolution concept and skill Marie taught. Though other inmates had expressed doubts about the usefulness of certain skills, no one had ever taken issue with every aspect of the course the way he did.

Marie tried to respond patiently to Joseph's constant arguments, but she was relieved when that ten-week course was finished. She decided to take a break for a few weeks before starting another one. When she got to the B Block classroom on the day she was to start the next course, Joseph was waiting in the classroom.

"I've signed up to take your course again, Miss Marie," he told her.

"I thought you found it all pretty useless, Joseph."

"It is. I'm gonna figure out what else is wrong with it this time around."

For another ten weeks, Joseph prodded and contradicted. This time, Marie issued challenges of her own. Each time he insisted his methods would work better, Marie said, "Let's talk about your idea. What if you did it your way? What might happen next?" She'd have Joseph talk through the situation step by step to visualize what the outcome might be. As he talked, she could see that he was starting to recognize the cause and effect of his aggressive tendencies. As the other men in the class added their comments to Joseph's analyses, Marie could see that these conversations were helping all of them.

By the end of the second ten-week course, Joseph had become the best advocate for nonviolent conflict resolution Marie had ever seen. He understood the skills and concepts inside out and could reason with anyone else who said it couldn't work. He became a one-man recruiting machine, convincing dozens of other men on the block to sign up for upcoming classes, often reserving one seat for himself.

Another B Block resident, Robert,[12] took the course only once, but it affected him profoundly. Robert had been in and out of prison for over thirty years and was constantly involved in fights. He signed up for the course, saying he knew something needed to change. By the time the course ended, Robert's entire outlook had changed and he stopped fighting.

Many of the men on the block took the course over and over.

"Miss Marie, did you know this is a ten-pack course?" one inmate asked her.

"Ten-pack? What does that mean?"

"It means if somebody wants to get into your class but it's already filled and he don't want to wait till the next one, he'll have to offer at least ten packs of cigarettes to get somebody else to let him take their spot."

The first time Hawk took the course, he deemed it goofy, saying he didn't need to be playing silly games at his age. But after a few more times, he admitted that the more he participated the better he felt about himself and his situation.

Jerry's friend, Brother Harry, took the course eight times, proudly posting his certificates for each class in his cell. Brother Harry had gotten his nickname due to his deep religious convictions and his involvement in the weekly Catholic services held at the prison. He was known and loved by both staff and inmates throughout the prison. Rockview's priest, Father Crouse, brought Harry into the chapel as a sacristan. John McCullough invited him into his office on Friday afternoons for a chat and a cigarette. Many of the men considered him a spiritual guide and mentor. Out in the prison yard, when he wasn't carrying out his self-appointed duties of picking up litter and keeping the yard neat and tidy, Brother Harry could be found in earnest conversation with another inmate, his bald head leaned in close, his comforting hand on the other man's shoulder. Brother Harry was a steadying influence within B Block.

The staff on B Block saw that some of the men like Brother Harry, Hawk, Joseph, and others who had completed the conflict resolution course were highly effective in mediating conflicts, and the staff encouraged the trained men to help keep peace within the block.

Some inmates on B Block had serious mental illnesses and, at times, Marie wondered whether they really grasped what she was teaching. An inmate named Dennis[13] taught her never to underestimate them. Dennis had Tourette syndrome. His face twitched constantly and his tongue stuck out the right side of his mouth. He seemed far removed from reality. However, he signed up for Marie's conflict resolution class.

Dennis' whole world revolved around an imaginary pet iguana. During class, when Marie asked, "Who do you most admire?" he answered, "My pet iguana." When Marie posed the question, "What was your most memorable experience?" he told a rambling tale about his pet iguana. The other inmates knew that whatever Dennis said, it wouldn't make sense, and they ignored his obsession with his pet iguana.

Partway through the ten-week course, Marie addressed the topic of nonviolence. As she often did, she shared a story from her own life to convey the power of nonviolence. She told the men that she had once been forced to the ground in a remote gravel parking lot by a man who had held a knife to her throat.

"It was an ugly and frightening moment for me," she told the inmates. "I knew he intended to rape me. I tried to stay very calm. I looked into his eyes with all the love I could show him. And I asked him the first question that came into my mind: 'Do you really want to hurt someone you want to love?'"

She looked around the room at the men. They were all wide-eyed.

"What did he say?" one asked.

"What did he *do*?" asked another.

"Well, what I said was so unexpected, my looking at him with love and concern was not at all what he expected. It completely disarmed him. He got up and threw down his knife and cursed and paced around the parking lot. But he did not hurt me."

Several of the men exhaled loudly. Others shook their heads in disbelief.

"The power of love I tried to show him was stronger than his desire for violence," she concluded. "If I had responded differently, I would have been badly hurt, maybe even killed, and he probably would have ended up in prison for the rest of his life."

From the corner of the room, a voice repeated, "You coulda been killed. And he coulda been in prison the rest of his life." It was Dennis. The other men turned and stared at him. It was the first time he'd said something that made sense and that didn't include his pet iguana.

Then, he blurted, "Miss Marie, I thinks your heart is bigger than your brains!"

The men laughed.

"Yes, Dennis," Marie told him. "You're exactly right."

During the remaining weeks of the course, Dennis participated in every discussion, offering his own ideas and comments. He never mentioned an iguana again.

A few weeks after the course ended, Dennis greeted Marie when she arrived on B Block.

"I made something for you, Miss Marie." Dennis handed her a colored drawing he'd made of a desert scene with a cactus and a brightly feathered roadrunner. There wasn't an iguana in sight.

Marie had received dozens of paintings and sketches as gifts from inmates over the years, many of them quite good. The drawing from Dennis gave Marie another idea. She contacted the inmates she knew who were talented artists and told them about the VAC's annual fundraising sale.

"We could have a special auction of artwork to raise money for the Volunteers in Prison programs," she explained to each man. "What a wonderful and important contribution you could make by painting or drawing something to sell at that auction."

Word spread among other inmate artists in other prisons and soon the VAC had a large collection of oil paintings, watercolors, ink sketches, and other artwork to auction.

The funds from the auction provided the seed money for another of Marie's big ideas. She wanted to expand conflict resolution training and victim offender mediation to every prison in Pennsylvania.

The Department of Corrections' deputy commissioner, Margaret Moore, provided an opening. Moore invited Marie to conduct a conflict resolution "Train-the-Trainer" program for staff from several different prisons. Moore then planned to have those staff members return to their respective prisons and teach conflict resolution to staff and inmates. Superintendent Bill Love from Huntingdon offered to host the Train-the-Trainer program.

Marie and Bob Olsen taught nineteen staff members from seven prisons how to teach the Creative Nonviolent Conflict Resolution course.

Within the first two hours of the class, some of the staff members showed such resistance to what Marie and Bob were teaching that it threatened to derail the rest of the group. Several of them weren't sure why they'd been told to attend the training and others said their schedules were too overloaded to teach it to others. Some staff rejected the idea of giving inmates affirmation, discussing feelings, or using "I-messages."

"With inmates, we only use 'you' statements," one staff member asserted.

"If we'd do the things you're teaching, we'd lose control of the prison," another claimed.

Finally, their negativity was so disruptive that Marie suggested that they take a break. She went to see Love.

"Does the DOC expect corrections staff to treat inmates and fellow staff with dignity and respect?" she asked, knowing that this was part of the DOC's code of ethics.

"Yes," Love replied.

"Would you come into the class and talk with the staff about this?"

Love talked with the group and the class proceeded more smoothly. But for Marie it highlighted a critical issue. In a summary to Love afterward, she wrote, "Staff needs clarity on the role of corrections: treatment or punishment? . . . If we are going to have staff who are proud of their job and an atmosphere congenial to providing treatment for inmates, we must start now and continue to work for a justice system that includes creating wholeness rather than one based on fear, punishment, and vengeance."[14]

She didn't know how many of the staff they had trained would teach the conflict resolution course to others. A couple of the staff members had remained resistant throughout the course. Fortunately, others had really taken it seriously and seen the value in the training. Marie felt confident they would promote peaceful conflict resolution skills in their prisons. Marge Holland, the chaplain from Muncy, had championed positive opportunities like the runathon for the women there, and she worked hard to foster positive relationships between inmates and staff. Marie knew she would implement the conflict resolution program. But what the others did with the training back at their own institutions was out of Marie's hands. She turned her attention to other restorative justice efforts.

Two of the Rockview lifers Marie had met, Victor and Bear, were actively promoting victim offender reconciliation within the Lifers Association at Rockview. They had invited Howard Zehr, author of *Changing Lenses* and an early pioneer in victim offender reconciliation in the United States, to present a seminar on the topic to the lifers. Zehr had visited Rockview to interview and photograph life-sentenced inmates, including both Victor and Bear, for a book he was writing.[15] While there, Zehr had introduced the men to restorative justice concepts, igniting a desire in the men to learn more.

In their proposal for a seminar at Rockview, Victor and Bear had written,

> It is our belief that the victims loss and suffering must be made known to every offender in an effort to kindle the divine deposits which are in all human beings. Only then can true rehabilitation begin to take place. Once offenders truly understand the injury they have caused, they will be less likely to violate others.[16]

Victor and Bear asked Marie to help secure additional speakers, obtain clearances, and organize numerous other details for the seminar.

MARIE WAS EXCITED by the inmates' interest in restorative justice. But she thought prison staff should understand the principles too. She asked Chris Power, her BVS volunteer, and Bob Olsen to help her create and teach a five-day training curriculum that they called "Healing Brokenness." The program would consist of two days of conflict resolution training, a one-day introduction to victim offender reconciliation, and two days of a new *Breaking Barriers* video series created by Gordon Graham.[17]

Graham was an ex-offender who had turned his own nearly twenty-year prison experience to good by creating educational programs to help inmates turn their lives around.

Several years earlier, the Voluntary Action Center had purchased a copy of Graham's *How to Do Life on the Streets* video series and had circulated it among the prisons to help inmates prepare for their eventual release.

Marie wrote to Graham at his Seattle office and told him about Pennsylvania's prison volunteer programs and what she hoped to do with Breaking Barriers. She invited him to be one of two keynote speakers at that year's statewide Serenade to Volunteers in Corrections. The other keynote speaker would be DOC commissioner Joseph Lehman. Marie further enticed Graham with an offer to introduce him to many of Pennsylvania's top corrections people and the promise of a visit to Rockview to meet with inmates. He accepted Marie's invitation.

Graham's visit gave him an opportunity to promote his Breaking Barriers program to corrections staff and to Lehman. During his visit to Rockview, he conducted a three-hour seminar with fifty inmates, including Bear and Victor.

Afterward, Graham wrote to Marie to thank her and to tell her how impressed he had been with both the Serenade and the work she and the volunteers were doing.

"I had a good conversation with Joe Lehman," Graham's letter concluded. "I think we will be able to do something about getting more support for expansion of the Breaking Barriers process there in Pennsylvania."

Within a few months after Graham's visit, the Pennsylvania Department of Corrections purchased copies of his *Breaking Barriers* video series for every prison in the state, giving Marie what she needed to start implementing her new program.

The VAC board gave Marie, Olsen, and Chris Power the go-ahead to offer the Healing Brokenness program to staff in up to five prisons and agreed to cover their travel expenses. Using an old sales trick she had learned, Marie sent a letter to Commissioner Lehman and all of the prison superintendents offering a free Healing Brokenness class to the first five prisons who responded. It worked like a charm. Her phone rang off the hook and she quickly lined up five classes around the state.

Within a span of two months, they taught the five-day program to prison staff at Rockview, Huntingdon, Cresson, and Retreat. Marie was encouraged by their response. After twelve staff members at Cresson completed the program, their superintendent, Frederick Frank, wrote a letter to Deputy Commissioner Moore, suggesting that the Healing Brokenness program be incorporated into the regular curriculum of the DOC's statewide Training Academy.[18] Frank Waitkus, a corrections records specialist at the Retreat prison, wrote to Commissioner Lehman and suggested that the program be made available at every prison.[19] Charles Zimmerman, superintendent at Waymart, who had attended the conflict resolution Train-the-Trainer program wrote to Marie, "The Department of Corrections certainly is indebted to you for the efforts you are making at helping us understand and manage conflict better."[20]

The superintendent at the Cambridge Springs women's prison was also interested in having his staff trained, but could schedule only two days of training at a time. Marie booked three separate sessions at Cambridge Springs, months in advance.

When the dates for the Cambridge Springs program finally arrived, Bob Olsen agreed to help teach the first segment, the two-day conflict resolution course. They made the four-hour trek to the remote prison situated in the northwestern corner of the state. When they arrived, they discovered that the staff had forgotten about the scheduled training. The deputy, Charles Utz, apologized profusely.

"We came all this way—could you just get a group of staff together to take the class?" Marie asked.

"Impossible. We can't just pull staff away from the cellblocks for two days. I'm sure you understand."

Marie and Bob looked at each other. Bob shrugged, but Marie wasn't about to give up.

"What about inmates, then? Could you get a group of inmates together—maybe fifteen or so?" Marie asked.

"Sure, we can do that. What types of inmates would you like to have?"

"Give us your angriest, toughest women—the ones you can't control."

Utz laughed. "Oh, you don't want our *worst*—we've got women here who are violent, manipulative, belligerent like you wouldn't believe."

"That's exactly who we want," Marie said firmly.

Utz shrugged. "All right, then. Let's give them to her."

The guard at the front desk started making calls to different cellblocks to get the inmates brought to the training room while Marie and Bob went to set up.

"After all the rough guys we've taught, how tough could these women be?" Bob said with a laugh. Marie laughed too as she wrote, "Welcome to Creative Nonviolent Conflict Resolution" on the blackboard.

When the first woman came into the room, she walked right up to Marie, leaned in with her face just inches from hers and said, "You think you're gonna teach us *what*?" Then she turned, stomped away, and slammed herself into a chair.

Another woman strutted toward Marie, stopping only when her body would have collided with hers and gave a menacing stare. "Who told you I was violent?" she demanded.

Throughout the morning, the anger and belligerence of the women made Joseph's challenges back on B Block seem like child's play. Bob and Marie pressed on, trying desperately to engage the women in discussions about values and feelings, to convince them of the power of good listening and problem-solving skills, even to get them to participate in the Light and Livelys. Marie sent up silent, pleading prayers throughout the day. *This one's for you, God.* The women remained sullen and defensive.

By the end of the day, Bob was ready to go home. Over dinner at the Cambridge Springs hotel, he said, "I'll take male inmates anytime."

Marie was exhausted, but she hated to give up. "Bob, do we believe in this stuff ourselves?" she asked. "We have to trust the course and what we're teaching. Let's stick it out. Tomorrow will go better, I just know it."

Bob sighed. "It certainly couldn't get any worse."

The next morning, the fifteen women filed into the classroom, glowering and silent.

Bob and Marie had decided to start with the group-on-one affirmation where everyone in the room said something positive about each member of the class, one at a time.

Marie explained the activity, then stood behind the first woman, Roberta,[21] with her hands resting gently on her shoulders. Roberta tensed at Marie's touch.

"Now, each of you look at Roberta. Think about the beautiful person who is inside her. Tell Roberta something positive that you know about her."

There was a long, awkward silence. Roberta stared at the floor.

"Well, I'm her cellie, so I'll start. Man, she is some kinda neat-freak! Everything around her just looks neat and clean. When I get outta here, I'm gonna ask her to come help me clean up my place!"

Everyone laughed.

The next woman spoke. "You hear that laugh Roberta has? That is the best laugh. When I hear it, I gotta laugh too."

As each woman in the circle talked about the good they saw in Roberta, Marie felt Roberta's shoulders relax. By the time each of her fourteen classmates, plus Bob and Marie, had given their affirmations, tears were streaming down her cheeks.

They repeated the process for each woman. Marie stood behind each one, her hands resting on each woman's shoulders, while others spoke. One by one, each woman's entire posture and demeanor changed as she heard sixteen other people say good things about her.

"I know if I ever needed anything, Teresa[22] would be there for me."

"Leah[23] is so smart. Every time I need help with my GED math, Leah helps me understand it."

"Janet[24] is a caring mom—she talks about her kids all the time."

By the time they finished, every person in the room was crying openly, including Marie and Bob.

"We aren't monsters," Roberta said, wiping her cheeks. "Even though they tell us we are."

"We're real people, beautiful people," Janet added.

"Yes, you truly are," Marie told them.

After the morning's catharsis, Marie felt like she was with a different group of women. They were lively, sincere, engaged. It was one of the best groups she'd ever taught.

At the end of the day, Marie told the women, "What we've covered these last two days is just the first part of the Healing Brokenness program. We're scheduled to come back here two more times to teach the rest of it. Of course, we were supposed to teach this whole thing to staff. But if we can get approval to teach all of *you* in those next two sessions, would you like to do that?"

The women enthusiastically agreed. Marie made the arrangements with Deputy Utz, and she and Bob returned two more times to Cambridge Springs.

At the end of their third session, the women asked if some of the staff could be invited in to see the women receive their certificates. Marie asked the staff members to stand with her and Bob to congratulate each woman.

"You constantly harp at us to get our act together," one woman said to the staff. "But it took this Healing Brokenness program to show us how."

"All of the inmates and all of the staff should take this class," another woman added.

Marie started asking to teach the toughest inmates in each prison. The women at Cambridge Springs had helped her understand that the toughest ones were probably the ones who were hurting the most and would soak up the compassion and love offered to them like a sponge.

THOUGH MARIE HAD enjoyed being the director of the Voluntary Action Center for nine years, her heart was with the men and women in the prisons. She wanted to step down as VAC director to focus full-time on the Volunteers in Prison programs. But Marie knew the VAC didn't have enough money for two full-time directors. The VAC board had been talking for years about the fact that the prison programs had become larger than all of the other VAC programs combined. They had often talked about splitting the prison programs off and creating a separate organization. But that, too, would take money they didn't have.

Then, one afternoon, Rev. David Vogan, a Presbyterian minister and VAC supporter, came to Marie's office.

"If you had a sum of money and could do anything you wanted with it, what would you do?" Vogan asked.

"How much money?" Marie asked.

"A *lot* of money."

Marie told him about her desire to focus full-time on the prison work and to expand it.

Vogan replied, "Well, write up a proposal and a budget to do that and the presbytery will fund it."

It seemed too good to be true. Marie went to her mentors, Ann and Rose, to tell them about his incredible offer.

"It sounds like an answer to prayer, Marie," Ann said.

"But it would mean I'd be leaving the Voluntary Action Center," Marie replied. "I couldn't be the director anymore."

Rose spoke up. "You've been a wonderful director for the VAC. But your heart is in prison work, Marie. We've always known that. It's time for you to pursue your dream. You have our blessing."

12
CENTERING PEACE

An eye for an eye and the whole world will be blind.
— Mahatma Gandhi (1869–1948)

When will our consciences grow so tender that we will act to prevent human misery rather than avenge it?
— Eleanor Roosevelt (1884–1962)

With encouragement from Rose and Ann, Marie wrote a detailed proposal to expand all of the prison programs and submitted it to Rev. Vogan.

"This shows what you need for one year. What will you do the year after that?" he asked.

"Well, I'll have to spend the first year raising money to keep it going," Marie replied.

"We're going to give you enough money for five years," he told her.

It was yet another miracle. Marie threw herself into planning. She wanted to continue weekly volunteer visits and the Family Visitation Assistance program at Rockview and expand the statewide programs, including the runathons, Christmas cards, PrayerMates, Healing Brokenness classes, and the Criminal Justice Advocacy and Support Directory. But there was another important piece she wanted to add.

She had seen so many offenders gain a sense of self-worth and make genuine contributions to the community by volunteering through

CACJ's Community Service program and the runathons. Marie wanted to create an inmate volunteering program. A decade earlier, she had attended a workshop at a National Association on Volunteers in Criminal Justice conference on the topic of "Inmates as Volunteers" and had always dreamed of creating such a program. She wanted the inmates to gain job skills and social skills, and she wanted their volunteer work to provide tangible benefits to the community so that plenty of people would support it.

She remembered the suggestion that Robert, one of the VAC's court-referred volunteers, had made to provide inmates with tools to repair donated appliances and furniture so they could be sold for more money. Marie drafted a proposal to teach furniture and small appliance repair to inmates from the county jail. Inmates would fix donated items to sell. The community would have a place to buy reasonably priced used furniture and appliances, keeping those things out of the landfill. And proceeds from sales of the donated items could keep the whole program going.

Marie sought advice from Ann and Rose, as well as members of the VAC and CACJ boards. She met with Warden Wilson at the Centre County Jail to get his approval to offer work-release and good-time credit to inmate volunteers. Warden Wilson had worked at Rockview and knew of Marie's work there. He said he thought her proposed program would be terrific for the inmates and promised his support. They discussed logistical details such as how many inmates to send to the program, how to select participants, and security and supervision guidelines for the inmates while they were away from the jail. After months of preparation, Marie took the proposal to the Centre County commissioners and received their approval.

Marie assembled a board of directors that included Rose, who was now ninety-three years old, and Ann, age eighty-two. They incorporated all of the prison programs under the name "CentrePeace, Inc." In part, the name reflected the influence of the Brethren, Quaker, and Mennonite peace churches that had been so instrumental in supporting her programs over the years. It also conveyed the mission they established to "center peace" in people's lives by "replacing walls built by fear and vengeance with understanding and reconciliation, and to contribute to a justice system based on creating wholeness and healing brokenness."

With funding from the Huntingdon Presbytery, the Middle Pennsylvania District of the Church of the Brethren, and a Centre County Community Development Block Grant, CentrePeace was in business. They rented a small garage on the outskirts of Bellefonte, near the county jail, to serve as a workshop. A small army of inmate and community volunteers fixed the place up. People donated tools and refinishing supplies for the workshop, as well as furniture, appliances, and household goods for the sales.

They dubbed the inmate training program "Project Restore" with the dual purpose of restoring material goods and restoring lives. They

Inmate trainees at CentrePeace work on furniture refinishing projects. The Project Restore motto is painted on the wall behind them: "In gratitude to those who donate items to Project Restore, we dedicate our time, our respect, and our creative abilities to recycle and restore." Photo courtesy of CentrePeace, Inc.

hired a supervisor to work with the five to ten inmates who would come to CentrePeace for five hours a day, six days a week. A volunteer named Dee Muller taught them how to refinish furniture. Dozens of additional volunteers sorted and priced the donated goods for sales, which they began holding in the parking lot outside the workshop.

Another volunteer, Vicki Garvin, served as Marie's secretary and took care of the office work for all of the prison programs. They soon realized that the jail wasn't providing bag lunches for the inmates, so Vicki and Marie took turns preparing daily lunches for the inmates.

Marie taught conflict resolution classes and the Breaking Barriers program to the inmates. She also had every volunteer and staff member take the conflict resolution course and stressed the importance of giving the inmates continual affirmation.

"We want to be sure that every inmate has seen and felt love before they leave our program," Marie told the volunteers and staff regularly.

Unfortunately, the neighbors didn't agree.

The Millers, an older couple living next door to CentrePeace, told Marie that they were terrified by having inmates walking around near their house. Marie explained the whole CentrePeace program and philosophy, and told them about the prison work she had been doing for nearly twenty years.

"We have support from a lot of churches," she told the Millers, "including Presbyterians, Quakers, Mennonites, and the Church of the Brethren, which I belong to."

"I didn't know you were Brethren. I grew up in the Sugar Run Church of the Brethren," Mrs. Miller said.

"Really? I attended that church when I was first married and led the choir there," Marie replied.

"Maybe you knew my parents, the Pletchers. My father is dead now, but Mother still goes there."

"Oh my goodness, yes, your mother asked me to sing 'In the Garden' at your father's funeral."

"That was you? You sang so beautifully for my father. I'll never forget that," Mrs. Miller said, clasping Marie's hand in hers.

As Marie left their house, she thought, *What are the chances?*

Within a week, Mr. Miller visited CentrePeace to check out the inmates for himself. He soon started visiting regularly, bringing cookies Mrs. Miller had baked for the men. The Millers quickly became surrogate grandparents for the inmates.

Another neighbor, Bill Schaeffer, called Marie to complain about inmates walking around freely outside the building.

"We're running a conflict resolution training for inmates and staff, and I always like to have people from the community in these classes," Marie told him. "Inmates need to hear the perspectives of people from the community. You'd be a good person to do that. Why don't you come in and take the course. I'll be happy to offer it to you at no cost."

Schaeffer agreed. Soon after completing the class, he became a dedicated mentor and GED tutor for one of the inmates. He offered to donate welding equipment and set up a welding training program for the inmates when CentrePeace had enough space for such a program. Schaeffer became a strong supporter and regular visitor to Centre-Peace.

Along with the successes came daily challenges. The inmates brought their own issues. For some it was struggles with drug or alcohol addiction; others had serious family issues that were compounded by their incarceration. Often, inmates were frustrated, angry, or depressed about conditions at the jail and delays in their court cases or parole process. The staff and volunteers were sometimes counselors, sometimes parent figures, always role models. They had to balance respect for the inmates with being attentive to possible signs of inmates taking advantage of the freedom they had at CentrePeace.

A few times staff discovered that an inmate had stolen something, or had stashed drugs or booze somewhere on the premises. Because the majority of the county jail inmates were locals, they sometimes knew, and occasionally hated, each other. Sometimes family disputes reared up: "your sister was the one who called the police on me," or "you had a fling with my girlfriend." Jail was an intense, highly concentrated, closed society where every issue was magnified dramatically and the inmates brought that drama to CentrePeace every day.

Marie welcomed these conflicts as they provided opportunities to model and prove the value of nonviolent conflict resolution skills. She, the staff, and volunteers were all tested daily to practice what they preached. They met regularly to brainstorm ways to handle the issues that arose between inmates, staff, and customers. Mediation became part of the fabric of CentrePeace.

Once CentrePeace was up and running, Marie was able to focus more attention on Rockview. After more than a year of planning, Victor, Bear, and Marie had organized a half-day Victim Offender Reconciliation Conference. Yusef, the inmate leader Marie had met years earlier through Graterford's runathon, was now at Rockview and had also helped with the conference. They invited nearly one hundred inmates, the entire Rockview staff, and over twenty community representatives from churches, victims' groups, CentrePeace, CACJ, and the Prison Society.

Eight speakers representing the courts, corrections, victims, and the community offered their perspectives on the impact of crime. Harvey Yancey, major of the guard at Rockview, spoke candidly about his own incarceration years earlier, and how his understanding of what it was like to be an inmate now informed his work as a member of the corrections staff. OJ, who was now working as a drug and alcohol counselor, and occasionally still volunteered for the VAC, told the men about his path from being in prison to making a life for himself on the outside. Judge Charles Brown provided a view from the bench. Representatives from several community organizations spoke candidly about how people in the community viewed inmates. Several crime victims shared their experiences.

The inmates' perspective was provided through videotaped interviews with ten offenders of varying ages, backgrounds, offenses, and sentences. Yusef had conducted the interviews with the inmates and edited them into a finished video. The men hoped that the video would help audience members see the human faces of offenders. After the conference, Victor wrote to Marie:

> I believe the seminar you brought into fruition here at Rockview has the greatest potential to inspire positive change in the men here. Even the most hardened men here were moved. . . . When you move lifers who have for the most part abandoned the outside world and their responsibilities to it, it is just short of a miracle.[1]

Victor and Bear also wrote letters of appreciation to each of the speakers, on behalf of all of the Rockview lifers.

> The men were profoundly moved by what they heard and saw. For many it was the first time they were required to face the extent of the tragedies they set in motion through their actions. Accountability is an integral part of human development and betterment. Your participation in the seminar has awakened in the men of Rockview a need to account for their actions. In so doing, you have begun a process that can only serve to benefit everyone. Thank you for your demonstration of true human concern and compassion. Thank you for daring to care about those who are so often forgotten.[2]

Bear

In the days and weeks after the conference, Bear prayed that the hearts and minds of victims, offenders, and people in the community would open to the possibility of reconciliation. Listening to crime victims talk about the devastation they'd suffered had been a kick in the gut for him and many of the other lifers. But they had asked the speakers for honesty and they'd gotten it.

Knowing that many people in the community supported sentences of life without possibility of parole, with no second chances, was crushing. If he let himself dwell on it, Bear knew it would extinguish the tiny flicker of hope he clung to that perhaps, one day, he would be free.

He'd been in prison for over half of his life, seventeen long years. He had been a scared, naïve kid when he'd come in. He had never been in trouble before and was shattered by the surreal turn of events that had led to him being charged as an accomplice in someone else's death. One night soon after he'd come to prison, Bear had knelt on the floor of his cell, sobbing and praying, begging Ms. Gabriel[3] to forgive him for his role in her death, whispering over and over again how sorry he was. He had written letters of apology to everyone he knew—his family, his football coach, friends, teachers, his attorney, the DA, the judge. He knew it could never be enough, but it was all he had to offer.

The finality of his sentence—life without possibility of parole—hadn't sunk in for a long time. But now he knew that, short of a miracle of commutation from the governor, he'd be here until he died. Bear had petitioned for commutation three times and had been denied a public hearing each time. He had to grow up in prison, and had decided to make the best of it. A few mentors— Mr. Snavely at Camp Hill, Pastor Larry Titus who had visited him regularly in prison for nearly a decade, and his good friend Victor—had helped along the way, teaching him how to do good and walk a straight path amid the evils of prison life.

Bear got involved in every educational and leadership opportunity that came his way. He worked as a clerk for the prison chaplain, and helped to plan weekly worship services in the prison. The Victim Offender Reconciliation Conference felt like one of his finest efforts. People like Marie Hamilton and Howard Zehr gave him hope for the future. And his faith in God kept him going, one minute, one hour, one day at a time. It was all he could do.

The atmosphere of hope created by restorative justice programs at Rockview was soon overshadowed by ominous changes in the winds of public opinion. The state's execution chamber, housed at Rockview, had lain dormant for over three decades. It appeared that was about to change.

A new governor, Tom Ridge, had taken office in January, and within the first month he signed the first of a staggering 220 execution warrants he'd eventually sign in his six-year term. Pennsylvania had the fourth highest number of death row inmates in the country.

The state's chosen method of execution had been changed from the electric chair to lethal injection several years earlier. Rockview's electric chair had been dismantled and the execution chamber was modified to carry out this new method.

Thirty-nine-year-old Keith Zettlemoyer was scheduled once again for execution, this time on May 2, 1995. Marie and the other members of the Centre Region Coalition to Abolish Capital Punishment organized a candlelight vigil for the night of the scheduled execution.

Marie called Dr. Mazurkiewicz to talk with him about their planned prayer vigil.

"I appreciate you calling me, Marie," Mazurkiewicz said. He sounded tired. "Though you won't be able to hold your vigil on the prison grounds, you can gather across the road from the prison. I'll see that there's a place set up for you."

There was a long silence. Marie couldn't imagine how he must feel, especially since he'd have to preside over the execution along with the doctor who would make the pronouncement of death. Though Dr. Mazurkiewicz had a reputation for being tough, Marie had seen a gentle, humanitarian side of the man in the twenty years she'd been working with him. She knew that he cared deeply about the men under his watch at Rockview. But Zettlemoyer's fate wasn't his decision.

"I'll pray for you, too, Dr. Mazurkiewicz," Marie told him before hanging up.

Jerry

From his cell on the third tier of East Wing, Jerry stood watch through the long night of May 2. The cellblock was unusually still, as most of the men sat, immobile, in front of their televisions, watching the news coverage of the pending execution.

The barred window in front of Jerry's cell faced the front door of the deputy warden's building. The execution chamber was housed there, on the second floor. Jerry sat in front of the window on his small wooden desk chair. Prison scuttlebutt was that Zettlemoyer had asked for a cheeseburger and fries for his last meal. *How could he eat, knowing. . . .* Jerry couldn't let himself finish the thought.

He watched as members of the press arrived, six of them, chosen by lottery. *Why is it offered like a prize?* he wondered. He watched as the six civilian witnesses arrived. *Who would choose to watch a man be killed?* He watched as state police vehicles pulled up and several officers ducked into the building.

Jerry tried to fathom how desperately alone Zettlemoyer must be feeling, knowing how close death was. *We're all afraid we might die in here, but he knows. Is he anxious to just get on with it, hoping this will finally pay his debt to society? Is he thinking of his victim? His family?*

Jerry looked at the clock on his old RCA television. 9:45 p.m. He tried to shake off the chill that took over his body and began to pray.

Help the victim's family find peace, God, but through some means other than this execution. Help Zettlemoyer's family find peace, too.

Silhouetted shadows moved across the upstairs windows of the deputy warden's building.

Be with Dr. Mazurkiewicz, Lord. May he never have to do this again. We know he doesn't believe in this.

The shadows disappeared. Movement stopped.

Be with the men and women on death row, God. May they find their way to you.

All of the lights at the front of the deputy warden's building went out.

Be with all of the people who are in favor of the death penalty and help them to see another way.

A black station wagon appeared out of the darkness. It backed up to the front door.

Be with the people out there who are protesting this execution, God. Don't let them be disheartened.

Shadowy figures carried a dark bundle to the waiting vehicle. The station wagon pulled away quickly.

Don't let the protestors give up. Give them courage, God, to keep fighting against this.

The lights in the building came back on.

Jerry watched as the state police, the witnesses, and the reporters all departed quickly.

Then he turned away from the window.

God, forgive us all.

In a small, roped-off area across from the Rockview prison, Marie stood watch and prayed with about a hundred other protestors. A little after 10:25 p.m., they got the word: Keith Zettlemoyer was dead. Marie wept, her candle flickering in the chilly darkness.

The following week, when Marie and the volunteers returned to B Block for their regular weekly visit, the entire prison felt eerie and unsettled. A staff member who Marie had gotten to know well had resigned the day after the execution.

"I just can't work in a place that kills people," she told Marie.

Marie felt the same way, but she knew the inmates needed her and the volunteers now more than ever.

Another death less than two weeks later deepened the immense sadness Marie was feeling. On May 14, 1995, at age ninety-three, Rose Cologne died. Rose had often said she thought the epitaph on her tombstone should read, "Off to another meeting." Marie couldn't imagine another meeting without her dear friend and mentor.

13

Forgiveness

Each of us is more than the worst thing we've ever done.[1]
–Bryan Stevenson, New York University law professor
and founder of the Equal Justice Initiative

The meetings did continue without Rose, as did the work.

A second execution was carried out in August 1995, of fifty-two-year-old Leon Moser. Governor Ridge had signed nineteen death warrants in his first eight months in office, nearly the same number Robert Casey had signed in his entire eight years as governor. Marie found it all profoundly disturbing.

Over the years, she had met with families of murder victims and heard their stories. She couldn't fathom the pain those families felt. She tried to imagine how she might feel if someone she loved was murdered and she prayed that she would find the strength to forgive.

She also saw how deeply many inmates yearned to be forgiven by their victims and families. In the conflict resolution course, one entire class session was devoted to the topic of forgiveness. But the first time Marie taught it on B Block after the summer's state-sanctioned executions, forgiveness was a highly charged and deeply emotional subject. She started with her usual quotations about forgiveness, and tried to explain the concept. But what had been done in a building within sight of their classroom overshadowed everything.

Hot tears rose to Marie's eyes and her throat constricted. The men shifted uncomfortably on the wooden benches. Not knowing what else to do, Marie prayed silently, *This one's for you, God.*

The room was silent except for the ticking of the heavy institutional clock on the wall.

Finally, one man cleared his throat. "Uh, Miss Marie?"

"Yes, James?"[2]

"Uh, well, I was just thinking about this buddy of mine. See, he killed a little girl years back. So he's been in prison a long time. And I guess that little girl's family had a really rough time for a lotta years. They wanted . . . uh . . . they thought my buddy should have been sentenced to death, too."

James stopped talking for a minute. Several of the inmates looked down at the floor.

He continued, "But then, that little girl's parents started visiting my buddy in prison, just, you know, to talk to him. They wrote letters to him and sent him books to read. And now they're even helping him with his parole plan so he can find a place to live and a job when he gets out. Miss Marie, is *that* what you mean by forgiveness?"

The other men sat silently, many with tears streaming down their cheeks, waiting for Marie's answer.

"Yes, James," she said quietly, after dabbing away her own tears. "Yes. That is exactly what we mean by forgiveness."

Marie knew that few inmates had the sort of opportunity for redemption that James' friend had. She also knew that many inmates had been victims themselves, of crime, abuse, neglect. Many of them had never forgiven their abusers.

She asked the men to think of a time when someone had wronged them. They discussed how they had dealt with their anger. Then she asked whether there were things they were still angry about. The men had a long list of grudges and resentments.

"If that anger is fresh in our minds, if we talk or think about it a lot, that isn't healthy. Even if our anger is justified, it will sap our energy and prevent us from being the kind of person we want to be," she explained. "Anger toward another person gives that person control over us, but by forgiving, we can let go of that anger."

She gave each man a laminated "forgiveness card" with a message she had found many years earlier:

> Not to forgive is to yield oneself to another's control. If one does not forgive, then one is controlled by the other's initiatives and is locked into a sequence of act and response, of outrage and revenge, tit for tat, escalating always. The present is endlessly overwhelmed and devoured by the past. Forgiveness frees the forgiver.[3]

Edward[4] had been unusually quiet during class. Finally, he blurted, "I'm angry with my parents and I will *never forgive* them! I won't even let them on my visiting list."[5]

"Why don't you want your parents to visit, Edward?" Marie asked.

"I'm here for doing the same thing my father did to me," he said, "but my father never went to prison for it."

Marie could tell by looking around the room that the other men understood exactly what Edward was talking about. She knew the statistics on inmates who have been the victims of abuse were staggering.[6]

"I will *never* forgive him!" Edward repeated.

"How painful that must be for you," Marie said quietly.

He stared at Marie for a minute, then put his head down. "Yeah," he muttered.

"Let's pretend for a minute," Marie suggested. "Let's pretend that your father is right here. And let's try practicing our 'I' statements. What would you like to say to your father if he were here right now?"

The other inmates all seemed to hold their breath.

"I wouldn't say *nothing*," Edward replied. "I'm not talking to him!"

"I know this can be very difficult to even think about," Marie said softly. "Take your time."

A few inmates looked at Marie, wide-eyed. One cleared his throat. Others stared at the floor. Marie waited patiently, and silently said a prayer for Edward.

Marie teaching conflict resolution in Rockview's B Block North. Photo courtesy of CentrePeace, Inc.

He looked at Marie. She nodded.

"I . . . I guess. . . ."

"It's okay, Edward," Marie said. "Start with 'I feel.' Just pretend your father is right here."

"I feel . . . so . . . so angry . . . because of . . . what you did to me. You hurt me over and over again. And you never got caught. And you . . . and. . . ." His voice broke and tears flowed down his sallow cheeks. Other inmates quickly looked away, some awkwardly brushing their own cheeks with roughened knuckles.

Marie wanted more than anything to give Edward a comforting hug. But she simply gave his hand a squeeze and nodded, then suggested they take a break. The men quickly stood up and moved around the room.

After the break, Marie told the men about the time she'd spoken to a support group for families of murder victims.

"This group met periodically to talk about their painful memories and their anger about their loved one's murder. They wrote letters to lawmakers and circulated petitions to deny pardons and support executions of inmates on death row. This was one angry group. And the more they talked about the murders of their loved ones, the more angry they got.

"I was introduced as the speaker for the evening, and I told the group that I work with prison inmates.

"'You're *nice* to those people?' one mother of a murdered child asked me.

"I tried to tell them about what we do here in the prisons, but a father interrupted me and asked, 'Who pays you for this?'

"I could tell these people were carrying a tremendous amount of anger—not so very different from the anger you were talking about."

Many of the inmates nodded.

Marie went on. "Well, I figured I might be tarred and feathered and run out of town that night. But I decided to forget the speech I had prepared and just tell them about another family I had met. That family had held on to their anger about their loved one's murder for years, and it weighed them down. But then that family went to the prison with a mediator to confront the person who had murdered their loved one and to ask questions—like 'Why did you do this?' and 'Are you going to kill again?'—and to talk about how much it had hurt to have their loved one taken away. And the person who had murdered their loved one told them how very sorry he was, and how much he wished he could take it back. And through that conversation, that family finally found peace. They could let go of all that anger when they were finally able to forgive."

The men in her class sat quietly for a few minutes, trying to take all of this in.

The day's session was nearly over. Marie closed with these thoughts: "Forgiveness doesn't mean that what the other person did was okay. In fact, what they did may have been absolutely horrible. But forgiveness lets you put your anger and the person who caused your anger in a place where they can no longer control you. We do not forgive for the sake of the other person. We forgive for our own sake. Forgiveness frees the forgiver."

As the group adjourned, Marie hoped that, despite the executions that had been carried out at Rockview, the message of forgiveness had somehow gotten through.

A FEW MONTHS later, Edward flagged Marie down during her weekly visit to B Block.

"I have a visit coming up, Miss Marie," he said, smiling.

"That's wonderful, Edward. Who's coming to see you?"

"My parents!" he reported proudly. "All the way from Arizona they're coming—just to see me!"

"Really? I thought you kept them off of your visitors list."

"Don't you remember, though, Miss Marie? Don't you remember, in class—the forgiveness we talked about?"

Marie smiled. "Yes, Edward. I remember."

Marie spoke often to churches, civic groups, and legislators about the need to move away from a punishment-focused criminal justice system toward restorative justice. In May 1996, she and Dr. Mazurkiewicz spoke together at a forum titled "Pennsylvania's Penal System: How Well Is It Working?". Dr. Mazurkiewicz spoke about the radical changes he'd seen in his twenty-five years at Rockview. Shifts in federal law[7] over the previous decade had expanded the use of prison sentences for many crimes, especially drug-related offenses, established mandatory minimums, lengthened sentences, and restricted paroles. Those legislative changes had led directly to the explosion of Rockview's population, from 425 inmates in 1970 to over 2,100 in 1996.

Mazurkiewicz told the assembled audience that investing more money in education and counseling for inmates would be far more effective than promoting laws to keep them in prison longer. As Marie listened to the superintendent's remarks, she realized that he had become part of a small minority within the system that was still calling for rehabilitation instead of punishment. Mazurkiewicz would retire within a year.

Between 1994 and 1996, Marie had served on the Pennsylvania Justice Fellowship Task Force,[8] which had held nine public fact-finding hearings with testimony from over 150 criminal justice experts on the critical issues in the state's burgeoning prison system and the urgent need for reform. The task force delivered a comprehensive set of recommendations to Governor Ridge that, if implemented, would reduce recidivism while still protecting the public. The task force estimated that the recommended reforms would also save Pennsylvania taxpayers over $850 million in the first four years of implementation.

Their recommendations included implementing community-based alternatives to incarceration for low-risk, nonviolent offenders; a comprehensive restitution system to make offenders accountable to their victims; and improving probation, parole, and offender reentry programs to ensure the success of those released from prison.

The task force also recommended that a greater number of inmates with life sentences be considered for commutation, especially those who had already served twenty years, had completed 60 percent of their sentence, or were over age fifty-five. Such inmates had been statistically proven far less likely to reoffend.

Unfortunately, at the same time the task force was making their recommendations, two highly publicized cases of Pennsylvania parolees committing additional crimes led to a public outcry to toughen commutation procedures, despite the fact that hundreds of other lifers had been successfully paroled. The impact was immediate, and commutations for lifers in Pennsylvania came to an abrupt halt.

It broke Marie's heart to think about how these changes would affect all of the lifers she had gotten to know—Lois, Bear, Victor, and dozens of others. Through the runathons, the VORP forum at Rockview, and annual Pennsylvania Lifers Association banquets and picnics, Marie had spent a lot of time with life-sentenced inmates over the past two decades. Lifers were usually the most mature and respected inmates, often serving as leaders and mentors for others. The changes in both public attitudes and commutation procedures left Pennsylvania's more than 2,500 lifers without hope.

Despite these setbacks, Marie took heart from two positive steps toward restorative justice taken in Pennsylvania.

In 1996, Pennsylvania became one of the first states in the United States to legislatively promote restorative justice for juveniles.[9] Initially, restorative justice was applied primarily to cases of nonviolent crime, often through victim offender mediations.

Then, in 1998, Marie was invited to serve on a task force with representatives from the Pennsylvania Department of Corrections, the Office of the Victim Advocate,[10] and restorative justice practitioners to establish procedures for mediations between victims and incarcerated offenders in cases of violent crime.[11] Marie was one of the few participants who understood inmates' perspectives and needs. Others in the group thought these mediations should focus only on victims' or survivors' needs. But Marie knew that many inmates longed for the opportunity to seek forgiveness for their crimes. She advocated for consideration of inmates' needs in the process. The group consented, but decided that the process could be initiated only by victims or their families. Inmates could not request such mediations.

The process would require intense preparation of both victims and inmates by a pair of trained mediators. In individual meetings with each party, they'd discuss their feelings about the crime, the impact of it, questions they might want to ask, what they might want to say to the other party, concerns about a face-to-face meeting, and their hopes for the outcome of a mediation. This advance preparation could take months, even years. The process would be completely voluntary for both victims and offenders, and either party could choose to end the mediation process at any point. In cases where either party didn't want a face-to-face meeting, a form of "shuttle mediation" could be used with mediators relaying messages between the parties. Inmates who chose not to participate would not be penalized. Conversely, those who did wouldn't receive any special privileges or reduction of their sentence. With procedures established, Marie looked forward to receiving her training for these mediations.

But for the moment, the work at CentrePeace was consuming her. In 1998, CentrePeace volunteers logged over 55,000 hours, and CentrePeace programs reached more than 44,000 people.

The statistics for the Eighteenth Annual Pennsylvania Prison Runathon were also impressive: 1,817 inmates, staff, and community members at eighteen prisons ran a total of 27,937 miles and raised $17,337. But the result that made Marie cheer the loudest was the number of runners who completed marathon distance that year—she awarded special marathon T-shirts to 571 inmates who had run twenty-six miles or more. Cliff Parris, activities chief for the Department of Corrections, told Marie that all street clothing had been banned in the state prisons except for the runathon T-shirts. The inmates across the state had now raised over $200,000 for youth and were honored as "Volunteers of the Year" by Big Brothers Big Sisters of America.

Project Restore was also growing rapidly. DeLois Fluke, from Stone Church of the Brethren in Huntingdon, had decided to close her upholstery business and asked Marie if Project Restore wanted her left-over fabric.

"I don't want your fabric, DeLois. I want *you*. Would you teach upholstering to the inmates?" Marie asked.

DeLois agreed.

A large upholstery company in Pittsburgh was closing and contacted Marie, offering to donate their equipment. With professional equipment, fabric, and a knowledgeable instructor, the inmates were soon converting dilapidated sofas and chairs into beautiful finished pieces that sold quickly. Dee Muller, their furniture refinishing

An inmate trainee works on a furniture reupholstery project with guidance from Centre-Peace volunteer Dee Muller. Photo courtesy of CentrePeace, Inc.

instructor, quickly learned upholstering so she could teach it too. CentrePeace began accepting custom orders for upholstery work.

They had quickly outgrown their tiny space on Benner Pike. Though it was a major financial stretch, the CentrePeace board approved the purchase of the building next door to serve as a sales showroom. Marie's long-time friend and fellow Brethren, George Etzweiler, and the Project Restore supervisor, Greg Piper, designed and built an addition to connect the workshop and the showroom, with the help of volunteers from the Pennsylvania Conservation Corps. At Marie's request, Rockview's new superintendent, Robert Myers, even allowed a workcrew of four prison inmates and a supervisor to help finish the addition.

However, around the same time, Myers halted the weekly B Block volunteer visits for the first time in twenty-three years, citing heightened security concerns and more labor-intensive processes for conducting background checks of volunteers. The men of B Block were crushed. Many of them wrote to Marie asking when she and the volunteers would return. Brother Harry wrote and included a five dollar donation to CentrePeace. Marie knew it must have taken Harry months to save that much money from his prison wages. She immediately sent a thank you letter and a copy of the latest CentrePeace newsletter to Harry, telling him he was now officially a "member" of CentrePeace. Marie had convinced the board to set membership dues at one dollar per year, though some had complained that a dollar wouldn't even cover postage to mail newsletters to members.

"I don't want to prevent anyone from joining," Marie had replied. "If dues are only a dollar, people have no excuse not to join. And once people join and learn about what we do, they'll be much more likely to get involved and make bigger donations." Annual dues have been one dollar ever since.

Hawk wrote to Marie too, saying he missed her visits and hoped she could come back soon. The last time she had seen him, months earlier, he had been deeply depressed. When Hawk had first arrived on B Block, he had shown Marie pictures of his young children every week. He'd been in prison so long that now his children were grown and had children of their own.

Marie wrote to the men, assuring them that she missed seeing them and that she was doing everything possible to get the weekly visits started again.

Meanwhile, she worked on promoting CentrePeace in the hopes of attracting additional financial support.

The Learning Channel's "Furniture Guys," Joe L'Erario and Ed Feldman, visited CentrePeace and gave the inmate trainees both tips and praise for their furniture refinishing and upholstery work.

"We could sell some of these pieces for big bucks if we had them in city showrooms," Feldman told the inmates.

The men beamed at the compliment. But it was compliments from their customers that meant the most to them. One inmate who had very little self-esteem and had never done any kind of work with his hands had learned furniture refinishing at CentrePeace. He worked on a single dresser for weeks, painstakingly stripping, sanding, staining, and finishing the piece. When he completed it, the Project Restore supervisor, Greg Piper, helped him carry the dresser into the showroom. A showroom volunteer put a price tag on it, along with a sign that read: "This piece was refinished with care by one of our inmate trainees." The inmate smiled shyly. A few days later, a woman came to Centre-Peace, saw the dresser, and decided to buy it.

Greg told the lady he'd get someone to help load the dresser into her van and brought out the inmate who had refinished the dresser. As Greg and the inmate wrapped the dresser in blankets and loaded it into her van, the lady commented on how beautiful the piece was and how excited she was to have such a fine piece of furniture for her home.

"This gentleman right here is the one who refinished it," Greg told her. The inmate blushed as the customer turned toward him and complimented him further. The woman ended up staying and talking with the inmate for nearly an hour. With the boost to his confidence, he quickly became one of CentrePeace's best furniture refinishers.

As groups of inmate trainees completed the Project Restore program, the CentrePeace staff organized "graduations" for them. When the weather was nice, they had permission from the jail to take the men to Spring Creek Park for all-day celebrations that included a picnic, speeches by the staff and volunteers commending the trainees for their accomplishments, and certificates for each graduate.

They invited each graduate to say a few words about his experience at CentrePeace. For many of the men, it was the first time they'd ever been asked to say anything in front of a group. Some mentioned the repair or upholstery skills they'd learned. Many were grateful for the good-time credit they had been able to earn to reduce their sentences at the jail. One trainee said he hadn't been thrilled about having to take the conflict resolution course, but then found it so helpful that he didn't like working with other trainees until they had completed the course too. All of the trainees thanked the staff and volunteers for the love and respect they had been given, sometimes choking up as they tried to express their gratitude.

At one graduation, a trainee mentioned the Thanksgiving meal the staff and inmates had eaten together at the home of John Yocum, another Project Restore supervisor.

"Being invited to a nice Thanksgiving dinner with all of you, laughing and talking and having a good meal together. . . ." He paused to compose himself. "I never had anything like that in my life. You all have been like the family I never had."

Marie (far right) with CentrePeace staff, volunteers, and inmate trainee graduates. Photo courtesy of CentrePeace, Inc.

Marie always invited the men to come back to CentrePeace after their release from jail, to let the staff know how they were doing. "We love each and every one of you," she'd always tell them. "Remember to be good to yourselves by *doing good* for others."

The circle of good begetting good became part of the fabric of CentrePeace.

One inmate trainee named Sherwood[12] had experience tuning and repairing pianos before coming to CentrePeace. Marie asked an organ tuner to teach him that skill as well. With Sherwood's expertise, CentrePeace was then able to accept donated pianos and organs, and repair, tune, and sell them.

One day, Mr. Miller, who lived next door, told Sherwood, "This whole building was a music store at one time, filled with pianos and organs. I ran the place." Then, Mr. Miller sat down at a piano and played. The staff, volunteers, inmates, and customers all stopped what they were doing, and stood together and listened, clapping wildly when he finished. After that, he regularly offered impromptu mini-concerts in the CentrePeace showroom until his health failed.

Later that summer, a group of teen volunteers from Camp Blue Diamond[13] worked at CentrePeace. One of the inmates told the teens about Mr. Miller's piano concerts.

"He's pretty sick now and can't come over to see us any more," the inmate reported.

"Let's go give *him* a concert," one of the teens suggested.

They invited Mr. and Mrs. Miller to sit on their back porch, then the teens, staff, volunteers, and inmates stood together on their lawn and sang old hymns and camp songs.

Along with music, art became part of the fabric of CentrePeace. After hearing about inmate art contests held in the state prisons, Marie offered space at CentrePeace to exhibit and sell the winners' artwork. Cliff Parris, from the Department of Corrections, gathered the artwork and brought it to CentrePeace. People from the community came in to see the artwork and to purchase the pieces that were for sale. Marie knew many of the inmates, so she could tell purchasers something about the artist who had created each piece. Proceeds from the sale went back to the artist.

Children's artwork had been an important part of CentrePeace through the Christmas Cards for Inmates program. In 1997, the 20,000 prison inmates across the state who received Christmas cards from children were finally given a formal way to express their gratitude to the children. Marie got permission from the Department of Corrections to start a "Valentines for Children" program. CentrePeace delivered blank cards to the prisons for inmates to decorate with their own artwork. Inside each card, a preprinted message read:

> *Before his execution,*
> *St. Valentine sent a note thanking a child*
> *who befriended him while he was in prison.*
>
> *He signed the card:*
> *Your Valentine*
>
> *Happy Valentine's Day with Gratitude for Your Christmas Card*

As children did with the Christmas cards, each inmate signed only his or her first name, with no other identifying information. CentrePeace collected and carefully screened the cards for appropriateness, then sent batches of the decorated cards in time for Valentine's Day to all of the childrens' groups that had provided Christmas cards. Marie knew that inmates needed opportunities to give love just as much as they needed to receive it. Now, she hoped that the children receiving the valentines would feel that love from the hearts of the men and women who sent them.

14
GRACE GOES TO PRISON

Without being forgiven, released from the consequences of what we have done, our capacity to act would, as it were, be confined to one single deed from which we could never recover; we would remain the victims of its consequences forever.[1]

–Hannah Arendt (1906–1975)
Twentieth-century political philosopher

The walls of fear between inmates and victims were the ones Marie had always thought most impenetrable. The new statewide Mediation Program for Victims of Violent Crime finally offered a way to start chipping away at those walls, one victim and one inmate at a time. Marie completed the specialized training for the program and was assigned to her first case, along with co-mediator Marcia Drew.

Through the Office of the Victim Advocate, Jenny[2] had asked to meet with Dave,[3] the man who had murdered her brother, Kenny,[4] nearly twelve years earlier.

Marie and Marcia scheduled the first of many preparation meetings with Jenny. Jenny had been told about Marie's work with inmates and immediately voiced concerns.

"Are you going to take Dave's side?" Jenny asked.

"Neither Marcia nor I will side with anyone," Marie replied. "As mediators, we are neutral. Our role is to help prepare both you and

Dave over the coming months, and to be with both of you during the mediation."

Jenny frowned. "Okay," she said hesitantly. "We'll see how this goes. So, where do we start?"

Marcia asked Jenny why she'd decided to request mediation with Dave.

"On the first day of the trial, I went to my brother's grave and made a promise that I would someday sit down face to face with Dave," Jenny explained. "Dave and Kenny had been best friends, and Kenny had been married to Dave's sister, though they were separated when Kenny was murdered. Kenny was my hero, as well as my big brother. He was always there for me. *Always.* When Dave murdered Kenny, I lost not only my brother but also my best friend."

Jenny described the brutal way Dave had killed Kenny, shooting him multiple times. Because Kenny had been married to Dave's sister, tangled family relationships had been torn apart by Kenny's murder. Jenny had become paralyzed with fear that affected every decision she made and permeated her relationships with her children and her husband.

"What are your expectations for the mediation with Dave?" Marie asked.

"I honestly don't know," Jenny replied. "I'm afraid that if I go into it with a lot of expectations, I don't know how I'll handle it if they don't happen. I feel like the safest thing is not to have any specific expectations."

Marcia asked Jenny what questions she had for Dave, and what she wanted to say to him, to let him know how Kenny's murder had affected her and her family. They discussed Dave's possible reactions and asked Jenny how it might feel to see him, and to listen to things he might want to say. Jenny made notes that would eventually help during the mediation.

Over the next six months, Marie and Marcia met with Jenny regularly to help her prepare for the mediation.

At one meeting, Jenny said her family was furious that she planned to meet with Kenny's murderer. "They're hounding me so bad, saying I shouldn't do the mediation. I've questioned whether I really want to go through with it. I'm scared to death, but I know it's something I have to do to save myself. I've become so consumed with all of my feelings about Kenny's murder—it's ruining me inside. It destroyed my first marriage. My second husband is putting up with a lot. I know I have to go through with it, for me."

Marcia explained the actual mediation process, inviting Jenny to decide on details like whether she wanted herself or Dave to enter the mediation room first and how she wanted to start their dialogue.

Marie explained prison security clearance procedures, and advised Jenny about what to wear and what to avoid. She'd be allowed to bring photos and other small items to the mediation, but had to submit a list in advance for security clearance. Marie described the general prison environment—the sights, sounds, smells—and the layout of the prison and the location of the meeting room they'd use for the mediation.

DURING THE MONTHS of preparation with Jenny, Marie and Marcia also met with Dave.

Marie asked how he felt about meeting with Jenny.

"I don't think I can do this," Dave said.

"What concerns do you have, Dave?"

"That she'll scream at me and just tell me how much she hates me."

"She may be very angry, and part of the process is to let her express her feelings. But part of our job as mediators is to set some ground rules. We ask that there be no shouting, name-calling, or put-downs, and that each person listen to what the other person has to say."

"The other thing is, the guys here are saying, man, don't do this—it's for wimps."

"What do *you* think?" Marie asked.

Dave shrugged.

"Does it feel like something a wimp would do—sitting down with someone they've wronged, and listening to them?"

Dave looked down at his lap and shook his head.

"No, I don't think so either, Dave," Marie said gently. "This definitely isn't for wimps. A wimp wouldn't be strong enough to do this."

Marie suggested that they rehearse a little bit. She asked Dave how he might respond if Jenny expressed strong feelings. They discussed questions that Jenny might want to ask and what it would be like for him to answer. Marie asked him how he'd feel if Jenny brought pictures of Kenny.

Dave turned pale and looked away suddenly. "Kenny was . . . he was my best friend. We had such good times together. And then . . . then . . . I . . ." He stopped talking. He dropped his head into his hands, sobbing quietly.

Marie waited. When Dave could speak again, he said, "I don't know if I could look at pictures of Kenny. What if I break down in front of her?"

"Well, that might happen. It often does. These are really difficult conversations for everyone. The mediation is a time for you to let Jenny know how you feel. Tears are fine. Jenny might cry too. She might even have some of the same worries you have about the mediation. But, you're the only person in the world who can answer her questions, Dave. There are things Jenny really needs to know that only you can tell her. If you're willing to try to answer whatever questions she has, that could really help her."

Dave sat quietly, then started nodding slowly. "Okay. If doing this could help Jenny somehow, then it's worth it. There's nothing else I could ever do to make up for what I did—but at least I can do this."

After six months of intensive preparation, both Jenny and Dave felt ready to meet.

Jenny

Jenny asked her husband to come along for moral support. She planned to bring photos of Kenny, photos of his tombstone, his class ring, and the new watch he bought on the last day he and Jenny had spent together. Marcia and Marie had submitted her list to prison staff for approval.

On the morning of the mediation, they had planned to meet Marie and Marcia early to review things one more time. But Jenny and her husband got a late start, then got lost on the two-hour drive and arrived at the prison half an hour late.

Jenny had never been in a prison. A potent mix of intimidation, stress over being late, and apprehension about the day ahead unsettled her as she walked in. Marcia met them inside. They went through the security checkpoint with its metal detectors and X-ray machines. Jenny handed over the photos and Kenny's class ring. She had forgotten to bring Kenny's watch. The security guard consulted the list, questioned her briefly about the watch, then waved her through.

After clearing security, Marcia said, "When we walk through this next door, Dave will be in there. I just want you to be ready."

Jenny's heart pounded as she looked at the thick steel door separating her from the man who had killed her brother. She took a deep breath and nodded. "I'm ready."

The guards buzzed them into the main visiting room. Marie sat across the room with a thin, gray-haired man in baggy brown prison garb. Jenny looked around. No one else was there.

"So, where's Dave?" she asked.

"There, with Marie," Marcia said.

"That isn't him."

Marcia frowned. "Stay here." She went across the room, spoke briefly with Marie and the man, and then returned.

"That's Dave," Marcia said.

The man looked up. Jenny saw that it *was* Dave. She hadn't seen him since his trial. He didn't look anything like the young, cocky, tough guy she remembered. Jenny did a quick calculation: Dave would be about thirty-six years old, but he looked sixty-six.

Dave and Marie stood and they all walked into the small meeting room adjoining the main visiting area. Marcia closed the door. Jenny sat down at the table.

"I have trouble with my hearing. Is it okay if I sit across from you?" Dave asked Jenny. "Unless you're afraid of having me that close."

"I'm not afraid of you," Jenny replied quickly. She realized with surprise that it was true. After years of paralyzing fear of the man who had murdered her brother, she felt nothing for this shriveled, beaten-down man.

Dave sat down. "I want to say how sorry. . . ."

Jenny stopped him. "First, before you say anything, I want you to see what you've done." She laid photos of Kenny, his tombstone, and his freshly covered grave on the table in front of Dave. "This is all I have left. This is what you took away from me."

Dave started to shake.

Jenny explained the image engraved on Kenny's tombstone. It was an eighteen-wheeler driving along a ribbon of highway. "He was about to pursue his dream of having his own rig. You put an end to that dream."

Dave began to sob. "I'm so . . . so sorry."

"That doesn't cut it for me," Jenny replied bluntly. "You should have been sorry a long time ago. You know, at the trial, I hoped you'd get a longer sentence. We were hoping for a first-degree murder conviction. Seems to me you got off easy with the argument that you were drunk and didn't know what you were doing."

"I did have a serious drinking problem," Dave admitted. "I had to detox here in prison without any help."

"You think I should feel sorry for you?" Jenny asked.

Marie spoke. "Jenny, it might be helpful if you could try to listen to Dave and understand where he's coming from."

Dave looked at Marie. She nodded for him to continue.

"No—I was just trying to say that I've gotten myself straightened out. I even have my GED now, and I'm taking auto mechanics classes here at the prison."

"You know, I really don't care about all of that," Jenny replied angrily. "My tax dollars paid for you to have all those great things."

Dave looked down at the table.

Jenny continued. "I hear you're up for parole soon. I don't want you anywhere near me if you do get out of here."

"I know," he said in a near whisper.

"I've been terrified for years—twelve years." Jenny's voice shook. "Terrified to go out of the house, terrified to let my kids out of the house, terrified to let them go to school. I pulled my kids out of school and homeschooled them because I was afraid something bad would happen to them, like happened to Kenny. Did you know that? That I took my kids out of school?"

Dave shook his head.

"Because I was terrified, my kids were terrified too. I've had nightmares, depression, crying jags that lasted for days. It affected my work, my marriage, my entire life. Even though I knew you were locked up, I was scared somehow you'd get out and then you'd come after the rest of us. Do you know what it's like to live that way every day for twelve years? Do you?"

Dave shook his head again, tears streaming down his rough, wrinkled cheeks.

Marie interjected, "Maybe we could let Dave say a few things now."

Jenny stared at Marie, then stood up. "I need a break." She walked out of the room into the main visiting area, which was now filled with inmates and their families, talking and laughing, children playing.

Marcia came out and stood next to her. "What's happening?" she asked.

"I've about had it with Marie saying I should listen to Dave's feelings and Dave's perspective. This man brutally murdered my brother! I couldn't care less how *he* feels. This isn't about Dave—it's about me! This meeting isn't for his benefit—it's for *mine*!"

Marcia listened quietly, then said, "Let me talk with Marie."

A few minutes later, Marcia motioned for Jenny to return to the room.

Jenny sat back down at the table and took a deep breath. She looked at Marcia. Marcia nodded for her to proceed.

Jenny launched into the questions she had about the murder. One question, especially, had been weighing on her for twelve years.

"How did you know where to find Kenny that night?" Jenny asked.

"I didn't really. I was just driving around and saw his pickup parked in front of a house, so I knocked on the door. It was a duplex. A lady came to the door and I asked for Kenny. She said he was in the apartment on the other side. So I knocked there and Kenny answered."

Jenny sank back into her chair and tried to still her shaking hands as she replayed a scene in her mind that had haunted her since the night of Kenny's murder. Earlier that day, Jenny had told a friend where Kenny was going to be that night. After Kenny was murdered, Jenny wondered if her friend had tipped Dave off about where to find Kenny. If she had, then Jenny was partly to blame for her brother's death. That guilt had been like a millstone around her neck for twelve years. Now, the crushing weight of blame was finally lifted by Dave's explanation. She struggled to refocus her thoughts.

Though she wasn't sure why, Jenny felt a need to know specific details of the murder.

In a shaky, nearly inaudible voice, Dave answered Jenny's questions, one by one.

"What did you do with Kenny's black cowboy hat?" Jenny asked.

"I don't know," Dave said softly. "I don't remember him having his hat when . . ." He stopped suddenly.

"Kenny's hat was his signature. Every state he had been to, he got a state pin and put it on his hat. He never went anywhere without that hat. But then, you knew that, right? He didn't go anywhere without you either. You were one of his best friends. . . ." Jenny broke into deep sobs. "Why, Dave? Why did you kill him?"

Dave broke down again and couldn't speak. When he finally composed himself, he told Jenny how the whole thing had started, with Dave's sister, who was Kenny's estranged wife. She had told Dave that Kenny abused her. She was in a wheelchair after a serious accident, and Kenny had been a big strong man. Dave's sister had played on his sympathies and made him believe that her husband beat her regularly, even though that didn't sound like Kenny. Dave admitted that his own drinking problem had messed up his judgment.

It wasn't until after he had murdered Kenny that Dave began to think his sister might have lied. The first time she visited Dave in prison, he confronted her, and then realized he had done this terrible thing based on lies and manipulations by his own sister.

"What I did was so wrong. I know that. And I am really, really sorry," Dave said.

"He was my hero," Jenny said. "And my best friend. And you took him away. It doesn't seem fair that you get to live and he doesn't—that you'll soon be free, and he'll never be."

Dave looked at Jenny, wide-eyed. "Am I going to have to watch my back for the rest of my life?" he asked quietly.

"You know, Dave, if I'd wanted to do something to you, I could have. But I'm not about to ruin my own life by coming after you. You're not worth it. So, no, you don't have to worry about that."

Dave sat back in his chair and let out a long breath.

"For a lot of years, I was afraid of you," Jenny admitted. "But I'm not any more. Look at you—you're locked up in prison. And when you're out, you'll have to put on job applications where you've been for the last twelve years and why. There will be plenty of people in society who won't want you anywhere around. What you've done is going to be with you for the rest of your life."

Finally, both Jenny and Dave seemed exhausted. They'd been talking for several hours. Marcia suggested that they break for lunch.

Marie, Marcia, Jenny, and her husband left the prison. Over lunch at a nearby diner, Marcia asked Jenny what else she wanted to discuss with Dave.

"I'm not really sure," Jenny replied. "I just know we're not done yet."

When they reconvened, Dave asked, "Did Kenny ever tell you about our Greyhound bus ride home together after we finished bootcamp?"

"No," Jenny replied.

Dave had fallen asleep on the bus and Kenny had left him sleeping, so Dave missed his bus stop. He woke up at a bus stop a hundred miles later and had to change buses to get back home. Jenny laughed out loud at her brother's prank, and Dave did too.

"That sounds just like Kenny," Jenny said. "He was a perpetual jokester, the life of the party."

Dave told Jenny other stories about their hijinks and escapades, about the little day-to-day things the two best friends had done together, their inside jokes and ideas about life. Jenny had never heard most of the stories Dave told. When he finally ran out of stories, he and Jenny sat quietly for a while.

There was a knock at the door and a guard stuck his head into the room. "I really hate to do this, folks, but visiting hours are over and you have to wrap things up."

They had spent over eight hours in mediation.

A part of Jenny felt like she couldn't leave. Dave had a connection to her brother that she could never have. She wondered what else he knew about Kenny that she didn't know. But she also realized she was just going to have to let some things go.

Marie asked, "Jenny, is there anything else you wanted to talk about?"

"I can't think of anything else right now," Jenny replied.

"Dave, how about you. Is there anything else you wanted to say?"

Dave looked at Jenny. "It kills me that I have nothing to offer to make it a little more bearable for you."

"I appreciate you saying that, Dave," Jenny replied. "But you're right. There's nothing you can give me."

"And I know there's nothing I can say that will be enough to make up for what I did," he continued quietly. "I know that saying I'm sorry doesn't even begin to take away the fact that Kenny is dead. I've had to live with that fact every day for the last twelve years. It's haunted me every night—how I could have been so messed up to do what I did. But for what it's worth, I am truly, truly so very sorry. I don't expect you to forgive me, but I do want you to know how sorry I am. Because of my own actions, I ended up losing my best friend, too. I miss him so much."

Jenny sat quietly, listening to Dave, with tears streaming down her face.

After a little while, she asked, "May I write letters to you, Dave?"

Dave turned to Marie and Marcia. "Would that be allowed?"

Marie promised to check with the prison administration and let Dave and Jenny know.

Jenny had one more thing she wanted to say to Dave and she finally felt ready. "I forgive you, Dave. I'll never forget what you did . . . but I forgive you. I'm hoping to move on with my life now and I hope you can too."

Dave's whole body shook as he wept again. Jenny had hoped to see Dave shattered as a human being. But when she saw just how shattered he really was, she didn't know what to do with it. After more than eight hours in mediation, Jenny finally felt she had gotten what she needed. She was ready to go home.

Marie and Marcia stood back as Jenny and Dave rose from their chairs on opposite sides of the table, approached each other, and stood for a long silent moment looking at each other.

"There is something you can do for me, Dave," Jenny said.

"Tell me. I'll do anything."

"When you get out of here, stay on the straight and narrow. Turn your life around and make sure you don't ever do anything like this again."

Dave nodded as his tears flowed again. He held out his hand. Jenny shook it.

Then the guard came to take Dave back to his cell.

Jenny and her husband, and Marcia and Marie walked out through the empty visiting room. They passed the security desk, the metal detectors, and the X-ray machines. The heavy steel door slammed shut behind them as they walked out into the strange reality of a hot, humid August evening.

They went to a restaurant to have dinner and review the mediation.

"How are you feeling?" Marcia asked Jenny.

"I'm flying—total euphoria," Jenny replied with a smile. "This is the best thing I could have ever done. The slam of that prison door when we walked out felt like a door closing on a whole part of my life. I'm finally ready to move on."

A FEW WEEKS after the mediation, Marie met with Dave at the prison to discuss the mediation. The weekend right after the mediation had been rough for him, and he had wanted to talk with someone about the roller coaster of emotions he felt. Instead, he had been harassed mercilessly by other inmates and even a few of the staff for having gone through mediation with Jenny.

When Jenny heard how Dave had been harassed, she said, "Dave did the right thing—and he did it for the right reasons. The right thing often isn't the popular thing. I'm glad he was willing to do the mediation. I give him a lot of credit for withstanding the harassment in the prison and going through with it. When you're an inmate, you don't know what the people harassing you are going to do. So I'm glad he was strong enough to make the decision to meet with me."

She also understood Marie's concerns for inmates a little better. "Inmates are looked at as useless castaways, toss-offs—that once they've done something bad, they're likely to do it again. But I believe that people can change—that you can take something terrible and make something good out of it. So, I understand why Marie would be so passionate about what she does with inmates. If doing this kind of thing can keep one guy from doing something terrible again, then it's worth it."

After getting permission from the Department of Corrections, Jenny and Dave wrote letters to each other after the mediation. Six months after the mediation, Dave was released from prison and later successfully completed all the terms of his parole.

Later, Jenny spoke at a victims' rights luncheon that Marie attended. Jenny said:

The mediation experience was more than I can ever explain in words. . . . I had to release my anger, grief, and rage over the murder; it was ruining me inside. Forgiveness does not mean that I don't continue to grieve and to suffer the impact of what he has done to me. . . . I feel that I need to be a very visible reminder to Dave of what he has done to my brother. At the same time, I feel Dave needs my forgiveness, not to forget what he has done, but to heal as much as I needed to heal.[5]

Marie had once heard Howard Zehr say that he thought victim offender mediations were hallowed ground. As she mediated additional face-to-face dialogues between victims of violent crime and offenders, she saw miracles unfold in each one.[6] She often told people she was becoming addicted to miracles and she felt a pull to invest more of her time and energy to promote mediation and restorative justice.

In a way, she felt everything they did at CentrePeace promoted restorative justice. If asked, she'd be hard-pressed to say which of their programs had the greatest impact. But it had all grown too big for her, the staff, and volunteers to manage.

The Pennsylvania Prison Runathon was, by far, the most labor- and time-intensive program. The statewide prison-building spree that had added sixteen new prisons and quadrupled the inmate population in the last twenty years meant traveling to more prisons for planning meetings and awards ceremonies; printing more T-shirts, awards certificates, and plaques; working with more charities to receive donations; contacting more newspapers, radio, and television stations for publicity; and recruiting more volunteers to handle the thousands of details that were part of CentrePeace's role as coordinator.

Marie was immensely grateful that their newest BVS volunteer, Matt Stauffer, had taken over a significant amount of the coordination for the twentieth annual runathon, participating in all of the planning meetings at the prisons and helping with the awards ceremonies.

The twentieth runathon broke new records, with 3,260 runners from twenty-four prisons logging 48,966 miles. There were 1,079 runners who completed marathon distance or more.

One inmate summed up what the runathon meant to the inmates, saying,

> I took from society. I want to give back. It's my responsibility to become a better person than I was before my incarceration. This is part of becoming a better person—considering another's needs above my own. If it means making some sacrifices of myself and of my time, then so be it. I'm not alone. There are 3,000 other prisoners who, by their participation in the runathon, feel the same way I do. We all have been physically, mentally, and spiritually challenged as we each have completed as many laps as possible within the allotted time. If . . . raising money for alternatives to incarceration for youth . . . keeps one kid from going to prison . . . then I deem the [runathon] a success.[7]

With the nearly $32,000 raised at that year's runathon, the inmates had reached a major milestone—since the runathon's beginning, they had raised over $250,000 to help children. But the work involved had become unmanageable. In order to keep the annual runathons going, something had to change.

Ann Cook suggested talking with the Pennsylvania Prison Society about taking over the runathon, since the Prison Society had established connections with every prison and active branches all over the state. However, the Prison Society's inmate advocacy and prison monitoring role often put them at odds with prison administrators.

"Giving the Prison Society something so positive to do with the prisons might help tear down walls between them and corrections staff," Ann observed.

"Brilliant idea, Ann," Marie replied.

It was to be one of Ann's last brilliant ideas. She died on June 2, 2001, at the age of eighty-nine. Marie's tribute to her mentor in that summer's issue of the CentrePeace newsletter revealed the depth of her grief.

> I never expect to meet anyone on this earth to compare with Ann. . . . Ann was an example of love in action. She worked with the most difficult situations and I personally saw her as a humble servant to whom I often referred as the most powerful person I've ever met. She was to my family and me a best friend, and made us feel as though we were hers. I am blessed to have had her as a mentor and friend for twenty-eight years.

Rose, Ann, and Marie had called themselves the Three Musketeers. Over the span of two decades, the three women had defied conventional wisdom, broken through barriers, and torn down walls. But there was still much to do. With both Rose and Ann gone, when Marie faced new challenges, she asked herself, *What would Rose suggest? How would Ann handle this?*

As Ann recommended, Marie met with Bill DiMascio, executive director of the Pennsylvania Prison Society, to discuss the possibility of the Prison Society taking over the runathon. DiMascio agreed they'd help coordinate the runathon in 2002, and then the Prison Society would assume full responsibility for the runathon in 2003.

For twenty-four years, a generous anonymous donor had covered the expenses of the runathon so that one hundred percent of pledges could go to the recipient organizations. Marie wrote to the donor expressing her gratitude and explaining the decision to turn the runathon over to the Prison Society.

"I can tell you that the runathon has been a miracle from the start and has produced more miracles than anything I've been a part of. . . . Your generous support of this event over its twenty-four years has been one of the most significant reasons for its longevity."[8]

With the transfer of the runathon, Marie could focus on more restorative justice work. She wrote articles and gave presentations to local, state, and national organizations. At a national victim advocacy conference, Marie, a co-mediator, and a woman whose family member had been murdered participated in a panel discussion about a mediation between the woman and the man who had committed the murder. The intense discussion that followed and the interest shown by many audience members gave Marie hope that more victims would seek restorative justice rather than vengeance.

Inmates, too, were becoming more interested in restorative justice. The Pennsylvania Prison Society was promoting restorative justice in the prisons. Barb Toews, Restorative Justice program manager for the Prison Society, invited Marie to the Smithfield prison to conduct a mock victim offender mediation for the Smithfield Inmate Organization. One inmate played the role of a victim, another played the offender, and Marie mediated. Even as a role play, it stirred deep emotions for the men as they revealed their own yearning for the opportunity to meet with their victims and seek forgiveness for what they'd done. It broke Marie's heart to tell them that only victims could initiate such mediations.

But she was encouraged by the positive efforts of the Department of Corrections to offer Victim Awareness Education and Impact of Crime programs to inmates. The DOC also collaborated with the Prison Society to present a play titled *Body in Motion* to inmates at eight prisons. The play was based on the book *Transcending: Reflections of Crime Victims* by Howard Zehr.

A group of lifers and sex offenders at Rockview attended the performance. It was a wrenchingly emotional experience for the men to watch actors playing a rape victim, parents of a murdered child, and other victims of violence. Afterward, Marie facilitated a panel discussion with the men, many of whom talked openly for the first time about their own accountability for their crimes. Victor and Bear told Marie they were encouraged by the men's response.

Marie often thought that lifers like Victor and Bear best understood the need for restorative justice. She wished she could do more for them. She had continued to write commutation recommendations for some of the lifers she'd gotten to know, including her dear friend Lois at Muncy. Lois was now seventy-eight years old, the oldest female inmate in the state, and had been in prison for over thirty years. All of her petitions for commutation had been denied, as had the petitions of virtually all other lifers. Only two lifers in Pennsylvania had had their sentences commuted over the past decade. Marie found the state's life-without-parole sentencing policies to be one of the most disheartening aspects of her prison work.

Yet, there was much to feel good about. Dedicated CentrePeace staff members like Greg Piper, Matt Stauffer, Tim Brown, and others, along with dozens of committed volunteers, had helped the organization flourish. Matt had decided to stay on after his BVS year and was now one of the supervisors for Project Restore. Many of the staff and volunteers had been with CentrePeace since the beginning, and some had even worked with Marie when the prison programs were part of the Voluntary Action Center. As they celebrated their tenth anniversary, Marie was immensely grateful for their commitment and all of the ways they had helped the organization grow.

While Marie enjoyed reflecting on all that they'd accomplished, she was more interested in looking ahead. In a report to the Centre-Peace board, she wrote: "As we go into the next ten years, we have great hopes and many challenges."

One great hope was promoting the use of alternatives to incarceration throughout Centre County. The political push to fill three hundred brand-new beds in the recently opened Centre County Correctional Facility would make it an uphill battle. Marie planned to assist other counties around the state that wanted to set up their own Project Restore program. She hoped to expand Project Restore and reentry mentoring, and she still hadn't given up on the idea of establishing a halfway house for ex-offenders. The CentrePeace board had already embarked on an ambitious capital campaign to raise one million dollars to fund these efforts.

CentrePeace shop supervisor Tim Brown teaches an inmate trainee the basics of chair caning. In the upper right corner is a photo of CentrePeace volunteer Paul Harrison (now deceased), who first brought the art of chair caning to CentrePeace. His widow, Mary, still stops by CentrePeace every Friday to teach current inmate trainees the art of caning. Photo courtesy of CentrePeace, Inc.

Within a year, they were close to realizing some of those dreams. At the CentrePeace board meeting and Thanksgiving dinner on November 21, 2005, Marie thanked the board for making it possible for her to take one last winter sabbatical in Arizona before the expansion projects started. The capital campaign had gone well and they hoped to have enough money to get started by the time Marie returned in the spring. She also thanked the board members and volunteers who would keep things going while she was away. She'd be leaving for Arizona later that week.

The board, CentrePeace staff and volunteers, community guests, and inmate trainees gathered in the showroom for their annual Thanksgiving celebration. Greg Piper, Matt Stauffer, Tim Brown, and the inmate trainees had rearranged the showroom and set up tables for the meal. Tonya Young, the new CentrePeace office manager, and sales coordinators Barbara Yingling and Evelyn Smith had decorated the showroom for the occasion. Judge Charles Brown attended and sat side by side with the inmates, as he always did. As Marie enjoyed the Thanksgiving meal, surrounded by many of the people who had helped to make CentrePeace a reality, she was reminded once again of how much she had to be thankful for.

15

Full Circle

The definition of grace is when God gives you what you don't deserve.

We didn't deserve Marie Hamilton here in prison, but God sent her to us anyway.

—Jerry

Jerry

Jerry's eyes popped open automatically as they did every morning at 5 a.m. and he stared at the ceiling of his dimly lit cell. *Tuesday*, he thought. *Two days until Thanksgiving.* He squeezed his eyes shut. *Nineteenth round of prison turkey and stuffing.* He opened his eyes, sat up abruptly, and shook his head to clear away those thoughts. Getting through one day at a time in prison was awful enough, without dwelling on how long you'd been at it.

It was November 22, 2005.

Jerry followed the same routine he had followed every morning, seven days a week, 365 days a year, for nineteen years. He dressed quickly in a clean pair of browns. He leaned in to his bottom bunk to straighten his sheets and blanket. As he walked through the silent corridor of E Block to the communal bathroom, he felt a mixture of gratitude and relief to be in the low custody level block. Unlike his previous quarters on East Wing, here he had the freedom to leave his cell when he needed to without being at the mercy of a guard to let him out. A nonsmoker, Jerry preferred to get in and out of the bathroom before it was clouded with nicotine fog.

Back in his cell, he carefully measured out a teaspoon of the instant coffee he'd purchased from the commissary, put it into his cup, and added hot tap water from the tiny sink in his cell. Then he picked up his faded Bible, switched on a lamp, and ducked into a sitting position on his bunk. His cellie was still snoring in the bunk overhead—Jerry's twentieth cellmate. Some had been considerate, clean, and, like Jerry, focused on improving themselves through work and education. Some had been rude, some lazy, some had terrible personal hygiene. A few had been downright dangerous. But there wasn't much choice, so you did what you had to, to get along with a stranger in a 7' x 13' cell.

He glanced up at the poster he'd hung on the green concrete block wall. "The Lord's Gym" was printed above an image of Jesus in a push-up position, with a cross—inscribed with "The Sin of the World"—on his back. It was Jerry's daily reminder of God's grace. It gave him some comfort even on the worst days. He opened his Bible to Romans 8 and spent the next hour reading and praying, until the first count of the day.

His cellmate rose just in time for count. A loud clank punctuated the automatic locking of all cell doors. Jerry switched on the overhead light in the cell and the two men stood until a guard made his way down the long corridor, stopping at each cell to be sure every man was accounted for, checking each name on his list.

After count, another clank announced the unlocking of the cell doors. Jerry joined the sea of men headed out of the block and across the compound to the dining hall. It was unseasonably warm and overcast—good weather for his outdoor job in the prison yard. The chow line was long and slow, as usual. Each man was given his allotted portion of cold cereal, hard-boiled eggs, toast, milk, coffee, and fruit. Jerry moved to the nearest empty seat in the long row of stainless steel tables with benches bolted to the floor. He ate quickly and left, relieved as always to get away from the noise and chaos of the dining hall.

Returning to the block, he passed the dozens of other men waiting in the dayroom for the announcement over the loudspeakers to line up for their work assignments. The men were clustered in their usual groupings—the young toughs who relished stringing together as many profanities as possible in every conversation, a group of older inmates stuck in a time warp, reminiscing about better days, a small group engaged in Bible study, some inmates studying for the academic courses they were taking, and some idly passing time as they did day after day, playing cards or staring into space.

Jerry went to the prison yard, where a guard unlocked the equipment shed for him. Jerry managed the athletic equipment used by inmates during their twice-daily yard time. He looked across the still-quiet yard to the track where, just two months earlier, eighty men with numbers pinned to their shirts had participated in the runathon. Jerry loved the positive energy and excitement of the runathon. It was one of his only opportunities to see people from outside the prison walls. He treasured the chance for conversations with people other than guards or inmates. In September, he had sat on the bleachers, counting laps with volunteers from Big Brothers Big Sisters and CentrePeace, including his dear friend, Marie Hamilton. They'd had a long conversation about all of the programs at CentrePeace and Marie's plans for expanding them.

Jerry had seen Marie and the other volunteers coming into Rockview every week for years. His close friend, Brother Harry, had been involved in many of Marie's classes on B Block and had told Jerry about them. He knew Harry thought the world of Marie, like he did.

Now, Brother Harry stopped by the yard, as he did every morning.

"How're you feeling today, Harry?"

"Not so good. But I'm not complaining. Any cleaning up I need to do out here, Jerry?"

Jerry knew how seriously Brother Harry took his job of keeping the bathroom area in the yard cleaned up, even when he was ill. "Lots of cigarette butts over there by the urinals, and a bit of trash was blowing around along the fence. Probably won't have many guys out here this morning. Everybody wants to get more work hours in before Thanksgiving."

"Another Thanksgiving," Harry said sadly. "Well, at least we'll get a decent meal. Guess I'll go see about that trash."

"Thanks, Harry."

Jerry sighed as he watched his friend shuffle away. Harry was in his late 60s and in poor health. Prison life took a heavy toll and men aged rapidly here. Illness, skin disease, and staph infections were rampant, and, with average wages of thirty cents per hour, most men couldn't afford the five dollars they had to pay to see the prison nurse, let alone the additional five dollars they'd be charged for each medication that might be prescribed. Jerry hated to see his friend suffering. *Harry probably won't see many more Thanksgivings*, he thought sadly, before turning his attention back to organizing the equipment in the shed.

Suddenly, a loud boom echoed across the prison field. Jerry ran outside and looked toward Benner Pike, which ran along the boundary of the prison property. A dark blue SUV had crashed into a utility pole. Jerry could see it clearly along the short stretch of road that was visible from the prison. Other cars pulled over. People ran toward the wrecked vehicle. Then an explosion shook the ground and the people turned and ran away from the wreck.

Jerry's heart pounded as he watched a ball of fire shoot into the air. Sparks crackled and rolled along the power lines toward the prison. They reached a transformer. Another explosion. Jerry felt like his own chest was exploding. Chills tingled down his neck and spine. He started praying. *Help them, God. Whoever's in that car. They must be terrified, all alone up there. Comfort them. Give them peace, Lord. Please don't let them die.*

Sirens screamed from both directions on Benner Pike. A fire truck, police car, and two ambulances roared up. *Please, please, God. Be with them. Help them get out safely.*

"What's goin' on, Jerry?" A few Christian brothers Jerry knew from chapel had gathered in the yard.

Jerry pointed to the scene of the accident, never taking his eyes off of it. "It's a bad one," he said, his throat tight. "Pray for them, guys."

"Sure will," one of them replied. The men watched for a few minutes, then moved on.

Jerry didn't budge. He kept praying. He could see the emergency crew surrounding the vehicle. People ran back and forth from the fire truck and ambulances to the wreck. Fifteen minutes passed. Then thirty. Then forty-five.

Several guards came over to where Jerry was standing and watched the scene.

It seemed like forever before the ambulance crew got someone out of the vehicle. *Please, Lord, let them be alive. Let them live.*

Jerry saw the crew wheel the stretcher to the ambulance and lift it in. They closed the ambulance doors, and the lights went on. *Go with them, God. Watch over them. Let them know you are with them.*

Jerry waited for the ambulance to pull away. It didn't.

The ambulance lights turned off.

Oh, no. Please, God. What is going on?

Jerry held his breath. *Please.*

After several minutes, the ambulance lights came back on. The siren echoed across the fields as the ambulance roared away toward State College.

Heal them, Lord. Be with them, whatever happens.

Another guard came by.

"Yard time's over, Jerry. Time to go in."

Please, God. Somehow turn this into a blessing or a miracle, Jerry prayed before turning away to go back to his cell.

Mrs. Hamilton?"

Marie tried to focus through the haze of painkillers she'd been given. She shifted her eyes so she could see the doctor standing by her bed. She couldn't turn her head.

"Looked at the X-rays . . . your back is broken . . . need surgery."

Her eyelids were heavy. She had to concentrate hard.

"Right leg . . . severe breaks . . . your arm . . . additional surgery . . . stabilize first."

He didn't say neck. I didn't hear neck. Thank you, God.

The accident replayed in her mind like an old movie reel. As she had headed north along Benner Pike, an oncoming car had crossed over the yellow line into her lane of traffic. Marie had swerved sharply and kept the other car from hitting her, but the sudden motion had caused her own vehicle to flip. Those first moments after the accident, when she was trapped in her car with shattered glass and blood everywhere, had been some of the loneliest she'd ever experienced. When she'd heard the explosions, she was sure she was going to die alone there in the prison field. *Just like the inmates,* she thought, *who fear they'll die alone in prison.*

She had been on her way to have breakfast with a friend in Bellefonte before going to the CentrePeace office, where she had a long list of things to do before leaving for her winter sabbatical in Arizona. Now, with a broken back, broken leg, and broken arm, she didn't know how she might have to spend her winter.

In her hospital bed, in the hours and days that followed, Marie was able to move in ways that seemed impossible, given the severity of her injuries. Her doctors ordered another round of X-rays. And then another. And another. They were baffled. The break in her leg now didn't look as severe. It wouldn't require surgery. Her elbow was dislocated, but her arm wasn't broken. She had a contusion and a punctured lung, but she wouldn't need surgery on her back, either. The new X-rays of her back showed a more minor break that could be allowed to simply fuse together.

After eight days in the hospital, and eight days in a rehab facility, Marie's son, Steve, moved her into his home, where he'd set up a hospital bed and arranged for visiting nurses. After two and a half weeks with Steve and his family, Marie was able to return to her own home the day before Christmas.

The holidays were a blur. Her days were consumed by pain and rehab. At first, she had to use a walker, then a cane. In January, she asked her doctors whether she could go to Arizona for the rest of the winter and continue her rehab there. They helped her make the necessary arrangements, and she made the trip. The palm trees, bright sun, and blue skies of Arizona were good medicine.

When she returned to State College in the spring, she tried to return to work at CentrePeace. There was much work to do to get their planned expansion projects underway. But Marie quickly realized she was unable to sit at her desk for very long and she couldn't go up or down stairs. The six-mile drive from her home to CentrePeace along Benner Pike terrified her. She was so petrified by the sight of oncoming traffic that she began seeing a psychiatrist for post-traumatic stress. She turned down speaking engagements. She had to ask other volunteers and staff members to go to meetings and teach conflict resolution classes in her place. Marie had to admit that she couldn't do the work that needed to be done at CentrePeace. She went to the board of directors and they agreed to begin searching for a new executive director. Meanwhile, the volunteers and staff kept all of the programs going and Marie did what little she could to help. The months of her recovery dragged from spring to summer and into autumn.

Nearly a year after her accident, it was time once again for the annual Rockview runathon. Though she was still recovering, Marie was determined to be there. She hadn't missed a runathon at Rockview in twenty-seven years. She wasn't about to miss number twenty-eight. When she arrived, her friend Jerry was the first person to greet her at the entrance to the yard, as he had done at every runathon since 1992. His lake-blue eyes twinkled at her under thick white eyebrows.

"How are you, Marie? We haven't seen you here in a really long time."

"I haven't been back to Rockview since my car accident, Jerry."

They sat down on the bleachers.

"You had a car accident? I didn't know that! When?"

"Last November. It was right out here, along Benner Pike."

Jerry stared at her, open-mouthed. "Marie, it was you, it was *you!*"

"What?"

"Was it last November 22? At about 8:15 in the morning?"

"Yes. . . . "

"You were in a dark blue SUV and you hit a utility pole."

"Yes, yes!" Marie exclaimed. "Jerry, how do you know that?"

"See that shed over there?" he asked, pointing to a small building across the yard. "I was working in the shed that morning. I heard the crash, ran outside, and saw a vehicle wrecked into the utility pole. I saw the balls of fire when the transformers exploded and watched the fire travel along the electrical wires right down here to the prison. The power was out for over two hours here in the prison that morning."

Marie shook her head as what he was saying slowly sank in.

"When I saw that accident, Marie, I had no idea who was in that car, but I knew that I needed to pray. I knew someone was out there, alone and probably afraid they were going to die. So I started praying, and I stayed right there and watched and prayed. It took over an hour for the medics to get the person out of the car. Then, they put the person in the ambulance. But then the ambulance didn't pull away and they turned the lights off. I . . . I was afraid that meant. . . ."

Jerry stopped talking, bowed his head, and sat quietly for a moment. All around them, the runners ran. The onlookers cheered. The volunteers counted laps. Marie blinked back tears.

"I didn't know what to pray for then," Jerry said, shaking his head slowly. "But I just kept praying anyway. I felt so strongly that, no matter what, I shouldn't stop praying. So, I prayed that somehow, some way, that accident would turn out to be some kind of a blessing, or a miracle. Finally, they turned the lights back on in the ambulance and it pulled away. So then I hoped maybe everything was going to be okay, the person was still alive. So I kept on praying and I didn't stop."

"I did think I was going to die out there," Marie admitted. "It seemed so strange—after all of the men and women I've talked to who fear dying, alone, in prison. And there I was, on the prison grounds, alone, thinking *I* might die here."

Jerry told Marie that he had asked the COs, the major, and others often in the days and weeks that followed if they knew who had been in that accident. But no one knew anything about it.

"It was me, Jerry. You prayed for *me!*"

Marie told him what had happened in the hospital—about the surgeries the doctors had told her she'd have to have, about the baffling changes in her X-rays, about how she'd healed without surgery.

"That's amazing!"

"It's a miracle, Jerry! What were the chances that you, my dear friend, would witness my accident from here in the prison? I thought I was alone and was sure I would die out there. But you were here, watching over me and praying for me."

"Just like you've done for us over the years, Marie. Just when we thought we were alone and forgotten in here, you showed up to watch over us and help."

Marie shook her head.

"Your accident happened right at the section of Benner Pike that's visible from down here. If it had happened half a mile further in either direction, I wouldn't have seen it. I might never have known there was an accident or prayed for the people involved. What were the chances of *that?*" Jerry added.

"Another miracle!"

"And now here you are," Jerry said, beaming.

"And now here I am."

"What an awesome God!"

"Yes, indeed, Jerry. What an awesome God!"

Marie felt like cheering, hugging Jerry, jumping up and down, and dancing around the track. Instead, she channeled her excitement into shouting encouragement to the men who ran lap after lap around the track for the sake of children. Throughout the long afternoon, Marie and Jerry sat side by side and watched, smiling, as the runners ran, the onlookers cheered, and the volunteers counted laps.

EPILOGUE

While there is a lower class, I am in it; while there is a criminal element, I am of it; while there is a soul in prison, I am not free.

—Eugene Debs (1855–1926)

Marie retired from CentrePeace on January 1, 2007, and continues to teach Creative Nonviolent Conflict Resolution for CentrePeace and for community groups. She divides her time between Pennsylvania and Arizona. She enjoys spending time with her two sons and two grandchildren and pursuing her hobby of creating gemstone art.

Her son, Mike, with the help of professionals, family, and friends, has learned to manage his bipolar disorder, primarily through physical exercise. He received meteorology and mathematics education degrees from Penn State University. He enjoys teaching part-time in local schools and frequently visits the same streams he fished since he was a boy.

Marie's father, Robert Fortney, is well at age ninety-two and enjoys recalling a blessed life during weekly visits and phone calls from his family. He often says the church in Curryville was *everything*. Her mother, Virginia, passed away in 2007, at age ninety-seven.

Jerry continues to serve his sentence in a Pennsylvania State Correctional Institution. He also strives to serve God and hopes to continue to do so after his release. "What's most important to me now," he says, "is not to start another business or build another house on a lake, but rather to help others build a solid foundation in Jesus Christ."

Bear remains incarcerated, but says he "feels free to pursue God's destiny for my life, in worship, discipleship, and evangelism." He is involved in a worship planning team, plays the keyboard, and leads others to a more intimate relationship with God through music and song. He also participates in creative drama for the ministry.

Yusef is now up for parole consideration after serving over three decades in prison. He is working on a program to have prisoners finance and rebuild inner cities, one neighborhood at a time—a prisoner-initiated "Marshall Plan."

Butch remains incarcerated in a Pennsylvania State Correctional Institution where he is involved in as many activities as his time permits, including helping to plan and participate in the annual runathons. His main focus is to keep working toward his eventual release.

Snooky is now retired and lives with his wife in Pennsylvania. He enjoys spending time with his children and grandchildren.

Lois died in prison in 2007. She was eighty years old.

Victor was found hanging in his cell in a Pennsylvania State Correctional Institution on Passover weekend, 2008. He had made another request to the state pardons board for merit review for possible commutation of his life sentence. He had just found out that it had been rejected.

Brother Harry died in February 2008 on B Block North. A memorial mass was held for him at Rockview. Jerry attended the mass for his friend.

Edward's parents made the cross-country trip from Arizona to visit their son four times before they died. Edward says that making the decision to forgive them and allowing them to visit him in prison was the most important thing he's ever done. He continues to take every class and training program that is offered in prison, where he remains incarcerated.

Joseph continues to promote conflict resolution skills within prison, where he remains incarcerated.

Hawk remains incarcerated. "It's been a long hard road . . . a nightmare," he says. But he tries to remain hopeful, concluding, "God will do the right thing at the right time." About Marie, he says: "Her smile, charisma, and wisdom touched a lot of people in prison, including me, and I bet a lot of people outside of prison too!" Hawk turned seventy-two in 2009.

Since Robert completed the conflict resolution course with Marie, he hasn't been involved in a single fight. He remains incarcerated.

OJ got married, received a degree from Penn State University, and continued to work as a VAC volunteer and as a drug and alcohol counselor for many years.

Lawrence was furloughed and then released, but later returned to prison, where he currently resides.

JT was last seen in another Pennsylvania state prison, sentenced on drunk driving charges, after five years of living successfully on the outside, drug- and alcohol-free. In one of his last letters to Marie, he wrote: "Took me 25 years to quit a life of crime, institutions, and failure. Now I'm right back where I started . . . but I've the hindsight to survive better than most. . . . Be constructive, dear woman. You've come a long way. Remember: *squares make it*! Much love, as always, JT." His current whereabouts are unknown.

Tony continued to help promote Marie's prison programs for many years. While he never directly apologized to Marie for his attack on her, she says, "In a way, everything he did to help promote the prison programs was an apology." Once Marie had told him, "You know, Tony, if a woman says 'no' and you proceed, that's rape." She didn't know whether the message sank in with him until months later, when she overheard Tony explaining to one of his friends, "You know, man, if a woman says 'no' and you go ahead anyway, that's rape." Marie says, "That was all the apology I ever needed—to know that he finally understood." Marie has since lost contact with him.

After Rocky's release from Rockview, he kept in touch with Marie for years by phoning about once a month to let her know that he was doing well. He had found a nice girlfriend. One day, a staff member from the Graterford prison called Marie and said, "Guess who we have in here? Rocky is back in prison." Marie asked, "What is he in for?" The staff member told her Rocky had been arrested for possession of a motorcycle that didn't belong to him. Marie considered it a success that Rocky had not committed another rape. Marie has since lost contact with him.

Dr. Joseph Mazurkiewicz retired in July 1997 after nearly forty years of service to the Pennsylvania Department of Corrections, including twenty-seven years as the superintendent at Rockview. He passed away in 2003.

Dr. John McCullough left Rockview to become the deputy superintendent at Camp Hill after the 1989 riot. He later returned to Rockview as deputy superintendent, then took a superintendent's post at Houtzdale before becoming the Western Region deputy secretary. He has since retired and has taught at the Pennsylvania Department of Corrections Training Academy and Penn State University.

Dr. Greg Gaertner has retired from the Pennsylvania Department of Corrections and teaches at Penn State University in the Rehabilitation and Human Services program.

Lou Matsick is happily retired and no longer involved in the corrections system.

Bill Love is now retired, but continues to be actively involved in public service through his work with the Beaufort County, South Carolina, Department of Special Needs, where he is director of a day program.

CentrePeace continues to grow under the leadership of the new executive director, Thom Brewster. Thom continues weekly sessions with the men of B Block North every Tuesday afternoon, providing either Nonviolent Conflict Resolution training and/or teaching *Breaking Barriers*, a videotaped series facilitated by an ex-offender turned communications guru, Gordon Graham of the Pacific Institute. Thom is currently the only volunteer visiting the men of B Block each week.

Greg Piper and Matt Stauffer continue to supervise Project Restore along with Ron Kilgus. Forty-four trainees from the Centre County Correctional Facility graduated from the Project Restore program in 2008.

For Christmas 2008, cards made by children were sent to 19,748 men and women serving time at twenty-four correctional institutions throughout Pennsylvania via the Christmas Cards for Inmates program. CentrePeace hopes to collect enough cards in 2009 to give one to each of the 76,000 men and women currently incarcerated in Pennsylvania's local, state, and federal correctional facilities. Over 329 children's organizations, vacation Bible schools, Sunday schools, home schoolers, and individual families throughout the United States help to create these cards.

The PrayerMates program continues to have a long waiting list of inmates wishing to be matched with a prayer partner. The program is still conducted on a first-name-only basis, with all correspondence from each party going through the CentrePeace office and being screened to protect the confidentiality and identity of both partners.

The Criminal Justice Advocacy and Support Directory is still published every two to three years by CentrePeace in collaboration with the Pennsylvania Institutional Law Project in Philadelphia.

The Pennsylvania Prison Runathon is no longer coordinated by the Pennsylvania Prison Society. There is no longer any central coordination of the runathon and it is now up to the administration of each prison to determine whether and when to hold runathons. In 2008, sixteen of Pennsylvania's twenty-six state prisons held one. Community support, sponsorship for runners, and volunteer involvement in the runathons have dropped off sharply.

Creative Nonviolent Conflict Resolution training is offered to churches, schools, prisons, and other groups regularly through CentrePeace.

Community Alternatives in Criminal Justice (CACJ) continues to offer mediation services, pre-trial intervention programs, and a bail program in Centre County, under the direction of executive director Bonnie Millmore, who has served in that role since 1984.

The Voluntary Action Center of Centre County (VAC) is now the Community Help Centre. They continue to recruit and train volunteers to work for numerous agencies in Centre County, Pennsylvania.

As of the end of 2008, Pennsylvania had a total of 47,968 people incarcerated in its state prisons, including 225 inmates on death row, and 4,570 inmates sentenced to life without possibility of parole. The 2008-09 annual Department of Corrections budget was $1.6 billion, the third largest line item in the state's $28 billion budget, after education and welfare.

Three additional prisons are slated to be built in Pennsylvania by 2011, at an estimated cost to taxpayers of $200 million per prison to build, and an additional $50 million per prison per year to operate.

EDITORIAL NOTE

At the conclusion of the author's interview with each inmate, she asked, "What would you like the world to know about your life now?" Many of the inmates wrote their own statements. Summaries of their words are presented here as a reminder of the need for ongoing restorative justice work in our prison system.

ACKNOWLEDGMENTS

Countless blessings have unfolded from this effort to put Marie's story on paper. Best of all are the many people who lent their voices to enrich the story. Jerry's "crazy ideas," prayers, and friendship have been gifts beyond measure. Bear is a gentle man of true faith who helped me to "speak truth, with love." John McCullough shared his extensive knowledge, his clear-eyed wisdom, and his humanity in generous portions. Jenny inspired me with her strength and grace in sharing her story of forgiveness. Butch, Yusef, Hawk, and dozens of other incarcerated men and women courageously opened their lives to a stranger's probing questions. Marie's family graciously opened their lives to the telling too, even when it was painful. George Snavely spent hours with us, calling up memories of the Camp Hill riots that he would have preferred to leave buried. His genuine compassion and concern for the men he taught at Camp Hill shone through it all. Superintendent Tennis, Mr. Rackovan, Mr. Schnars, Officer Gentzel, Ms. Williams, and other Rockview staff opened doors in myriad ways and allowed me to witness firsthand the miracle of the Rockview runathon. Ms. McNaughton, DOC press secretary, helped me track down historical details and offered wise counsel.

As I interviewed dozens of the dedicated volunteers and corrections staff who worked closely with Marie over the past three decades, it was immediately obvious why she loved and respected each of them: Betty Bergstein, John Brighton, Judge Charles Brown, George Etzweiler, Eleanor Ferguson, Greg Gaertner, Ed Hall, Marge Holland, Ireen Jones, Angus Love, Bill Love, Birgit Maier-Katkin, Lou Matsick, Father Francis Menei, Bonnie Millmore, Phil Mullen, Martie Musso, Cliff Parris, Cynthia Schein, Barb Seibel, David Stickell, Nathan Tobey,

Harvey Yancey, and Tonya Young are only a few of the hundreds who worked side by side with Marie over the years to tear down walls, heal brokenness, and offer hope and humanity.

The work of CentrePeace carries on, thanks to the vision and leadership of Thom Brewster and his staff: Mel Coble, JoAnne Fischer, Ron Kilgus, Greg Piper, Kay Skies, Evelyn Smith, Matt Stauffer, and Barbara Yingling. They, along with dozens of CentrePeace volunteers, bless the lives of thousands more forgotten men and women in Pennsylvania's prisons every year.

I couldn't ask for more supportive fellow writers than those in the York Writers Group—their spot-on critiques and constant encouragement sustained me over the past two years. Treasured friends at the Elizabethtown Church of the Brethren have held me and this project in constant prayer—I'm so grateful to them. Pastor Greg Davidson Laszakovits gently, yet persistently, encouraged me to venture beyond my comfort zone, and continues to remind me to stay open to possibilities.

My editor at Brethren Press, James Deaton, must surely be the most affirming, thoughtful, collaborative, and conscientious editor in the entire publishing industry. Wendy McFadden, the publisher, embodies the ideal combination of practical, down-to-earth business savvy and visionary leadership. I'm humbled and thankful that she was willing to take this leap of faith with me. And Jeff Lennard, my marketing guru, has incredible creative energy and enthusiasm for what he does to shepherd books out into the world, this one included.

My dad read so many drafts of the manuscript, he knows the stories nearly as well as I. His loving critique at every stage was exactly what I needed, while my mom proudly told everyone she knew that her daughter was spending a lot of time in prison. Fortunately, she also told them why. My husband has bravely stepped into this world along with me, educating himself along the way and adding his wise and thoughtful perspectives to the book and everything that has followed. Through their unwavering support, incredible patience, and heavy dose of good humor, he and my two amazing kids made it possible for me to immerse myself in this project for the past two years. Cliché or not, I truly could not have done it without them. I want to thank and acknowledge Jean Moyer again here—what a gift she is to the world. And, of course, without Grace Marie Fortney Hamilton there would be no *Grace Goes to Prison*. Her story has opened my eyes, and her example has opened my mind and my heart. I pray it will do the same for others.

Notes

Preface

1. The Lancaster Area Victim Offender Reconciliation Program (LAVORP) provides mediation services to victims and offenders and works to effectively resolve, reduce, and prevent conflict through teaching and implementing principles of restorative justice.

> Lancaster Area Victim Offender Reconciliation Program
> 53 North Duke Street
> Room 303
> Lancaster, PA 17602
> (717) 397-2404
> http://www.lavorp.org/

2. Restorative justice focuses on four basic questions:
   - Who has been harmed by a crime?
   - What are their needs?
   - Who should be accountable for addressing those needs?
   - What can be done to address those needs?

In restorative justice, victims, offenders, and community members all have an active role in answering these questions. By contrast, traditional criminal justice focuses on who has broken a law and what punishment should be meted out for breaking the law. Law-breaking is seen as a crime against the state (i.e., *Commonwealth of Pennsylvania v. John Doe*) and thus, the actual victims of the crime are typically cut out of the entire criminal justice process, unless they're needed as witnesses in a trial. And plea-bargaining often results in offenders being sentenced for something other than the actual crime they committed. Information on restorative justice adapted from Howard Zehr, *Changing Lenses: A New Focus for Crime and Justice*, 3rd ed. (Scottdale, PA: Herald Press, 2005).

3. This encapsulates the mission of CentrePeace. To find out more information about CentrePeace and its work today, visit http://www.centrepeace.org/.

4. The Pew Center on the States, *One in 100: Behind Bars in America 2008*, February 2008. To view this report in its entirety, visit http://www.pewcenteronthestates.org/.

5. Recidivism is relapse into criminal behavior.

6. *Webster's Revised Unabridged Dictionary,* s.v. "grace," http://dictionary.reference
.com/browse/grace.

Prologue

1. Pseudonym

1. Path to Prison

1. Brethren Volunteer Service (BVS) is a volunteer service agency established by the
Church of the Brethren in 1948 to provide an intentional way to share God's love
through acts of service. For more information about BVS work all around the
world, visit http://www.brethren.org/.
2. Nickname
3. In the B Block therapeutic community, staff and inmates tried to remember to use
the term "residents" to refer to the inmates, as a more respectful way of referring
to the men.
4. The story of that strike was detailed in the book *Caged: Eight Prisoners and Their
Keepers,* by Ben H. Bagdikian, published in 1976, the year after Marie and the
VAC volunteers started their weekly visits in Houser's Hall at Rockview.
5. Furloughs provided an opportunity for inmates to gradually reacclimate to life in
the community prior to their release. Not all of the men in B Block were permitted furloughs. Some were not allowed because prison staff or administration did-
n't trust what they might do in the community. Some didn't meet the basic criteria,
and some were turned down by judges. In order to be eligible for furlough at that
time, B Block residents had to meet the following criteria:
   a.   have a minimum security status
   b.   have served half of his minimum sentence
   c.   have served nine months in a state institution
   d.   have his A (honor) rating
   e.   have participated in recommended programs
   f.   be misconduct-free
   g.   be considered by prison staff to be a good risk for the community
   h.   have a good reason for a furlough
   i.   does not have a detainer of two years or over

In addition, while on furlough the men were to adhere to a strict set of rules and
regulations. Any violation while on furlough could result in suspension of their
pre-release status and, hence, could delay their release from prison. The furlough

program was curtailed in the mid-1990s amid political and legislative changes that were oriented toward a "tough on crime" stance. Information about Rockview's furlough policy adapted from "Furlough Procedures and Rules" from John McCullough, director of treatment, November 15, 1976.

6. Marvin (real name), letter to Marie Hamilton, December 9, 1975.

2. Life Behind Bars

1. The Heifer Project (originally called "Heifers for Relief") was begun by Dan West, a Brethren volunteer from northern Indiana, in 1942 after assisting in relief work in Spain during the Spanish Civil War (1936–1939). Now known as Heifer International, its mission is to end hunger permanently by providing families with livestock and training so that they "could be spared the indignity of depending on others to feed their children." For more information on its work today, visit http://www.heifer.org/.
2. Phoenix Indian School was a boarding school for Native American children. The school had opened in 1891 to assimilate Indian children into white culture. Despite a change in the school's guiding philosophy in 1935, from assimilation to cultural pluralism, when Marie arrived the school still emphasized conversion of students from their native beliefs to an approved Christian denomination. Catholic, Mormon, and Baptist missionaries conducted weekly religion classes at the school to instruct students in their denomination's beliefs. Robert A. Trennert, Jr., *The Phoenix Indian School: Forced Assimilation in Arizona, 1891-1935* (Norman: University of Oklahoma Press, 1988).
3. *Houser Hall Resident Handbook: Working Together,* January 1976.
4. John Brighton, "Remarks to the Men, Staff, and Volunteers of Houser Hall." July 6, 1976.
5. Real name
6. Marie Hamilton, letter to residents of B Block North, December 7, 1976.

3. Breaking Barriers

1. Real name
2. Jeffrey A. Beard, letter to Marie Hamilton, May 23, 1977.
3. Founded in 1787, the Pennsylvania Prison Society is a social justice organization that advocates on behalf of prisoners, formerly incarcerated individuals, and their families. For more information, visit http://www.prisonsociety.org/.
4. Nickname

5. Rocky, letter to the volunteers of B Block North, March 1, 1978.

6. At that time, Pennsylvania was one of only three states where all life sentences carried no parole eligibility. In Pennsylvania, any inmate with a life sentence can ever hope to be released only by receiving a "Commutation of Sentence" from the state governor. The complicated process for commutation involves submission of extensive documentation by the inmate to a pardons board, review of the inmate's case by the pardons board, then a vote by the members of the board to either recommend to the governor that the inmate's sentence be shortened or deny the request. If the pardons board recommends commutation, the governor may then choose either to follow their recommendations and commute the inmate's sentence or deny commutation.

7. Tyrone (real name), letter to Marie Hamilton, January 18, 1978.

4. Maxed Out

1. Pseudonym

2. Pseudonym

3. Pseudonym

4. Pseudonym

5. Pseudonym

6. "Maxed out" is when an inmate has served his or her maximum prison sentence and, by law, must be released from prison.

7. Marie Hamilton, letter to the residents of B Block North, March 1979.

8. Rocky, letter to Ann Cook, March 1979.

5. Common Ground

1. Real name

2. Real name

3. Lawrence, letter to "To Whom It May Concern," 1979.

4. The VAC team, in addition to Marie Hamilton, included Robert Ayer, Dave Colton, Ann Cook, Gregg Cunningham, Don Ealy, George Etzweiler, Robert Farrell, Campbell Lovett, Norm MacMillan, Madhu Sidhu, Helen Small, and David Stickell.

5. At that time, jobs for inmates in the prison paid an average of 16¢ per hour. A $5.00 pledge required over thirty hours of work. Current wages for inmates in Pennsylvania's state prisons average 25¢ per hour.

6. Michael (real name), letter to the Voluntary Action Center, June 14, 1979.

7. Every day, at various times, all inmates are required to return to their cells, which are then locked while guards take a count to be sure every inmate is accounted for.

8. Browns are the brown, standard-issue prison uniforms worn by every inmate in Pennsylvania's state prisons.

6. Committed

1. Real name
2. Marie Hamilton, letter to Ronald Marks, July 11, 1980.
3. Ronald Marks, letter to Marie Hamilton, July 14, 1980.
4. Rocky, letter to Marie Hamilton, August 4, 1980.
5. Rocky, letter to Marie Hamilton, December 8, 1980.
6. Real name
7. Real name
8. Real name
9. David, letter to Marie Hamilton, May 1981.

7. A Ray of Sunshine

1. David, letter to Marie Hamilton, June 1981.
2. Marie Hamilton, letter to Julius Erving, April 6, 1982.
3. The divestiture movement began as a United Nations resolution calling on all Western nations to stop investing in or doing business in South Africa and to impose various economic and other sanctions on the country, to protest the apartheid policies of the South African government.
4. All letters coming into Pennsylvania state prisons are opened by staff and examined for contraband, which includes "prohibited correspondence." Pennsylvania Department of Corrections, *A Handbook for the Families and Friends of Pennsylvania Department of Corrections Prison Inmates*, November 2006, p. 18. http://www.cor.state.pa.us/portal/lib/bis/Handbook_for_Families_and_Friends.pdf.
5. The "Hole" is solitary confinement, usually called "Segregated Housing Unit" or "Restricted Housing Unit" by prison staff.
6. Real name
7. Pseudonym
8. Real name
9. Real name
10. Real name
11. Real name
12. Real name
13. Real name

8. Love in Prison

1. English Standard Version of the Bible
2. The organization is now called VIP Mentoring. For more information, visit http://www.vipmentoring.org/.
3. Dr. Benjamin Rush (1745-1813) was a Philadelphia Quaker, physician, and social activist who had been one of the signers of the Declaration of Independence. The Benjamin Rush Award was established in 1948 by the Medical Society of Pennsylvania. The annual awards recognize outstanding contributions to community health and welfare.
4. Butch, letter to Margaret Moerschbacher (Benjamin Rush Committee), October 17, 1982.
5. Marie Hamilton, letter to Butch, November 5, 1982.
6. Real name
7. James, letter to Marie Hamilton, June 19, 1983.
8. Marie Hamilton, letter to Bob Gross, July 25, 1983.
9. Keith J. Leenhouts, letter to Mackinac Island Conferees, May 14, 1985.
10. Real name
11. Nickname

9. No Chicken Tonight

1. "B," prayer request to Volunteers in Prison, 1987.
2. Frank (real name), letter to Marie Hamilton, undated.
3. "E," prayer request to Volunteers in Prison, 1987.
4. Volunteers in Prison, PrayerMate brochure, 1987.
5. Marie Hamilton, PrayerMate letter to congregations in the Middle Pennsylvania District of the Church of the Brethren; undated.
6. Marie Hamilton, letter to Governor Robert Casey, March 3, 1987.
7. Glen R. Jeffes, Pennsylvania Department of Corrections Commendation to Marie Hamilton, May 2, 1987.
8. Marie Hamilton, letter to Commissioner David S. Owens, Jr., October 23, 1987.
9. Pseudonym
10. Real name
11. Real name
12. Real name
13. Pseudonym
14. Marie Hamilton, letter to J. Harvey Bell, February 1, 1988.

15. As reported in Volunteers in Prison newsletter article, "Serenade to Volunteers in Corrections," 1988.
16. David S. Owens, Jr., letter to Marie Hamilton, July 19, 1988.
17. Lawrence S. Apsey (1902-1997) was a Quaker and the founder of the Alternatives to Violence Project.
18. Real name
19. Lawrence S. Apsey, "Elements and Suggestions for Non-Violence Rap" (handout), Alternatives to Violence Project. Visit http://www.avpusa.org/.
20. Douglas, letter to Marie Hamilton, January 21, 1989.
21. Michael J. Leidy, letter to Marie Hamilton, February 17, 1989.
22. To learn more about the Victim Offender Mediation Association, visit http://www.voma.org/.
23. Victim offender mediation is based on the concept of restorative justice. See note 2 in Preface.
24. David S. Owens, Jr., Remarks to Serenade to Volunteers in Corrections, Elks Country Club, Boalsburg, Pennsylvania, April 16, 1989. Provided by Kenneth G. Robinson, press secretary, Pennsylvania Department of Corrections to Volunteers in Prison.

10. Violence Stops Here

1. Pseudonym
2. Pseudonym
3. Pseudonym
4. Pseudonym
5. Pseudonym
6. Nickname
7. White hat refers to a high-ranking corrections officer—typically a lieutenant. The name came from the white hats these officers wore.
8. George Snavely, Post-riot documentation. "Progression of Events at SCIC, October 25–October 29, 1989."
9. Information from telephone interview with Robert Morck, former director of the Chemical Abuse Department, Camp Hill SCI, who was in charge of the "New Values" therapeutic community at the time of the riots (March 7, 2008) and testimony from Douglas to the Senate Judiciary Committee Public Hearing on Recent Incidents at Pennsylvania State Correctional Institutions before Senator Stewart J. Greenleaf, Chairman, Senator John D. Hopper, Senator John J. Shumaker.

Transcript of Proceedings, dated February 27, 1990, Capitol Building, Harrisburg, Pennsylvania.

10. Nathan (real name), letter to Marie Hamilton, November 10, 1989.

11. Marie Hamilton, letter to inmate residents, Drug and Alcohol Unit c/o Mr. Robert Morck, Camp Hill, November 13, 1989.

12. Marie Hamilton, letter to "To Those Who Are Caught Up In The Conflict Within Prison Walls," November 4, 1989.

13. Honorable Arlin M. Adams, Honorable George M. Leader, and Honorable K. Leroy Irvis, *Final Report of the Governor's Commission to Investigate Disturbances at Camp Hill Correctional Institution,* December 21, 1989.

11. Healing Brokenness

1. Real name

2. Angel Tree is a program of Prison Fellowship International whereby churches purchase and deliver Christmas gifts to children in the name of their incarcerated parents. Visit http://www.angeltree.org for more information.

3. Victor (real name), letter to Volunteers in Prison, December 26, 1991.

4. Yasin (real name), letter to Volunteers in Prison, undated.

5. Real name

6. Nickname

7. Nickname, previously at Camp Hill

8. Real name

9. Marie Hamilton, speech to On Earth Peace Assembly, July 1992.

10. Real name

11. Real name

12. Real name

13. Real name

14. Marie Hamilton, letter and training summary to Bill Love, November 8, 1993.

15. Howard Zehr, *Doing Life: Reflections of Men and Women Serving Life Sentences* (Intercourse, PA: Good Books, 1996).

16. Victor and Bear, letter to Howard Zehr, April 2, 1992.

17. See http://www.ggco.com/correctional.html for more information about Gordon Graham and his training programs, or visit his blog at http://www.gordysthoughtsonchange.blogspot.com/.

18. Frederick K. Frank, letter to Margaret A. Moore, October 6, 1993.

19. Frank Waitkus, Jr., letter to Joseph D. Lehman, November 30, 1993.

20. Charles H. Zimmerman, letter to Marie Hamilton, November 3, 1993.

21. Pseudonym
22. Pseudonym
23. Pseudonym
24. Pseudonym

12. Centering Peace

1. Victor, letter to Marie Hamilton, November 15, 1994.
2. Rockview Lifers Association, letter to seminar participants, November 21, 1994.
3. Pseudonym

13. Forgiveness

1. See http://www.pbs.org/wnet/religionandethics/week344/profile.html.
2. Pseudonym
3. *Time* magazine, undated.
4. Real name
5. Inmates are permitted to place a limited number of people on their visiting list, and this list must then be approved by the prison administration. Most inmates have so few people willing to visit them in prison that almost no one would purposely exclude a person from their list.
6. The U.S. Bureau of Justice Statistics reports that over 16 percent of male inmates and more than 57 percent of female inmates in state prisons were victims of abuse at some point before their incarceration. In contrast, 5-8 percent of males and 12-17 percent of females in the general population have been victims of abuse. See http://www.ojp.usdoj.gov/bjs/pub/pdf/parip.pdf.
7. Federal Comprehensive Crime Control Act of 1984, Federal Anti-Drug Abuse Acts of the late 1980s, and the 1994 Violent Crime Control & Law Enforcement Act.
8. See http://www.restorativejustice.org/articlesdb/articles/714.
9. Act 33 amended Pennsylvania's Juvenile Act to require that the courts give balanced consideration to youth who committed crimes, the victims of their crimes, and the community at large. See Pennsylvania Commission on Crime and Delinquency—Juvenile Justice at http://www.pccd.state.pa.us/.
10. The Pennsylvania Office of the Victim Advocate was created in 1995 to represent the rights and interests of crime victims before the Board of Probation and Parole and the Department of Corrections. See http://www.pbpp.state.pa.us/ova/.
11. Find out more information about Pennsylvania's Mediation Program for

Victims of Violent Crime by visiting http://www.pbpp.state.pa.us/ova/cwp/view
.asp?A=3&Q=152848.

12. Real name

13. Camp Blue Diamond is a Church of the Brethren camp and retreat center located in central Pennsylvania near State College and Altoona.

14. Grace Goes to Prison

1. Hannah Arendt, *The Human Condition* (Chicago: University of Chicago Press, 1958): 237.

2. Pseudonym

3. Pseudonym

4. Pseudonym

5. Speech, 2002 Pennsylvania Department of Corrections luncheon commemorating Crime Victims' Rights Week.

6. Andrew Barnes, the current Victim Assistance coordinator in Pennsylvania's Office of the Victim Advocate, explains, "Forgiveness is not necessarily the goal of all participants in the victim offender mediation program. And it isn't a requirement for participation. Instead, each mediation is a unique and individual journey for both the victim and the offender. Each party brings their own expectations and goals to the process."

7. Letter from inmate participant as reported in the CentrePeace newsletter, Fall 2000.

8. Marie Hamilton, letter to donor, January 15, 2003.

SELECTED BIBLIOGRAPHY

The author conducted interviews with many of the people mentioned in this book between October 2007 and July 2009. In addition, she exchanged numerous e-mails and/or letters with the interviewees, asking them to review, fact-check, and confirm the accuracy of stories referencing them in the book.

In addition to interviews, e-mails, and letters, she also spent hours conducting research in the extensive archives of the Voluntary Action Center of Centre County (Pennsylvania), Volunteers in Prison, Inc., and CentrePeace, Inc. All of these archives are housed at the Centre-Peace headquarters in Bellefonte, Pennsylvania.

Additional sources listed below provided historical details, background information, and context for this book.

Adams, Arlin M., George M. Leader, and K. Leroy Irvis. *Final Report of the Governor's Commission to Investigate Disturbances at Camp Hill Correctional Institution.* Harrisburg, PA: the Commission. December 21, 1989. Available from the State Library of Pennsylvania.

Bagdikian, Ben H. *Caged: Eight Prisoners and Their Keepers.* New York: Harper and Row, 1976.

Beyond Conviction. DVD. Directed by Rachel Libert. San Francisco: Tied to the Tracks Films, 2006. http://www.beyondconviction.com/.

Freeman, Robert M. "Pre-Emergency Planning for Post-Emergency Litigation." *Corrections Today* 58, no. 4 (July 1996).

———. "Remembering the Camp Hill Riot." *Corrections Today* 59, no. 1 (February 1997).

McCullough, John. "Institutional Pre-Release Services: A Year Later. April 1975–April 1976," 1976. Unpublished.

————. "A Seven Year History of B Block North, A Therapeutic Community at the State Correctional Institution at Rockview," 1983. Unpublished.

McWilliams, John C. *Two Centuries of Corrections in Pennsylvania: A Commemorative History.* Harrisburg, PA: Pennsylvania Historical and Museum Commission, 2002.

Pennsylvania Commission on Crime and Delinquency. "Juvenile Justice." http://www.pccd.state.pa.us/.

Pennsylvania Department of Corrections. "Death Penalty." http://www.cor.state.pa.us/.

————. *Correctional Newsfront Special Edition: Bringing Honor to Victims.* 28, no. 4, April 2002.

————. "Policy 7.4.1—Alcohol and Other Drugs Treatment Programs," issued January 19, 2006.

Pennsylvania General Assembly. Senate. *Senate Judiciary Committee Public Hearing on Recent Incidents at Pennsylvania State Correctional Institutions before Senator Stewart J. Greenleaf, Chairman, Senator D. Michael Fisher, Vice Chairman, Senator John D. Hopper, Senator John J. Shumaker. Transcript of Proceedings.* Harrisburg, PA, February 1, 1990.

Pennsylvania General Assembly. Senate. *Senate Judiciary Committee Public Hearing on Recent Incidents at Pennsylvania State Correctional Institutions before Senator Stewart J. Greenleaf, Chairman, Senator John D. Hopper, Senator John J. Shumaker. Transcript of Proceedings.* Harrisburg, PA, February 27, 1990.

Pennsylvania Office of the Victim Advocate. http://www.pbpp.state.pa.us/ova/.

Pennsylvania Prison Society. http://www.prisonsociety.org/.

Pew Center on the States. *One in 100: Behind Bars in America 2008.* http://www.pewcenteronthestates.org/uploadedFiles/8015PCTS_Prison08_FINAL_2-1-1_FORWEB.pdf.

Residents of the Institutional Pre-Release Unit at Rockview State Correctional Institution (Bellefonte, Pennsylvania). *Houser Hall Resident Handbook: Working Together.* January 1976.

United States Department of Justice. National Institute of Corrections. *Critical Analysis of Emergency Preparedness: Self-Audit Materials,* May 1996. http://www.nicic.org/pubs/1996/013223.pdf.

United States Department of Justice. Office of Justice Programs. United States Bureau of Justice Statistics. *Prior Abuse Reported by Inmates and Probationers,* April 1999. http://www.ojp.usdoj.gov/bjs/pub/pdf/parip.pdf.

Victim Offender Mediation Association. http://voma.org/index.html.

Zehr, Howard. *Changing Lenses: A New Focus for Crime and Justice,* 3rd. ed. Scottdale, PA: Herald Press, 2005.

———. *Doing Life: Reflections of Men and Women Serving Life Sentences.* Intercourse, PA: Good Books, 1996.

———. *Transcending: Reflections of Crime Victims.* Intercourse, PA: Good Books, 2001.

DISCUSSION QUESTIONS

These discussion questions provide an avenue for book clubs, faith groups, and others to engage in the story of Marie Hamilton and the issue of restorative justice in our prison system. For an additional set of discussion questions geared toward faith groups, visit the author's website at www.melaniegsnyder.com or the publisher's homepage at www.brethren.org/brethrenpress.

1. The first time Marie went into a prison she experienced shock at seeing human beings in cages. *We do this in America?* Have you ever visited a prison? If so, what was your initial reaction?

2. What did you observe about the way Marie dealt with problems in the prison—with the staff and the volunteers, or the staff and the inmates? Why was she so successful as a mediator and advocate? What were the walls that began to come down as a result of the volunteers' visits to the prison?

3. When the volunteers were told that "prison reformers" weren't welcome at Rockview, Marie and others formed Community Alternatives in Criminal Justice (CACJ). Their vision was "meaningful change in the criminal justice system." What changes do you believe are needed? What would be the effect on society?

4. Did you experience any discomfort as you read about Marie's first mediation assignment with Dave and Jenny? Were your sympathies with Dave, the offender, or Jenny, the victim? What did Howard Zehr mean when he called victim offender mediations "hallowed ground"?

5. Marie observes: "Restorative justice means responding to . . . in-justices in a way that is genuinely meant to help rather than to hurt back. As we learn better how to heal our brokenness and how to help the offender so the cycle does not continue, we will be learning how to center peace." What would it mean for prisons to be focused on treatment and restoration instead of punishment? What are the challenges and obstacles? How might an effort to heal and educate offenders affect the recidivism rate?

6. How can Marie's style of working with people be applied in your own life? What universal values do you take from her story?

7. What is your personal response to *Grace Goes to Prison*?

To invite the author, Melanie G. Snyder, to speak to your group about Marie's work, restorative justice, or how to get involved locally, visit her website at www.melaniegsnyder.com.

To learn more about the work of CentrePeace contact:

> CentrePeace, Inc.
> 3013 Benner Pike
> Bellefonte, PA 16823
> Website: www.centrepeace.org
> Phone: (814) 353-9081
> Fax: (814) 353-9083
> E-mail: contact@centrepeace.org